Event-Driven Architecture

Event-Driven Architecture

How SOA Enables the Real-Time Enterprise

Hugh Taylor, Angela Yochem, Les Phillips, and Frank Martinez

✦✦ Addison-Wesley

Upper Saddle River, NJ • Boston • Indianapolis
San Francisco • New York • Toronto • Montreal
London • Munich • Paris • Madrid • Cape Town
Sydney • Tokyo • Singapore • Mexico City

Many of the designations used by manufacturers and sellers to distinguish their products are claimed as trademarks. Where those designations appear in this book, and the publisher was aware of a trademark claim, the designations have been printed with initial capital letters or in all capitals.

The authors and publisher have taken care in the preparation of this book, but make no expressed or implied warranty of any kind and assume no responsibility for errors or omissions. No liability is assumed for incidental or consequential damages in connection with or arising out of the use of the information or programs contained herein.

The publisher offers excellent discounts on this book when ordered in quantity for bulk purchases or special sales, which may include electronic versions and/or custom covers and content particular to your business, training goals, marketing focus, and branding interests. For more information, please contact

> U.S. Corporate and Government Sales
> (800) 382-3419
> corpsales@pearsontechgroup.com

For sales outside the United States, please contact

> International Sales
> international@pearson.com

Visit us on the Web: informit.com/aw

Library of Congress Cataloging-in-Publication Data

Event-driven architecture : how SOA enables the real-time enterprise / Hugh Taylor ... [et al.].

   p. cm.

Includes bibliographical references.

ISBN-13: 978-0-321-32211-1 (pbk. : alk. paper)

ISBN-10: 0-321-32211-8 (pbk. : alk. paper) 1. Service-oriented architecture (Computer science) 2. Discrete-time systems. 3. Business--Data processing. 4. Business enterprises--Computer networks. I. Taylor, Hugh.

TK5105.5828.E94 2009

004.6'82--dc22

                                2008055032

ISBN-13: 978-0-321-32211-1
ISBN-10: 0-321-32211-8

Text printed in the United States on recycled paper at RR Donnelley in Crawfordsville, Indiana.
First printing March 2009

Editor-in-Chief
Mark Taub

Acquisitions Editor
Greg Doench

Development Editor
Michael Thurston

Managing Editor
Kristy Hart

Project Editor
Betsy Harris

Copy Editor
Karen Annett

Indexer
Ken Johnson

Proofreader
Debbie Williams

Technical Reviewers
Cliff Berg
Kevin Davis
David Kane

Publishing Coordinator
Michelle Housley

Cover Designer
Chuti Prasertsith

Senior Compositor
Gloria Schurick

To our children:
Joy, Grace, Julian, Anthony, Noam, Ezra, Gavriel, Maggie, and Benjamin

Contents

PART I   THE THEORY OF EDA

PART II   EDA IN PRACTICE

Foreword

It's been 15 years since the dawn of the Web, and we are still absorbing the lessons it teaches us about decentralization, loose coupling, standards, and resource representation. Even when technology seems to move quickly, it can take a long time to understand, appreciate, and apply the core principles it embodies.

The roots of event-driven architecture run even deeper. Twenty-five years ago, the graphical user interface forever changed how we think about applications. Suddenly, the event loop became a central organizing principle. Programs listened to events, processed them, and responded to them—sometimes by firing new events. There was no other way to effectively support fickle and unpredictable users who are liable to do anything whenever they want.

Enterprise software systems, of course, serve whole populations of fickle and unpredictable users. Some are customers, some are suppliers, and some are business partners. Here too, effective software has to listen well and respond intelligently.

It sounds simple, and conceptually it is. But while the stream of events produced by a GUI application is defined by the operating system, and is well understood by the programmer, an enterprise application lives in a connected world. Just as the resource-oriented Web architect has to learn how to design stateless resources, so must the event-oriented enterprise architect learn how to design stateless events.

But if EDA presents new challenges, it also emerges in an era of new opportunity. The tools and techniques of service-oriented architecture are becoming more mature, more interoperable, and more manageable.

With a strong SOA skeleton in place, EDA can weave the enterprise's nervous system. This book explains why event-driven architecture yields smart and resilient enterprise software, and shows you how to start "thinking EDA."

—Jon Udell

Preface

About This Book

As professionals in the enterprise architecture field, we have observed the recent and spectacular rise of the concept of service-oriented architecture (SOA) with excitement tempered by concern. The new standards-based architectural paradigm promises great advances in interoperability among previously incompatible software applications. In turn, it has the potential to deliver gains in agility and IT cost control. Perhaps most exciting, though, is the potential for SOA to make possible the realization of event-driven architecture (EDA), an approach to enterprise architecture that yields a high level of agility by increasing systems' awareness and intelligent responses to relevant events.

At the same time, it became clear to us that the steps required to design and deploy an EDA, or an SOA, its master set of architectural characteristics, were far from obvious. Even going beyond the fact that the technology and standards are immature and, thus, challenging, the practice of uniting software with an overarching standards-based approach that extends outside the enterprise is a new field, lacking in many of the guiding principles of infrastructure, governance, and best practices that hold together most traditional forms of architecture and development.

For better or worse, some software vendors are now bringing what they call EDA suites to market. However, the commercial offerings in EDA tend to be quite narrowly defined and vendor-centric. As such, they are inadequate on their own to offer much in the way of instruction on the overall best practices required for EDA.

We perceive a need among architects for a book that combines both the theory of EDA—the grand vision that led to its formation and the essential nature of the paradigm—with a practical look at building an EDA over an SOA implementation in the real world. This book is neither all theory nor all practice. It is a blend, with the idea that true success with EDA depends on a good understanding of both aspects of the paradigm.

To understand how this book is set up and what it contains, we thought it would make sense first to take a quick look at the definition, history, and context of EDA and SOA. These two related architectural styles are not as new as they seem, though recent developments in standards have led to breakthroughs in their potential realization.

Inside This Book: The Path to EDA

Even for a lot of experienced architects and developers, the implicit connection between EDA and SOA has not been intuitively obvious. A lot of IT pros react to SOA with a sentiment akin to, "That's really cool. Now what?" These questions are completely legitimate. Imagine someone handing you a violin and declaring, "Oh, good, now I get to hear Mozart." That person is making several assumptions, including that you know what the violin is, how to play it, and how to play Mozart in particular. In many IT situations, it is not always evident how loose coupling and a service orientation will take you to an EDA. If your boss drops a Visual Studio 2008 pack on your desk and says, "Now you will deliver an EDA," you might not necessarily know how to get from here to there. That is the purpose of this book.

Much of this book is dedicated to helping you understand where the rubber meets the road in turning the vision of EDA into a reality. In so doing, we delve into detail on the subject of SOA, providing the essential building blocks of the most versatile and effective EDAs. We address one of the great unanswered questions posed in the wake of SOA's high-profile arrival on the IT scene: How do you actually get to the achievement of business goals that EDA enables using the actual technologies that make up SOA? The leap from Web services and SOA to the fulfillment of EDA, and its attendant agility and IT cost savings, requires some serious discipline.

Part I—The Theory of EDA

This book consists of two parts. Part I, "The Theory of EDA," covers the theoretical aspects of EDA. The path to EDA, which we guide you through in this book, starts with an understanding of what EDA is. Part I begins with a thorough theoretical definition of EDA. We cover the core components of EDA, such as event consumers and producers, message backbones, Web service transport, and so on. We also describe the basic patterns of EDA, including simple event processing, event stream processing, and complex event processing.

From this definition, we then explore the current context of EDA, which is the jungle of interoperability challenges that we all face in large enterprises. Having thus set up the situation that we face—we want EDA (or at least, we should consider it)—we see how difficult it can be to attain. Enter SOA, and its open interoperability, which paves the way for the realization of EDA.

In addition to defining EDA, we explore the SOA-EDA connection in depth. In our view, any serious attempt to develop an EDA today will rely on the use of SOA technology as it is emerging in the marketplace. The EDA of tomorrow will run on Web services and enterprise service buses. The EDA components—the event producers, consumers, and processors—will all be Web services. We will flesh out this vision of EDA.

The conclusion of Part I consists of examples of EDAs and how they might function. We explore examples of how businesses and other organizations might ideally use EDA to further their objectives. This set of examples provides a transition to Part II, "EDA in Practice," of the book, which moves you into the reality of EDA and how it might be approached in an actual enterprise setting.

Part II—EDA in Practice

Part II begins with Chapter 6, "Thinking EDA." This chapter explores ways to identify the ideal use of an EDA, or a partial EDA in realizing a set of business objectives. Chapters 7 and beyond present a set of case studies of EDA. Some of these case studies are based on real companies. Others are partially hypothetical, but based on real-life experiences we have had in the world of enterprise architecture.

In each case study, we describe the organizations involved as well as the technological and business challenges and objectives that they have. We look at the ways in which the business and technological situation would benefit from an EDA approach. We look at the practical issues that arise in its design and implementation. Our goal is to include, where relevant, some organization and non-IT issues, such as project management and communication. Of course, we get into depth on the technologies required to birth the EDA.

Throughout the case studies, we look at a number of related topics in the field of enterprise architecture that have relevance for learning about EDA. These include SOA infrastructure, governance, and security. Wherever possible, we try to point out business issues that are relevant, but perhaps not apparent to the technology reader, as well as technology issues that might not be noticed by the business reader.

One of our other goals is to instill in you a good sense of when to use an EDA approach and when not to, for the paradigm is not a panacea for all IT and business problems. This issue reminds of the story of a man who once approached a famous surgeon and said, "You make more money in a week than I make in a year. I don't think it's fair. Is what you do so special?" The surgeon replied, "Surgery itself isn't that complicated. I could probably teach you to do it in a few weeks. What takes the training and skill is knowing when not to operate, and what to do when something goes wrong. Learning those two things can take years."

So it is with EDA. Developing a Web service is not hard for an experienced developer. Knowing how to use the functions of an SOA to create an EDA, though, is another matter. And, like the surgeon, you would be well served by understanding when to use and not use the EDA approach. If you take away nothing else from this book, consider that there are many cases where an EDA is not the optimal solution to a business issue.

Who Should Read This Book, and How They Should Read It

If you're holding this book in your hand, you are probably involved with information technology. If you are not in technology, we really admire your desire to be a broadly informed citizen. We have written this book in fairly deep, but not excessively detailed, technical language.

This is not a book that is awash in code or extensive jargon. We have made the choice to skip the deep, deep techie language because of the likely blend of readers that we expect to find. The subject of EDA can be of interest to the work of a vast audience. EDA itself is an area that is inherently interdisciplinary. EDA naturally throws together developers, line-of-business people, IT managers, security specialists, architects, and network operations people. There is probably a whole EDA book for each of those disciplines. Luckily for us, someone else will write them. We want to present the topic in a unified approach that a multiplicity of readers can absorb.

Our other guess is that you probably work at a large organization or with an entity that interfaces with large organizations. Whether you work at a corporation, public sector organization, or educational institution, the issues for EDA are the same. We come from the corporate world, so we have a tendency to talk about "business value" a lot. If you can't relate to this, we are sorry, but for stylistic reasons we need to use just one measure of efficiency, and in our world, that measure is usually dollars. So, when we talk about "business value," we mean the economy of effort required to produce a result. It's a concept that can translate into any organizational agenda.

Acknowledgments

Thanks to our colleagues, Max Poliashenko and Chris Hart.

About the Authors

Hugh Taylor is a social software evangelist for IBM Lotus Software. Previously, he worked at SOA Software and Microsoft. He is the author of *The Joy of SOX: Why Sarbanes Oxley and Service-Oriented Architecture May Be the Best Thing That Ever Happened to You* and coauthor of *Understanding Enterprise SOA*. He is a lecturer at UC Berkeley's School of Information and a frequent presenter at technology industry conferences. Hugh earned his BA and MBA from Harvard College.

Angela Yochem is an executive in a multinational technology company and is a thought leader in architecture practices and large-scale technology management.

Angela has held senior leadership roles in Fortune 50 companies where she drove technology transformation based on business objectives. Prior to her executive roles, Angela specialized in design and delivery of large-scale distributed systems and solutions to complex integration and convergence challenges. She has extensive B2B and B2C commerce implementation experience, with a foundation in systems design and network design and management of multicampus networks.

Angela is the author of *J2EE and WebLogic Server, 2ⁿᵈ Edition* and is an IASA Fellow and an US Patent holder. Angela serves on executive boards and is a regular speaker at events and forums in the United States and abroad.

Les Phillips is a VP of enterprise architecture at SunTrust Banks Inc. Leveraging more than 15 years of industry experience, Les lays out the strategic and business foundation for many enterprise areas.

Throughout his career Les has applied smart strategies and inventive ideas on pressing business objectives in fields such as supply chain, telecommunications, banking, retail, and education. He's passionate when discussing his business transformation experience. Focusing on enterprise concerns and event-driven analytics, Les inspires and effectively helps businesses transform their DNA to achieve their market potential and performance goals.

A longtime cyberspace veteran, Les specializes in system integration. He has enabled numerous Fortune 500 businesses to expand their awareness by integrating their systems with the outside world. On these engagements, he led many initiatives to maximize current IT investments by exposing their inherent strengths as business services.

Les combines his skills with a twist of logic and a dash of creativity to form mouthwatering architectural cocktails.

Frank Martinez is a recognized expert in the area of distributed, enterprise application, and infrastructure platforms. Mr. Martinez is focused on driving development of scalable service-oriented infrastructure software that integrates business processes and information enterprisewide. Mr. Martinez's reputation as a technological visionary is demonstrated by his record of bringing innovative and commercially successful software solutions to market. He has had operating roles as a senior executive of several VC-backed firms and was instrumental in building Intershop Communications into a multibillion dollar public company in less than three years. Mr. Martinez was recently named an InfoWorld Innovator by *InfoWorld* magazine and has also been named one of 25 leading IT innovators by CRN.

Introduction

Event-Driven Architecture: A Working Definition

Event-driven architecture (EDA) falls into the maddening category of a technology paradigm that is half understood by many people who claim to know everything about it. Although we recognize that we, too, might not know absolutely everything there is to know about EDA, we believe that it is necessary to set out a working definition of EDA that we can adhere to throughout this book. Getting to an effective working definition of EDA is challenging because EDA must be described at a sufficiently high level that is comprehensible to nontechnologists, but at the same time not so high level as to sound vague or irrelevant.

An event-driven architecture is one that has the ability to detect events and react intelligently to them. For our purposes—and we discuss this in great detail later on—an *event* is a change in *state* that merits attention from systems. Brenda Michelson, a technology analyst, writes, "In an event-driven architecture, a notable thing happens inside or outside your business, which disseminates immediately to all interested parties (human or automated). The interested parties evaluate the event, and optionally take action."[1]

One of the simplest examples of an event-driven system is actually from the noncomputer world. It is known as a thermostat. The thermostat is a mechanical device that turns the heat on or off based on its programmed reaction to an event, which is a change in temperature. The shift in temperature is the event, the "change in state" that triggers the reaction of the thermostat, which, in turn, affects the action of the heater.

We can see another simple example in the evolution of the automobile. Cars are becoming increasingly intelligent by reacting intelligently to their surroundings. If rain hits the windshield, the automobile recognizes the rain event and automatically turns on the windshield wipers, turns on the headlights, and adjusts the front windshield defroster. All of these things were formerly the driver's responsibility, but now the car's internal system uses its intelligence to react. An EDA is an architecture that acts in the same way: It detects events and reacts to them in an intelligent way. To be able to detect events and react to them intelligently, an EDA must have certain capabilities, including the ability to detect events, transmit messages among its components that an event has occurred, process the reaction to the event, and initiate the reaction to the event if that is called for. In generic architectural terms, these capabilities translate into the concepts of *event producers, event consumers, messaging backbones,* and *event processors.* These go by many different names in practice, and this is one of the great hurdles to getting a feel for what an EDA is at its core.

Many examples of EDAs occur in the realm of information systems, though most of the ones currently deployed are limited in scope. For example, if your credit card is simultaneously used in two separate geographical locations, those two events can be "heard" by the credit card processing systems and examined for a potential fraud pattern. The credit card fraud detection EDA is set up to listen for events that indicate potential fraud and respond—or not respond—depending on a set of rules that are programmed into the event processors. If the charge occurring out of state is at a mail order merchant where you have shopped before, the system might not deem the event pattern to be a fraud. If the second charge is for a high-dollar value at a merchant where you have not shopped before, the EDA might trigger a response that places a warning or "watch" status on your credit card account. Or, the activity might prompt a person to call you and find out if you have lost your card.

Or, imagine that an FAA air traffic control application needs to know the probability of rain in a certain location. At the same time, the Air Force needs the same data, as does NASA. Assuming that the weather data is collected and available on a server somewhere, it is possible to tightly couple that server, and the software running on it, with the FAA, Air Force, and NASA's respective systems. Although this type of approach is frequently used, it is far easier to arrange for the weather application to *publish* the weather data and enable the *subscribers* (the FAA et al.) to get the data they need and use it however they need to use it. The *weather status event* of the weather application publishes the weather data so that the data subscribers can use it to drive the architecture. This is an event-driven architecture.

In this EDA, the FAA, Air Force, and NASA are integrated with the weather system by virtue of the fact that there is no specific coupling between the applications. Of course, they exchange data, but the applications are completely separate and have no inherent knowledge of one another. The developers do not need to know each other, and there is no need to coordinate. However, for it to work, they do need standards. To effectively disseminate and process events, the publisher and the subscriber might agree to use a commonly understood message format and a compatible transport mechanism.

One commonly used technology that is analogous to EDA is the Web itself. When you use a browser, you are initiating an integrated session with a remote system of which you have no specific knowledge. In all probability, you have no idea who programmed it, what language it's written in, where it is, and so on. Yet, your browser can pull whatever information it is permitted to get and show it to you in a format that you can understand. The event of requesting the uniform resource locator (URL) triggers the action that results in the display of the Hypertext Markup Language (HTML) content in your browser window. As we develop our explanation of EDA, though, you will see that the Web is a very simple EDA.

An EDA consists of applications that are programmed to publish, subscribe, or take other actions upon events triggered by applications with which they share no formal coupling. For this reason, EDA has been likened to a "nervous system" for the enterprise.

The Enterprise Nervous System

Where would the IT industry be without metaphors? Even the idea of using the word *architecture* to describe how Byzantine networks of hardware, software, and data are configured shows how reliant we are on abstraction to achieve an understanding of what we are trying to accomplish in enterprise IT. In the spirit of metaphors, then, we shall borrow a concept from human physiology, the central nervous system, to further our understanding of EDA.

If your cat steps on your toe, how do you know it? How do you know it's a cat, and not a lion? You might want to pet the cat, but shoot the lion. When the cat's paw presses against your toe, the nerve cells in your toe fire off a signal to your brain saying, "Hey, someone stepped on my toe." Also, they send a message that says something like, "It doesn't hurt that much" and "It was probably a cat." Or, if you saw the cat, the signals from your optic nerve are synthesized with those from your toe, each invoking your mental data store of animals and likely toe steppers, and you should know pretty quickly that it was, indeed, a cat that stepped on your toe. Your central nervous system is a massively complex set of sensory receptors, wires, and integration points, known as synapses. The nervous system is critical to your functioning and survival in the world. Just imagine if your central nervous system didn't work well and you confused the cat with the lion. As Figure I.1 shows, you might shoot your cat and pet the lion, which would then eat you.

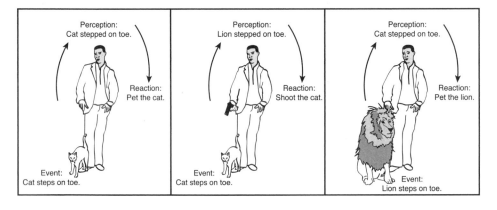

Figure I.1   The human nervous system as a metaphor for the enterprise. When the cat steps on your toe, do you recognize it as a cat, or mistake it for a lion?

Our enterprises have their own nervous systems, too. Our Web sites, enterprise resource planning (ERP) systems, customer relationship management (CRM) systems, databases, and network infrastructures, for example, all work to feed the corporate equivalent of sensory information to the corporate "brain." The corporate brain, in turn, assesses the input and reacts. Of course, the corporate brain might contain a few actual brains as well, in the form of employees, but their sensory input is determined by the enterprise nervous system. For example, if there is an increase in cash withdrawals at a bank, the banking systems, acting like nerve sensors in our toe, fire off withdrawal data to the corporate brain. The neurons in the corporate brain then route the data to its destination, which could be an automated bank cash reserve management system, the executive management team of the bank, or a combination. As our brain assesses and reacts to the cat stepping on our toe, the corporate brain of the bank must assess the input of the withdrawal spike and react.

If our enterprises were living beings, most of them would need some pretty intensive neurological care. Unlike a well-functioning person, whose nervous system can learn how to react to different stimuli and determine the best way to handle a given situation based on sensory input and mental processing, the typical enterprise has a nervous system that is hardwired to react in a specific set of ways that might not be ideal for every situation. In the cat-on-toe situation, most of our enterprises would probably expect the worst and then shoot in the general direction of the cat. Or, perhaps a more realistic version of the metaphor—the enterprise wouldn't even know that anything had stepped on its toe, or that it even had a toe. It would be completely unaware most likely because it was never given the ability to be aware.

Like the person whose knee-jerk reaction is to shoot the cat regardless of what is going on, most of our enterprises have a nervous system that is not well set up to receive the data equivalent of sensory input, process it, know what it is, and react in an appropriate way. Event-driven architecture is an approach to IT that gives the enterprise the ability to improve its nervous system and have a level of adaptability and awareness that it needs. This is what we typically hear described as *agility*: the ability to react intelligently to stimuli and also continually reshape the reaction as circumstances change.

Data is powerful, if you can see it and know what to do with it. To paraphrase Levitt and Dubner and their great book, *Freakonomics*, an EDA provides potential adaptation data that exists in streams that we can't possibly see on our own. Levitt and Dubner characterize the Internet as a "gigantic horseshoe magnet waved over an endless sea of haystacks, plucking the needle out of each one." Similarly, an EDA—the nervous system—gives us a way to acquire data and to make the data we have meaningful. For example, if we knew that every day we experience what it feels like to have a lion stepping on our toe, followed by no negative reaction, we might learn to ignore it as unimportant—or begin to assume that it's not a lion. That's fine, until a lion does step on our toe…

Building an EDA to instill good functioning to the enterprise nervous system involves getting the various sensors, message pathways, and reacting logic processors to work together. In broad terms, this is known as interoperation, and it is the heart of the new EDA discussion going on today.

The "New" Era of Interoperability Dawns

Reading about EDA as a "new" idea might give you a sense of déjà vu. As we saw with the familiar credit card fraud example, EDA is not a new concept. However, the current crop of EDAs uses proprietary standards for communication, and although they work well, they are, in effect, tightly coupled EDAs that can only share information among systems that use a compatible standard. For instance, it is possible to set up a fairly effective EDA if all systems are built on the same platform. Vendors have long provided high-performance pub/sub engines for compatible systems. The only problem is, as we know, not everyone is on the same platform, despite the dramatic sales efforts of some of Silicon Valley's best and brightest minds. The good news is that many platform vendors have released new service-based EDA products, which do not rely on tight coupling.

The quest for a well-functioning enterprise nervous system has been the catalyst for the development of EDA for many years. Why, then, is EDA receiving such renewed and intense interest today? The reason has to do with the explosion in interoperability and the standardization of data across multiple enterprises, which changes the game of EDA.

Ultimately, the existence of an EDA is dependent on interoperability among systems. You can't have awareness and reaction to events if the systems cannot communicate with one another. Existing EDA setups are invariably tightly constrained and narrow in their functionality because it has been so difficult, or costly, to achieve the level of interoperation of EDA components needed for any kind of dynamic or complex EDA functionality. That is now changing. Today, with the advent of open standards and the breakthroughs in system interoperability from service-oriented architectures (SOAs), it is now possible to establish EDAs that are far more intelligent, dynamic, and far-reaching than ever before.

To put the interoperability evolution in context, we will share a lunch conversation we had recently with a man who had been responsible for designing and implementing the basic underpinnings of the worldwide airline reservation and automated teller machine infrastructures. In the last few years, he has been involved in other pursuits, so he was eager to learn about SOA and EDA, the new tech trends that he had been hearing so much about in the industry media.

When we explained how the related concepts of SOA and EDA allowed, for the first time ever, truly open interoperation among heterogeneous software applications, regardless of operating system, network protocol, or programming language, he gave us a perplexed look. "That's new?" he asked with a slight smirk. "That idea has been around since 1961."

And, of course, he was right. The idea of open interoperability has been in the air for decades. Just like the automobiles have been around since the late 1800s. Even today, we still use a combustion engine to drive the wheels, so the essence hasn't changed much. However, never before have cars been so reactive to our needs and their surroundings.

The same evolution is true for the software and the circumstances that we find ourselves in now, in 2009. Over the last eight years, from 2001 to 2009, we have seen an unprecedented shift in the IT industry toward the use of open standards for the purpose of integrating diverse software applications. Also, more and more companies are exposing their data in a standardized fashion further expanding the circle of opportunity.

This all started back in 2001.... An unusually broad group of major IT companies, including IBM, Oracle, Microsoft, BEA, and others, agreed to conform to a specific set of Extensible Markup Language (XML) standards for interoperation between software applications. These standards, known collectively as the Web Services protocol, provide a technological basis for any application in the world to exchange data or procedure calls with any other application, regardless of location, network, operating system, or programming language.

Specifically, the major standards that were ratified included Simple Object Access Protocol (SOAP), which is the message formatting standard, Web Services Description Language (WSDL), which sets out a standard document format with which to describe a Web service, and Universal Description, Discovery, and Integration (UDDI), a Web services registry application programming interface (API), that are available for use in a particular domain.

Thus, Web services are software-based interfaces that are universally understandable, self-describing, and universally discoverable. As our colleague Jnan Dash, the legendary lead engineer of the Oracle Database, puts it, the combination of the Internet and Web services makes possible a kind of "universal dial tone" for all applications. (The Internet is the dial tone and Web services give you the ability to "dial.") With Web services, it is entirely possible for an application written in C to interoperate with a J2EE application without the need for any proprietary middleware. As a whole, the large-scale development and integration of Web services is a key step toward developing a service-oriented architecture (SOA). SOA represents a model in which functionality is decomposed into small, distinct units (services—for example, Web services), which can be distributed over a network and can be combined together and reused to create business applications. These services communicate with each other by passing data from one service to another or by coordinating an activity between two or more services.[2] The industry vision that is fueling the SOA trend is that one day virtually any application needed in your enterprise (whether it is inside your firewall or not) will be available as a Web service and will be freely interoperable with other applications, enabling the decomposition of application functionality into small units that can interoperate or be orchestrated in composite applications. This vision is idealized, and it is likely that a full-blown SOA of this type will never actually come into existence. However, many are approaching the paradigm in steps.

Many enterprises have begun to introduce service-orientation in their architectures, selectively exposing capabilities through Web services in configurations that suit specific business needs and selectively service enabling core legacy systems. This is a remarkable achievement for an industry that was very much in the doghouse after the Y2K panic and dot.com fiascos of 2001. The most striking thing about SOA, beyond the fact that Web services standards were adopted simultaneously by many large IT vendors, is the fact that it actually works. SOA is very much the technological trend of the moment, and it is everywhere. You see SOA as a prominent feature set in products from Microsoft, Oracle, IBM, SAP, and so on. Virtually every major technology company has announced an SOA strategy or even shifted their entire market focus to being service-oriented. A sure sign that SOA had reached prime time was when Accenture announced that it was going to spend $450 million on an SOA consulting initiative for its global clients.

SOA removes much, if not all, of the proprietary middleware and network compatibility blockages that inhibit rapid changes in application integration. As a result, they can loosen the coupling between applications. Given how important agility is, tight coupling is rightly held out as the enemy of agility. Loose coupling is the enabler of agility and SOA delivers loose coupling. Changes become simpler, faster, and cheaper. As integration agility becomes reality, so does EDA and its increased awareness. Therefore, SOA delivers the necessary agility required for an EDA. However, achieving this goal of EDA through loose coupling without destroying a range of security, governance, and performance standards requires a great deal of planning and work. And, as we start to see, the path from where we are now, to SOA and then EDA, is not always clear.

The ETA for Your EDA

This is not a cookbook, but it can put you on track for finding the right use for EDA in your organization and getting it started. At the very least, our intent is to familiarize you with this exciting new technological paradigm—and you will need this familiarity if you are a professional working in technology today. EDA and SOA are appearing in a myriad of commercial IT offerings and technological media articles. You need to know about EDA.

How you approach EDA is up to you, and if your career has been like ours, you might agree that rushing is seldom a good idea, especially when a new technology is involved. Our goal is to inform and stimulate your thinking on the subject. Whatever the ETA is for your EDA, only you will know the right way to proceed. Our wish is to give you the knowledge and insight you need to make it a success.

Endnotes

1. Michelson, Brenda. "Event Driven Architecture Overview." Paper published by Patricia Seybold Group (2/2/2006).
2. Wikipedia, http://en.wikipedia.org/wiki/Service-oriented_ architecture.

The Theory of EDA

CHAPTER 1

EDA: Opportunities and Obstacles

The Vortex

In the 1974 film classic *Blazing Saddles*, Mel Brooks, playing Governor William J. LePetomaine, struts around his office complaining, "Harrumph, Harrumph, Harrumph…" When one of his cohorts does not reply, he adds, "Hey! I didn't get a harrumph outta that guy!!" To us, this scene epitomizes the current state of enterprise architecture. There's a lot of complaining going on, and we have a big menu of issues that we can harrumph about if we choose to. For almost everyone in the architecture field, today represents an agonizing best-of-times/worst-of-times scenario. There is so much we want to do with our architecture, so much we need to do, and indeed, so much we can do—if we can solve certain core architectural problems.

Event-driven architecture (EDA)—and by this, we mean the modern, dynamic, and agile kind—presents a superb solution to a range of major organizational IT challenges. Yet, despite its desirability, its attainment has been frustratingly out of reach for many years. This has changed, though, with the advent of service-oriented architecture (SOA).

We see the EDA as existing in a kind of systemic vortex at the present moment. There are those who want EDA, and there are forces that block its realization, namely tightly coupled integration and interoperation. To set the stage for the rest of this book, then, this first chapter is devoted to establishing a thorough and workable definition of EDA, and explores the reasons it can be an effective solution to many business and

IT challenges. This chapter also describes how an EDA works, what it can do, and what it might be able to do as the paradigm matures. At the same time, this chapter introduces the subject of interoperability and integration of systems, the area of IT that has stymied those of us who seek EDA. The purpose of this chapter is to refine your sense of that goal of EDA—where we are headed (we hope) and the obstacles that stand in the way, to be solved as we progress in the sophistication of SOA.

EDA: A Working Systemic Definition

As we noted in the Introduction, an event-driven architecture is one that has the ability to detect events and react intelligently to them. Brenda Michelson, a technology analyst, writes, "In an event-driven architecture, a notable thing happens inside or outside your business, which disseminates immediately to all interested parties (human or automated). The interested parties evaluate the event, and optionally take action."[1] To be able to learn about how EDAs work and how we can build them, though, we need a more specific and workable definition of what Michelson's definition means in concrete terms. This book refrains from technologically specific concepts or brand names, as these terms (such as enterprise service bus [ESB]) tend to distract us from gaining a useful working definition of EDA and drag us into debates that take us off course.

Defining an Event

First, let's define what we mean by an *event*. In life, an event is something that happens: a car drives by, a ball flies through your window, someone falls asleep—an action occurs. Alternatively, for our purposes, an event can also be an expected action that does not occur. If the temperature does not go down at night, that could be an *event*. In systemic terms, an event generally refers to a change in *state*. A change in state typically means that a data value has changed.

For example, if you exceed your allowance of minutes of cellular phone time, your wireless carrier bills you for the overage. In EDA terms, the state of your minutes goes from "Under" to "Over," and that change in state triggers the billing of the overage charge. The value of your account balance changes as you exceed the minute allowance. The shift from *minutes* = *under* to *minutes* = *over* is an event.

An event has three levels of detail. At one level, there is the basic fact that an event has occurred. An event has either occurred or not. This takes us to the second level of detail, which is the event definition. To recognize an event, an EDA must have a definition of what the event is. In the cell phone example, the EDA must work with a definition of an event that says, in effect, a "change in minutes" event has occurred whenever the allowance limit is exceeded. Then, there is the detail of the specific event. By how much has the minute allowance been exceeded? In our example, the three levels of event detail would look like this: (1) An event has occurred, based on the following definition, (2) an event is defined as "minutes=over," and (3) the event detail says "So-and-so's minutes have been exceeded. Amount =10 minutes." All three factors—event notification, event definition, and event detail—are necessary when designing an EDA.

For an event to occur in an EDA, it must be in a form that a computer can understand. However, that does not mean that an EDA is exclusively the preserve of digital information. A change in state can also result from nondigital information being translated into digital form. For example, a digital thermometer typically has some kind of analog temperature sensor that inputs temperature information into the sensor and results in a digital value equated to temperature. The edges of an EDA might be full of analog information that is translated into digital data to trigger events.

A key learning point here is to understand that virtually anything can be an event or trigger an event. Rainfall in Chad could be an event, if it is quantified and made available as a source of data. Stock market activity in Tokyo could absolutely be an event, assuming you know why you are interested. The examples are endless. An ideal EDA can be easily adapted to recognize events that occur anywhere. The trickiest word in the preceding sentence was *easily,* a simple idea that can generate a lot of discussion and complexity.

EDA Overview

Armed with a sense of what an *event* can be, we can now add some flesh to the basic EDA definition. If an event is any "notable thing" that happens inside or outside our businesses, then an EDA is the complete array of architectural elements, including design, planning, technology, organization, and so on, which enables the ability to disseminate the event immediately to all interested parties, human or automated. The EDA also provides the basis for interested parties to "evaluate the event, and optionally take action."

The reason that EDA is a challenging concept is that it is so potentially broad. Just as almost any piece of data, analog or digital, can be an event, and any system in the universe can potentially be part of your EDA, where do you begin to draw the boundaries and definition of an EDA that makes sense to your organization? Though there is no bulletproof way to answer the question, we think that it makes sense to identify the main ingredients of an EDA, and build the definition from these constructs.

Event Producers or Publishers

To have an EDA, you must first have events. That might seem obvious, but a lot of otherwise sophisticated discussions of EDA either neglect or muddle up this central enabling concept. The EDA cannot work unless it has the ability to perceive that an event has occurred. For that to happen, the event must be created and then disseminated for consumption to EDA components called listeners (see next section) to "hear" them.

The technologies that do this are known as *event publishers* or *event producers*. With the broad definition of an event, event publishers can take many different forms. Most are software programs, though an event publisher can also be a dedicated piece of hardware that translates analog data into digital form and feeds it into software that can detect an event. You should keep the following core ideas in mind about event publishers.

Event publishers can be anywhere. Because events can occur outside of your enterprise, event publishers that relate to your EDA can be pretty much any place. Imagine the relationship between an airline EDA and the FAA radar tower. The radar tower, which serves many purposes, one of which is to be an event publisher, is completely separate from the airline's systems, yet it is part of the EDA.

Event publishers might or might not originate the data that is contained in the event itself. In their purest form, an event publisher generates a piece of data that is formatted to be "heard" as an event in accordance with the EDA's setup for this process. For example, a credit card processing system typically generates data that is EDA ready—it contains the card holder's identifiers, the time of the transaction, the amount, the merchant name, and so on. Of course, the data was created for the purpose of charging the card, not feeding the EDA, but it serves that purpose quite readily. In contrast, other event publishers need to translate data into a format that constitutes an event according to what the EDA requires. For example, there is no inherent event pattern in the Tokyo stock exchange index unless you specifically instruct an event publisher to transmit data about the index in a manner that makes sense to your EDA's purposes.

Event Listeners or Consumers

Like event publishers, event listeners can be anywhere. In theory, the event listener (or consumer) has a communication link with the event publishers. That is not always the case, but we will work under that assumption for now. The event listener is a piece of technology—typically software based, but also hardware—that "knows" how to differentiate an event, as it is defined, from other data it receives.

In the simplest form of EDA, the event listener can only receive the specific event data that it is meant to hear. For example, an EDA for building security might be based on a burglar alarm whose event listeners can only hear one kind of event—the kind created by a break-in. Window monitoring hardware will produce a break-in event in the occurrence of a breakage for the burglar alarm system to consume. The real world, of course, is more complex, and as we progress, we get into more involved EDA setups.

Event listeners also need to know what they are listening for. An application that reads the data stream of the Tokyo stock market average is not an event listener until it has been instructed to listen for some specific type of event. For instance, the event listener must know that a gain of 5% or more in the average is an event. A 4% gain is not an event. The event listener must be able to detect the event and be capable of interpreting the event. The criteria for interpretation are known as business rules.

Event Processors

After an event has occurred, and after the event has been published and consumed by an event listener, it must be processed. By processing, we mean determining the event's potential impact and value and deriving the next action to take. It does little good to have an event that is perceived, but not handled. An EDA without event processors is like the Tower of Babel—lots of event voices chattering at each other without interpretation yields nothing. An EDA should have the capacity to interpret the events it hears.

An event processor is invariably a piece of software. Although it might or might not be part of some larger, more comprehensive suite of applications, an event processor is distinctive because it has the ability to assess events, determine their importance, and generate a reaction of some kind, even if the reaction is "do nothing."

Event Reactions

Following our chain of activities, we have an event, which is published by an event producer, heard by an event listener, and processed by an event processor. Then, something (or nothing) needs to happen. Because "something happening" is inherently more interesting than "nothing happening," let's look at event reactions that require action.

Reactions to an event in an EDA vary widely, from automated application responses, to automated notifications sent either to applications or people, to purely human reactions based on business processes that occur outside of the EDA itself. In the purely automated application response category, we might see an EDA that reacts to an event by initiating an application-level process. For example, in the credit card fraud example, the EDA might modify a variable value from `Normal` to `Warning` based on an event that suggests that fraud is occurring. If this reaction is coded into the event reaction, it happens without any human involvement. Following this, another related branch of processes might handle new charge requests on the account differently based on a `Warning` value than it would in a Normal state. Event processors and reactions can be linked and interdependent.

The event reaction might be machine-to-human. Continuing with our example, imagine that there is a customer service representative who sees all the new `Warning` value changes and is prompted to call the cardholder to inquire about the status of their card. This approach to EDA is dependent on the human reaction to an event, a situation that might be good or bad, depending on the desired outcome. For example, many intrusion detection systems that monitor networks for unauthorized access attempts generate a great deal of false positives. Indeed, there are many intrusion detections that are not monitored at all. What these defectively implemented systems do is generate logs consisting of thousands of possible intrusion records, which are essentially useless. The takeaway here is that the human reaction might be very much part of the EDA design, even though it does not involve technology per se.

Finally, there are EDAs where the event reaction is based on an entirely human set of processes, following the detection and processing of the original event. For example, an EDA might generate a number of alerts that arise from a number of stock market indicators. An investor then reviews the alerts and decides whether to buy or sell. Once again, the EDA design must take into account the human reaction as part of its eventual success or failure. And, with this type of complex human decision making, it can be quite challenging to determine what the "right" reaction should be. Experts might differ on how to react to identical sets of event alerts. As they say on Wall Street, these differences of opinion make for a good horse race...

Messaging Backbone

The final core component of an EDA is the messaging backbone, the communication infrastructure—inclusive of hardware, software, network protocols, and message formats—that enables each piece of the EDA to communicate with one another. To serve an EDA effectively, a messaging backbone must have several characteristics. These characteristics are explored in great detail throughout the rest of the book, but for now, at a high level, let's use the following baseline to describe an optimal EDA messaging backbone.

The EDA messaging backbone does not necessarily have to be one single piece of infrastructure. Rather, the backbone refers to the ability of any number of separate pieces of messaging infrastructure to exchange messages using either common message transports or translators. For the purposes of illustration and simplicity, the backbone is shown in the illustrations in this book as a single connector, though the messaging backbone in real life might comprise many different pieces.

An EDA messaging backbone needs to be as near to universal as possible, meaning that it should enable messaging across multiple network transport protocols and data formats. In other words, it should be standards based, or have the ability to mediate across multiple messaging standards. It should be pervasive, that is, far-reaching and universally accessible. In reality, this means that it might be based on the Internet for EDAs that span multiple enterprises or on an IP-based corporate network for EDAs that exist within a single enterprise. It should be

highly reliable and inexpensive to develop, maintain, and modify—
which is, perhaps, a lot easier said than done, but this is a critical. Cost is
the "invisible hand" that has killed many great EDA initiatives. Finally, it
should enable a high level of decoupling between event producers and
event consumers. In reality, this usually translates into a *publish/sub-
scribe* or *pub/sub* setup.

The messaging backbone is arguably the most essential piece of the
EDA puzzle, for without it, there can be no EDA. Without the ability to
communicate, the event listeners, producers, processors, or reaction
processes, cannot work. Now, you might be thinking, "Yes, of course they
can—you can always create communication interfaces between systems." Of course, this has been true for many years. The reality, though,
is that proprietary interfaces, which have been the traditional way to
achieve connections, are costly to develop, maintain, and modify. So
costly, in fact, that they have rendered the concept of a dynamic EDA
virtually impossible to realize. This is now changing, and this shift is discussed in great detail throughout the book.

Assembling the Paradigmatic EDA

To get to the paradigmatic EDA—the one we use as the reference point
for the rest of this book—involves connecting event producers, event listeners, event processors, and event reactions using a common messaging
backbone. Figure 1.1 shows what this looks like in the plainest terms.
Obviously, things can get wildly more complex in real life, but it is best to
start with a very stripped-down paradigm example.

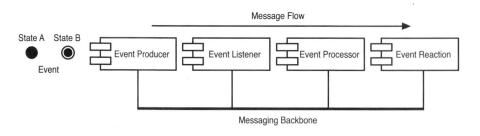

Figure 1.1   The paradigmatic EDA—consisting of event producer, event listener,
event processor, and event reaction, all connected through a unified messaging
backbone.

Like our "enterprise nervous system" that we discussed in the Introduction, the EDA works as a whole, taking in signal inputs in the form of event data, processing it, and reacting to it based on some kind of intelligent model. Like the nerve endings that tell us when we are hot or cold, being touched, or falling through the air, event listeners in the EDA quantify information from the world and order it into a form that the EDA can understand. The messaging backbone of the EDA is like the nerve cells themselves, transmitting signals back and forth from various places in the body and toward the brain. The brain is like the EDA's event processing components. It takes in event data and decides how to respond to it. The event reaction components are like our limbs. Based on the input, we take action, or not.

The Flavors of EDA

There's an old joke about Las Vegas, where a guy wants to be seated at a restaurant and is asked, "Which section would you prefer, smoking or chain smoking?" EDA is the same. Almost every type of computer system has some degree of event orientation in it. After all, computing is essentially a matter of input, processing, and output, much like an EDA. Following from this, discussions of what an EDA actually looks like can be confusing because they tend to get overly broad and encompass, well, just about everything in the IT universe. To keep our focus, let's look at several prime models of EDA that are in use today.

Dr. Manas Deb, a thought-leader in the Oracle Fusion and middleware space, once suggested that there are two essential types of EDA: explicit and implicit. In an explicit EDA, the event publishers send event data to known event listeners, perhaps even by direct hard-coding of the event listener destination right into the event producer. Many current implementations of EDA are either partly or wholly explicit. As such, they tend to rely on tight coupling of event producers and event listeners.

In contrast, an implicit EDA does not specify any dedicated connections between event producers and event listeners. The event listeners, or the event processors even, may determine the events to which they want to listen. The coupling between the event producers and listeners will be loose, or even completely decoupled in an implicit EDA. As you might imagine, an implicit EDA is more flexible and dynamic than an explicit EDA. Historically, they have proved too complex to implement. This has changed with the advent and adoption of open standards.

Of the two types, the implicit EDA is more agile; however, that agility comes with a price. As we implicitly process events, it becomes difficult to predict the outcome and monitor the success. For example, this form would not be ideal for processing multiphase transactions because the atomicity cannot be guaranteed due to the implicit processing—that is, the unknown processor of the state change can make it harder to understand or validate the origin of the state change.

Within EDAs themselves, there are three basic patterns of event processing: simple event processing, event stream processing, and complex event processing, which is known as CEP. In simple event processing, the EDA is quite narrow and simple. The event producer's function is to generate event data and send it to the event listener, which, in turn, processes it in whatever manner is required. The thermostat example is emblematic of a simple event processing design. The furnace gets the signal and switches on or off, and that's about it.

Event stream processing involves event processors receiving a number of signals from event producers (via the event listeners) but only reacting when certain criteria are met. For example, the thermometer might send the temperature data every two seconds, but the event processor (thermostat) ignores all but the relevant "switch on" data point, which activates the furnace only when it is observed.

Complex event processing (CEP) takes the EDA to another level, enabling it to react to multiple events under multiple logical conditions. So, for the sake of argument, let's say that we only want to buy U.S. Treasury bonds when the Nikkei hits a certain number, and unemployment figures dip below 5%. The CEP listens to multiple event streams, and knows how to correlate them in a logical manner according to the objectives of the EDA. In other words, the CEP starts to "think" like a person, taking in data from unrelated sources on the fly, differentiating between useful and useless information, and acting accordingly. This is the ideal of the complex, implicit, dynamic EDA.

In another example, complex event processing can also be instructed to do, in essence, the reverse of the previous example—meaning the processor could be instructed to determine the events that caused a particular outcome. In this case, the processor monitors for a particular outcome then derives the causality of the event or event sequence that created the desired event. This is highly valuable in proving hypothetical situations through simulation.

Without going too far off subject, we want to point out here that there is a natural match between CEP and artificial intelligence (AI). AI systems have the capacity to recognize patterns of information and suggest reactions to patterns of events. Later in the book, we delve into this under the rubric of business rules and automation of corporate decision making using CEP.

EDA Then, Now, and in the Future

Older EDAs have typically been event-stream or simple-event oriented and reliant on explicit or nearly explicit designs. Complex event processing, married with implicit capabilities, is really what most people mean when they talk about modern or futuristic EDAs. When you hear someone talk about how, for example, the Department of Homeland Security should be able to instantly know that John Smith, who has bought a one-way ticket for cash, has a fingerprint that matches that of a known criminal based on records kept in Scotland Yard—we are talking about an implicit CEP EDA.

This last example highlights why people are so interested in EDA. The paradigm has the potential to serve many business and organizational needs that are now unmet with existing enterprise architecture. The pressure to build EDAs comes from a desire to bring together information from disparate and unpredictable sources and process it in intelligent ways—even if the information is not in digital form at its creation. In business, the desired result might be agility, or improved profitability. In government, the goal might be tighter security or improved knowledge of the economy.

In addition, the EDAs that everyone seems to want are not only CEP based and implicit, but also highly malleable and dynamic. The world is not static, so EDAs can never stand still. It seems like a lot of hoops for an architectural paradigm to jump through, but the demand for the capability is quite real and the value that an EDA can realize is not hard to discern. However, we are not quite there yet. Though the future is looking pretty bright for complex, implicit, dynamic EDAs, a few enormous challenges exist, mostly residing in the world of system interoperation and integration, the gating technological factors of EDA.

The (Not So Smooth) Path to EDA

Years ago, one of us got profoundly lost while on vacation in the tropics. Driving a rented Jeep, he pulled into a small village and asked someone how to get to the rental cottage on the other side of the island. The local man gave him a funny look and said, "You can't get there in a vehicle." That concept, of being stuck in a place from which you can't get to your desired destination, should resonate with anyone who has contemplated transitioning an existing set of systems into an EDA or building one from scratch.

Taking a huge step back to gain perspective, let's identify the one architectural feature that you need to have an EDA. That feature is interoperability. Interoperability—the sum total of software and hardware that enables applications, systems, machines, and networks to connect with one another and communicate productively—is either an inhibitor or enabler of EDA. Without simple, cost-effective interoperability, there simply cannot be any EDA. Or, at least, there cannot be the kind of dynamic, implicit, complex EDA that we want now and in the future.

Given that EDAs are utterly reliant on interoperation between systems to work, we need to know where we, as architects, stand in the realm of interoperation. We must have a good grasp of how we have progressed (and not progressed) in the whole endeavor. To get started, we need to first agree on where we are now. That way, when we hear that we "can't get there from here," we will know that it is likely an untrue statement. There is always a way to get from here to there. It's all about knowing what path to take and how to move yourself.

We often tell our children, "Don't cry over spilled milk." In enterprise architecture, we should take that sentiment to heart. If your enterprise is anything like the ones we've seen in our 50 years combined experience, it's not quite spilled milk in that data center. It's more like a dairy that got hit by a tornado. You're drowning in spilled milk—and, you probably weren't the one who did the spilling. That guy is playing golf at a retirement community in Tucson while you tear your hair out.

Don't blame him, though. The current state of enterprise IT is not anyone's fault, and that's kind of the problem. Most of us are coping with the legacy, in the broadest sense of the term, of years of poorly thought through decisions and imperfect management. A lot of smart people made the best choices they could under the circumstances they were in at the time. We are living in the misshapen structures that their architecture afforded them. We call this *accidental architecture*, and it's all around us.

To illustrate accidental architecture, take the example of a phone company. As shown in Figure 1.2, this highly simplified phone company has three groups of systems, one for each of its core areas of operation: order management, line management (the provisioning and management of phone lines and service), and billing. At some point in the primordial past, the architecture of the phone company looked something like this. The order management systems connected with customized clients used in call centers and branch outlets. The order management systems connected with a service center and field service terminals used by traveling line installation personnel. The billing system connected with call centers, print server farms, and data entry terminals. In the dark ages when these systems were created, transfers of data from one system to another were either manual or completely hardwired. An order for phone service would be entered in the order system, but the request for phone service would be sent to the line management system and its personnel in a paper form. A hardwired connection transferred line use data to the billing system for output of printed phone bills.

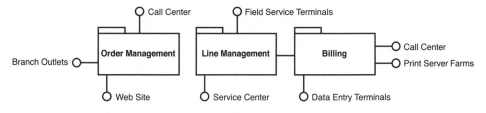

Figure 1.2 The original architecture of a phone company, which consisted of three separate sets of systems for order management, line management, and billing.

In the enterprise architecture shown in Figure 1.2, it made little difference how each group of systems was developed or configured. Each group could run using operating systems, programming languages, or message formats that were completely incompatible with the others. There is nothing inherently wrong with this kind of setup, either. It's just a nuisance when you want information or procedures from one group to be available with another. That's interoperation.

The milk got spilled when well-meaning IT people used the best tools and knowledge at their disposal to try and get such separate, incompatible systems to work together. Before we get into the mechanics of how interoperation has worked traditionally, and the reasons it can cause difficulty for IT today, we want to first go over the drivers of interoperability. After all, interoperability and its various clumsy incarnations over the years have all been done in the name of serving business needs.

Defining Interoperability

We say we want interoperability. Okay, but what is it, exactly? At its essence, interoperability is just what its name implies. It's two or more systems performing an operation together. If you and a friend pick up a heavy box together, you are interoperating. Both of your efforts are needed to lift the box. The reason we go over this seemingly obvious explanation is because interoperation in IT is often confused with integration.

For many of us, there is no distinction between interoperation and integration. The two concepts are often linked, and deeply related. However, we like to differentiate between the two because understanding how EDA components such as event listeners and event processors work together becomes easier when the two ideas are treated separately.

Interoperation means making two or more systems communicate or exchange information together, whether or not the systems are connected by any dedicated integration interfaces. In contrast, integration is a scenario where two or more systems are linked by a software interface that bridges the two systems. Integration is the technically specific means of getting two applications to connect, whereas interoperation is the broader scope view of the entire situation. To relate it to a real-world parallel, think about the difference between driving a car and taking a vacation. Of course, you might drive a car to take your vacation. Yet, there is far more to the trip than just sticking the key into the ignition and turning the steering wheel. To go on vacation, you need to know where you are going, why you want to go there, how to get there, and so on. In enterprise architecture, interoperation is the complete set of business and technology factors that make two applications come together. Integration is the conventional, but not exclusive means to that end. In essence, integration can be thought of as "interoperability by any means necessary."

Figure 1.3 shows a basic point-to-point interoperation scenario at the phone company. For reasons that we explore in the next section, the company finds it necessary to make the order management, line management, and billing systems work together to accomplish specific business functions. There already was one point-to-point interface between the line management and billing systems, but the company wants more connections to serve more business needs. The specific ways that the interoperation is achieved might involve application-to-application connections, network connections, physical connections, user interfaces, database updating, and so on.

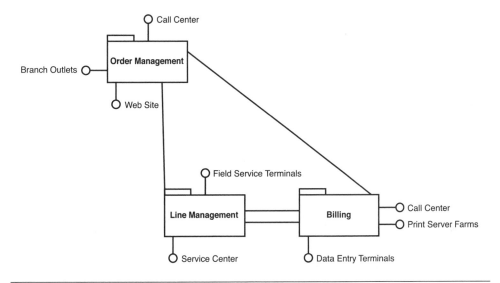

Figure 1.3 Interoperation results from a business requirement for two or more systems to exchange data or procedure calls. In this case, the order management system must connect with the line management and billing systems. This is a classic point-to-point style of interoperation.

Interoperation—A Basic Definition

A situation where two or more software components must work together to perform a function. Usually, interoperation involves two or more software applications exchanging data, processing those inputs, and sharing outputs with one or more applications.

Drivers of Interoperability

Having a discussion about interoperability issues in IT can often feel like walking in on a movie halfway through. You kind of understand why Mel Gibson is slapping the perp around, but you missed the part where he took the bribe.... In all of our nerdy ruminations about architecture, we often forget a core truth: IT systems and solutions we develop for interoperability all serve some kind of business objective. "Of course," you say. "That's obvious." Yes, it is, but interoperation can get so complex that it becomes its own topic, evolving in its own separate domain.

Although there are myriad reasons why IT needs to get systems to interoperate, we find that there are two essential groups of business requirements that drive the need for interoperability. **Business functional requirements** are a major driver of interoperation between systems. Business functional requirements are business situations that demand that two or more systems or applications work together to achieve a business objective. In the phone company example, a goal of providing real-time access to any customer account activity, whether it is related to a new order, a billing problem, or a service problem, necessitates interoperation between multiple separate and incompatible systems.

The second driver of interoperation is what we call **business extension**. Business extension is a situation where management wants to take advantage of data or system functionality to increase the scope of services offered or drive sales growth. For example, the phone company in our example might want to conduct telemarketing of cell phone plans to its landline customers. To attain an optimal marketing result on an ongoing basis, it would make sense for the telemarketers to be able to update the landline account holders' records with their marketing activities. Assuming the telemarketers were using the order management system as their basis of interacting with customers, the requirement to have the telemarketers update landline customer records—who was called, whether they wanted cell service, and so forth—could result in a requirement for interoperation between the order management and line management systems.

Classic solutions to these requirements are in the form of an abstraction layer—either product-based or custom—that pulls information from (and populates) a shared data store. These solutions are typically specific to a given business function and might not provide the generic interoperability required for long-term agility in an enterprise or product environment.

Application Integration: A Means to Interoperate

There is no law of nature that commands us to integrate systems that need to interoperate. We could always rebuild everything and achieve interoperation by smashing separate systems into one, new, unified system. Although that is sometimes the best path to take, it is usually not the one we choose because it is too costly and time consuming. Thus, short of unifying the systems through a significant rebuild effort, some forward-thinking IT organizations defined enterprise integration strategies to allow applications and systems to share data and functionality to better meet the needs of the business community. Historically, such strategies were built around vendor-based enterprise application integration (EAI) suites, also known as *middleware*. Figure 1.4 shows a basic middleware component that connects the order management, line management, and billing systems in our phone company example.

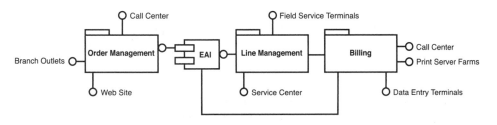

Figure 1.4 Integration typically involves the use of middleware, as shown by the enterprise application integration (EAI) module that connects the order management, line management, and billing systems at the phone company. The EAI approach contrasts with the point-to-point approach shown in Figure 1.3.

Middleware introduced an isolation tier to buffer the application changes from the integration logic. Typically message-bus based, this form of integration led to the idea of loosely coupled composite systems. The concept was simple, but initially the effort associated with bus-enabling an application proved to be difficult. Developers had to have in-depth knowledge of the target system to build bus connectors, just as they did for case-specific interfaces. Middleware vendors recognized the drawback, and in an effort to promote adoption, built application connectors to give their customers a cheaper alternative to hand-coding connectors. Of course, buying prebuilt connectors meant buying the vendor's middleware software, and although often cheaper initially than building from scratch, this investment led to long-term business constraints, including limited ability to upgrade or modify applications, insurmountable connector functionality restrictions, and classic vendor lock in. Figure 1.5 shows these adapters and connections in a perhaps more realistic version of what Figure 1.4 presents.

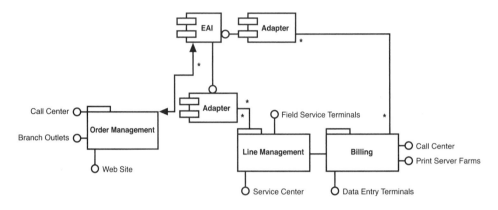

Figure 1.5   In reality, integration using middleware such as EAI tends to involve the purchase and maintenance of adapters, which can become costly and time consuming.

Integrating a middleware suite has typically required deep pockets and willingness to endure significant technical difficulty and organizational fallout. It is unfortunate, but the pain associated with incorporating these middleware suites into an enterprise architecture has prejudiced many technical managers against today's integration suites, including those based on industry standards (like the Java 2 Enterprise Edition [J2EE] Connector Architecture) and including frameworks that implement common integration design patterns.

To understand how complex and costly EAI can get, look at Figure 1.6, which represents a classic "islands of integration" problem. As is often the case, especially in companies with highly autonomous divisions or postmerger situations, there might be multiple EAI vendors in place in the enterprise architecture. Each EAI suite requires its own adapters to connect to each system. Thus, in the example shown in Figure 1.6, connecting the order management system to the line management system requires the use of an adapter from Vendor B, while connecting that same system to the billing system requires one from Vendor A. License and maintenance fees can add up quickly in this scenario, but the biggest cause of trouble is usually the personnel required to keep it all going and scheduling lags caused by multiple layers of integration and testing.

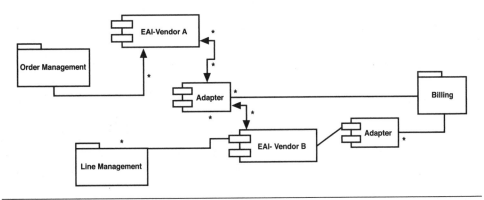

Figure 1.6   In many cases, especially in the wake of a merger, an enterprise architect might have to contend with multiple EAI vendors, with an increasing number of adapters required for integration.

The kind of situation shown in Figure 1.6 is quite common, and it is generally referred to as a *tightly coupled* architecture. The applications are bound with one another tightly, and making changes can be costly and time consuming. As a result, the expensive and painful lesson learned by many technical managers and architects is that banking an enterprise integration strategy on a proprietary vendor product can show a very small, if any, return on investment (ROI), and can ultimately limit the agility of an architecture.

Interoperation and Business Process Management

As integration strategies evolved to include process integration, middleware vendor software suites began to include business process management (BPM) or workflow-oriented integration. Promoting the idea that integration is driven by the business processes, these packages provided a better way to think about combining system functionality. However, as the sophistication of each integration approach increased, the complexity introduced also increased. The increased complexity required more implementation time and resources with a high skill level.

As Figure 1.7 shows, it is possible with certain EAI suites to map business process steps to the specific IT system that supports that step. The process shown in the figure is deliberately blank—we have shown it to get across the general concept. If it helps, you could imagine the process describes how to open a cell phone account as an add-on to a landline account, for example. The process touches each of the company's major systems.

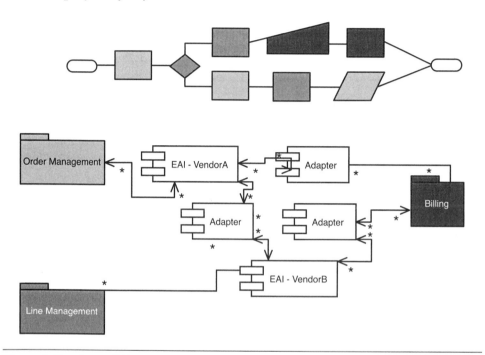

Figure 1.7   Some EAI suites include a business process modeling function, which enables a business analyst to map business process steps to IT systems. The respective shading of each process step reflects the system that supports it.

Business process modeling tools and technologies are helpful because they enable businesspeople and IT people to come together with a common communication vehicle that helps lay out specific requirements and solve business issues in ways that are often more streamlined than conventional discovery and requirement iterations. The added complexity that adding BPM to EAI creates, though, can drive cost and delays to an unsustainable pitch.

Ultimately, costs for such configurations increased to the point where leveraging existing components (reuse) became a priority. Relying on reuse to decrease implementation time is a valid approach, but without clearly identified techniques (like those introduced by SOA and EDA) is a pipe dream.

What Your COO Is Thinking

Your COO probably has a big jar of aspirin sitting on his or her desk waiting for those times when you come in to explain the IT organization's lack of agility. The irony of the situation is that the BPM tools that you deployed in Figure 1.6 were meant to ameliorate these tensions. And perhaps they did. If they did not, you might have some explaining to do. Unfortunately, IT tends to get blamed for being slow in scenarios where business process modeling is meant to speed up the pace of IT fulfillment of changing business requirements. What you might need to explain to the COO is that BPM only works if everyone can dance to the same tune: The business managers need to understand what their business processes actually are (which they might not). They need to agree among themselves, and disparate business units, about who does what, how it works, and who is in charge (also rare), and they must have a good understanding of the dependencies between IT and BPM. That understanding must be documented and modeled so it can be made repeatable or even automated. In turn, the IT people need to have a similarly broad knowledge of the relationship between business processes, IT systems, and their interoperation. If all of these conditions are met, the BPM approach can work well. However, as your COO might learn, it often doesn't work, and it is usually an organizational or even interpersonal problem at its core.

All of this brings us back to our spilled milk scenario. The unplanned growth in information systems and IT organizations in the '90s and the tactical, short-term-focused culture of this decade have combined today to create a consistent situation among enterprises of any meaningful scope: multiple disparate systems in various production environments supporting an organization's business goals. The sharing of data and functionality between applications might be today's primary technical architectural challenge for IT groups. The default solution for interoperability is often a point-to-point implementation optimized for a particular case; application teams seldom have the appropriate authority to define an overarching solution for more than the case at hand. The problem is that without an application interoperability strategy, point-to-point integration is often the standard and the coordination of decisions and processes across an enterprise becomes unmanageable over time.

Figure 1.8 shows what a lot of enterprises have come to resemble over the years. Integration between systems is excessively complex and poorly governed. Dependencies between systems that interoperate are either unknown, invisible, or very challenging to modify—resulting in a situation where something will always get "broken" when the IT department attempts to change system architecture in response to shifting business requirements.

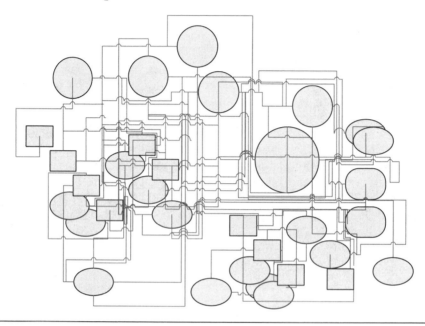

Figure 1.8 For many organizations, years of expedient point-to-point integration and heterogeneous EAI approaches has resulted in the "spaghetti" scenario depicted here. Complex integration and dependencies between systems makes it very costly and time consuming to change interoperation.

The bottom line with the spaghetti approach is that it wreaks havoc on agility and the potential for a complex, dynamic EDA. Business needs requiring visibility or coordination between disparate systems become more difficult (and more costly) to meet. As a result, a general dissatisfaction with IT groups abounds in the business community. Business managers grow frustrated with IT for being "slow," and IT gets stressed with business clients who seem to change their plans too much. Those tasked with managing all the interfaces that connect the pieces together get weary of the constant struggle to keep it all running right as unfinished changes pile up in queue. This hinders developing new revenue opportunities ultimately limiting business growth.

Is There a Diet for All This Spaghetti?

We have all probably wished at one point or another for some kind of IT version of the ultra low-carb diet that will forever banish spaghetti from our lives. If only such a thing existed. What we have actually found, though, is that a lot of us can't even articulate what it is we would want in its place. To set the stage for the rest of the book, then, let's try to think about what an ideal enterprise architecture might look like.

If you've ever looked at a personal ad, you've probably seen how picky people can be about a potential mate. Everyone is looking for that magic someone: tall, handsome, nonsmoker, football fan who loves his mother but not too much...right? Maybe that's crazy, but in our situation, we think it is healthy to dream about what IT could actually be like if things were different. How would your enterprise architecture "personal ad" read?

If it were up to us, our personal ad might say something like:

"**Seeking**: An enterprise architecture that's flexible; highly performant; adapts to changes easily, cheaply, and quickly; enables access to data in near-real-time; enables agility; can scale without pain; and doesn't require maintenance overhead that breaks the bank. Availability, resilience, security, supportability, testability required. 'High maintenance' is a turn off."

Whew, talk about picky! To put it succinctly, to get to the EDA we want, we ought to be looking for enterprise architecture solutions that are *flexible* and cost effective to change. The big challenge for most of us, though, is to understand the underlying architectural, technological, and organizational factors that have to come together to realize the level of flexibility and cost effectiveness we desire.

To relate flexibility and cost effectiveness to a concept that your line-of-business clients might understand, it might help to think in terms of business agility. As we mentioned in the preface to the book, agility is the lifeblood of business management today. Executives are preoccupied with being able to make strategic and operational changes to suit their shifting management objectives. As your IT architecture becomes more flexible and cost effective to maintain and change, you will be more able to enable agility than you are in your current spaghetti state.

Just how we get to that state of flexibility is a matter of lengthy discussion throughout the book. But, at least now we know what we want. We might never be swept off our feet by Prince Charming of the IT world, vendor pledges of eternal love notwithstanding. Yet, the exercise of thinking out loud about what we want is educational because it gives us a baseline of requirements against which we can measure proposed solutions and approaches to enterprise architecture. The process can also guide us as we think about designing and updating our existing architecture.

The important takeaway here is that any future architecture plan for EDA should ideally be matched up with this idea of flexibility and cost effectiveness before it is put into action. You might think, "Of course—this is so obvious," but if you take a look around your department, you will probably see quickly that it hasn't been so obvious to everyone. Or, to be fair, the technologies just haven't been available to make it all work. The first important step to take, though, is to understand how to assess the myriad underlying factors that come into play in discovering the optimal architectural state for an enterprise.

For purpose of focus, we concentrate on IT governance, policy definition and enforcement, system development life cycle, business process modeling, and standards. Though these factors might seem to be a layer removed from the goals of flexibility and cost effectiveness, they are, in fact, the foundations of these capabilities. Although we can say with confidence that the SOA approach and the EDA implementation of SOA are the paradigms most able to deliver the optimal architecture, the path that will make an SOA/EDA right for your enterprise will depend on how underlying factors relate to the unique circumstances of your enterprise.

For example, you cannot attain a state of agile application integration if you have not tackled IT governance. If your systems are poorly governed, or governed by an inappropriate set of policies, people, and organizational structures, it will be difficult to modify systems and their interoperation with any flexibility or cost effectiveness. Only you will understand how this relates to your specific situation.

Continuing on this thread, the system development life cycle must take interoperation into account throughout its entire process chain. Otherwise, attempts to introduce new systems, integrate existing ones, or make changes to integrations will experience delays and uncertainty (translating into costly problems). Business process modeling is a basic necessity for getting to a state of flexible, cost-effective enterprise architecture. There has to be a way for business and technology stakeholders to communicate with one another and map requirements to IT assets.

Finally, standards are the glue that holds it all together. Governing enterprise architectures should include adherence to the standards adopted by the enterprise so that the EDA model can evolve unencumbered. To be flexible and cost effective, an enterprise architecture must evolve based on standards, or at the very least have the ability to be tolerant of differences in the capabilities of its constituents to mediate and resolve impedances between systems with differing standards.

How Architecture Promotes Integration

The remainder of this book is devoted to showing you, through a mixture of theory and practice, how to move from where you are now (we guess in the spaghetti bowl) toward an EDA, using the SOA approach. With that goal in mind, we now turn to a theme that will recur through the rest of the book: the need for a unified architecture planning process to ensure progress toward the objectives of SOA and EDA as they best suit your enterprise needs.

It's important to understand that interoperability between applications and components is difficult to achieve without overarching, uniform technical direction. With the assessment of our underlying factors in mind, there are some things that your application groups can do now to promote interoperability before your formal strategy is in place. Your application group needs to define coarsely grained, cohesive interfaces (service-based integration). If the predicted evolution includes interaction with other systems, interfaces should be designed to support that direction. Some of these steps in the right direction will become clear to you as you read this book.

Regardless of the interoperability mechanism(s) available to you in your architecture, building your systems with interoperability in mind from the start is the easiest way to achieve long-term system integration. Of course, few of us have the luxury of starting with a blank slate because most enterprises rely on proprietary or homegrown legacy business-critical systems. Unfortunately, interoperability is one of the more difficult things to add to an existing architecture (hence the popularity of middleware solutions).

So how can we tailor our application and system design activities to promote long-term interoperability? As is often the case, the first thing we need is a plan. An effective enterprise interoperability and integration strategy is typically the result of a joint effort between the technical and business architects in your organization. It is the job of the technical leadership in an organization to understand how new and existing systems or products will evolve over time, based on their understanding of both market trends and emerging technology. Understanding this predicted evolution will help you determine the appropriate structure of your system, whether it should be service-oriented and/or event-driven, whether it will leverage enterprise service bus (ESB) technology, whether it should support dynamic discovery of services, whether it must leverage Java Connector Architecture (JCA)-based (or other) integration technology, how the architecture will be monitored and governed, and the like.

The questions of how services and components will be governed and managed and what interface requirements each new component or application will need to meet—such as what policies should be applied to Web Services Description Language documents (WSDLs) or interfaces, what test cases must be applied per interface, and so on—are typically in the domain of the technical architect. These details can be defined after the overall strategy is defined.

This book strives to clear up the confusion associated with defining an optimal strategy for your case. If your organization is like most, your physical infrastructure maps closely to your organizational layout. In an organization with many silos, systems in a single silo are tightly coupled and heavily interdependent, and the level of reliability, maintainability, and extensibility varies widely between silos. When systems need to interoperate across silos, integration is achieved on a case-by-case basis. Alternatively, if your organization is matrixed or "flat," every system might be independent of the others, with integration techniques defined and applied for specific endpoints. In both cases, business logic is buried deep inside of the applications and exposed only on a case-by-case basis to other applications. Interestingly, this holds true for large software product companies as well. You'll notice vendor products sold as consolidated suites that might not share underlying frameworks—usually the result of disparate development teams building the products in a given suite or platform.

In either case, defining a service-oriented architecture requires overarching technical direction and visibility into the multiple silos or application groups as well as a good understanding of the business needs per group. If your organization falls into either category and does not have an enterprise architecture team, you have your work cut out for you. Achieving an elegant enterprise architecture environment through grassroots activity across a large organization can be done, but takes an inordinate amount of time and relies on the goodwill of key people in the right places. In either case, applying SOA principles in the context of a business solution is a necessary step in the journey to enterprisewide SOA and achieving the promise of an EDA. Applying SOA scoped to a specific business problem, distributing your work, and evangelizing the methods will go a long way toward defining a cross-functional strategy. Ultimately, it's far better to aim for a business-driven, solution-specific SOA rather than one that mirrors a siloed approach to IT. Much of one's success or failure in this area depends on the way that the EDA/SOA is managed and governed.

Management and Governance

You will hear references to the process and organizational impact of defining an SOA. The impact is felt in a number of ways, but most painfully in the world of management and governance. Later in this book, we look at specific examples of management and governance issues, but for now we consider them at a high level. Good governance is about applying the minimal set of constraints required to encourage the desired behavior required for a targeted business outcome or regulatory requirement. Management and governance pose the biggest challenge for organizations planning to implement an SOA-based EDA, mainly because of the changes that might be required to the existing development processes. Before we talk about the challenges, let's describe what managing and governing an SOA can entail.

What Your COO Is Thinking

Governance is one of those classic words in business—constantly used, constantly misunderstood. The problem is that *governance* can mean many different things. It can even have multiple definitions for people in the same field. As a result, there can be great confusion about governance. We recommend taking the time to define governance in the context you intend to use it, regardless of how much you think other stakeholders understand it. For your COO, or top IT business partner, governance might have an instant connotation of corporate boards and "governing" the entity known as your corporation. This is the province of bylaws and shareholders, not IT. IT governance, in general, refers to the rules that the corporation sets out to govern the IT function at the business. Your COO might assume you are talking about the organizational structure and accountability of the IT function to the board of directors when you discuss governance with him or her. Alternatively, the COO might think you are talking about Information Security Governance, which typically involves a board-level commitment to securing the information assets of the business. However, in this book, we are concentrating on the "none of the above" governance, which is the way that the business governs the systems it uses to accomplish its business mission. You might need to explain this to the COO so he or she can get where you are coming from. Governance, in the SOA/EDA context, is a body of policies, standards, technological setups, and organizational rules that enable IT systems to make the business run the way it is meant to, while allowing the IT environment to evolve and function optimally.

The term governance is commonly used to define "...the processes and systems by which an organization or society operates."[1]

Information technology governance (or IT governance) is a subset discipline of corporate governance focused on information technology systems and their performance and risk management. Weill and Ross have further refined this definition as follows: "Specifying the *decision rights and accountability framework* to *encourage desirable behavior* in the use of IT."

In contrast, the IT Governance Institute expands the definition to include underpinning mechanisms: "...the leadership and *organizational structures and processes* that ensure that the organization's IT *sustains and extends* the organization's *strategies and objectives*."

Accordingly, SOA Governance can be thought of as

- A *decision rights and accountability framework*
- Specifying a set of *domain-specific extensions* to commonly utilized IT governance methodologies (such as Information Technology Infrastructure Library [ITIL], Control Objectives for Information and Related Technology [COBIT], COSO [from the Committee of Sponsoring Organizations of the Treadway Commission], and so on)

SOA governance is most effective when

- The decision rights and accountability framework is combined with the *effective operationalization of processes and supporting systems*.
- It is required to *encourage the desirable behavior of participating constituents* in the use of IT-enabled capabilities in a service-oriented enterprise environment.

In short, we can describe SOA governance as

- The models and structures we use to *create balance between constituent needs* typically satisfied by an SOA CoE (Center-of-Excellence)
- The mechanisms utilized to achieve *visibility and coordination* typically satisfied by an Integrated SOA Governance Automation solution
- The key decisions we *make, record, and (in some cases) digitally execute* in support of the guiding principles for an IT organization in the form of plan-time, design-time, change-time, and run-time policies

Additionally, SOA governance systems would be expected to support the end-to-end life cycle of an SOA—including planning, analysis, design, construction, change, and retirement of services—combined with the requisite mechanisms (processes, systems, and infrastructure) that support the definition, negotiation, mediation, validation, administration, enforcement, control, observation, auditing, optimization, and evolution of policies and service contracts in an SOA environment.

Whereas service contacts represent the scope of a contextual binding between the constituents leveraging a set of capabilities in an SOA environment, the policies represent the constraints (or checks and balances) governing the relationships, interactions, and best interests (or motivations and incentives for behavioral change) of the participating constituents, processes, and systems.

Governance of an SOA/EDA includes the definition and enforcement of policies and best practices. The definition of best practices can be achieved through the creation of templates, design patterns, common or shared components, semantic guidelines, and the like. Enforcing the usage of these practices, often a step toward measuring compliance, can be achieved through the definition of policies that are applied to services as they are designed, developed, and deployed. Governance toolsets may have their own method of defining a policy (typically through the use of assertions to be applied to WSDLs at various stages of the development process), or you could create your own through an assertion-based policy definition and application approach (not recommended). In any case, a governance vehicle of some sort should be defined as part of your SOA strategy, and this typically involves an architecture team responsible for defining best practices and policies.

After teams or individuals are assigned responsibility for best-practice definition and ongoing governance of the services, your software deployment process must adapt to include the application of policies to the services developed by your application teams. In other words, a review process, preferably a programmatic review, must be executed to ensure conformance to the policies set by your design team.

Management of an SOA includes a number of things: registries in which services can be referenced, service brokers or buses, service-level monitors, intermediaries or agents to support the abstraction of non-functional or enterprise concerns from the application layer, directory servers, and the like. Vendors offer product suites with all or many of these components for management of an SOA, but as mentioned earlier, applying any solution requires careful architectural design, definition of optimization goals, and clear assignment of responsibility and ownership. Managing an SOA is just as complex as a network management solution or a systems monitoring.

To summarize, the primary differences between management and governance of an SOA can be viewed as follows: SOA management focuses on whether the systems and processes (machines) in your SOA environment are behaving correctly relative to operational governance policies that have been specified. Are the machines behaving correctly? SOA governance focuses on whether the people, policies, processes, and metrics supporting the SOA program (people AND machines) are producing the desired business outcomes. Is the organization doing the right things? Both are important, and an integrated model tends to work best.

Chapter Summary

- The pursuit of event-driven architecture (EDA) brings into focus a tension between the goals of many IT organizations—including flexibility and EDA—and the realities of system interoperation, which must be solved to proceed to EDA.

- An EDA working definition is as follows: EDA is an approach to enterprise architecture that enables systems to hear events and react to them intelligently.

- An event is an occurrence, in either the digital or analog world, that is of interest to the EDA.

- For an EDA to work, it must be able to detect events and react to them. To do this, an EDA requires several components, including the following:

  - Event producers—software/hardware/logic that either generates event data or transforms it into a format that the EDA can understand

  - Event listeners—software/hardware/logic that can hear the event producer's output

  - Event processors—processor that interprets the events and generates responses, if one is required

  - Event reactions—entities that translate the event processor's response into an action; can be an application or a person

- EDAs can be either implicit or explicit. An explicit EDA is deliberately set up to process event data. In contrast, an implicit EDA may be based on a number of system elements that were not specifically designed to be an EDA. An implicit EDA is a great deal more dynamic and agile.

- There are three basic types of EDA processing:

  - Simple event processing—for example, a thermostat; the event leads to a direct action.

  - Event stream processing—the EDA must listen for specific event data and react.

  - Complex event processing (CEP)—the EDA hears events from multiple sources and processes them according to dynamic rule sets.

- When we talk about EDA today, we are really talking about modern, implicit, CEP EDAs. They offer the most potential for EDA, though they are the hardest to develop mostly because of constraints on system interoperability.

- Interoperability and integration are related concepts in IT that can cause confusion because they are commonly misunderstood. Although in the old days, systems might have existed in a state of isolation, today, it is necessary much of the time for one system to exchange data or function procedures with multiple other systems. This is known as interoperation, and it can be achieved through a variety of technological modes, including direct integration of systems. Integration is a type of interoperation that has each system with a specific, technological "hook" into another system or systems.

- There is nothing new about integration and interoperation. Over the years, most large enterprises have seen their systems connected by a multitude of technological approaches, including a direct point-to-point arrangement, as well as enterprise application integration (EAI) hubs and adapters that connect systems on a common platform. Though there is nothing inherently wrong with these approaches, they tend to result in complex, overly interdependent enterprise architectures that resemble spaghetti. Changing one element in such an environment can set off a chain reaction of related changes and modifications—a situation that slows down agility and adds costs to IT budgets.

- To get at a solution for the spaghetti problem, we establish objectives for an enterprise architecture that is both flexible and cost effective to maintain and change. The objectives are, in turn, supported by underlying factors that include IT governance, policy definition and enforcement, system development life cycle, business process modeling, and standards. We recommend an architectural approach to attaining SOA/EDA that is based on assessing your enterprise for its unique characteristics for these key underlying factors.

■ Overall, with the assumption that SOA/EDA is the approach to enterprise architecture that can deliver the desired flexibility and cost effectiveness (also known as business agility), in this chapter we begin to define how architecture can promote integration. Specifically, we begin a discussion of how an enterprise must identify and embrace a unified approach to planning and executing architecture design and subsequent implementations. This theme continues throughout the rest of the book.

Endnote

1. Michelson, Brenda. "Event Driven Architecture Overview." Paper published by Patricia Seybold Group (2/2/2006).

CHAPTER 2

SOA: The Building Blocks of EDA

Making You an Offer You Can't Understand

By now, you have a good general sense of what an EDA is, how it works, and what's getting in the way of its realization. The good news is that help is on the way. Service-oriented architecture (SOA), the broad move toward the use of standards for system integration, offers a true path to the kind of dynamic, implicit EDA that we seek. If our current enterprise architecture is the spilled milk, SOA is the "mop."

Of course, getting from here to there is not so easy. The whole subject of SOA brings to mind the classic joke about what you get when you cross a lawyer with a mob guy: someone who makes you an offer you can't understand… Yes, SOA is truly a breakthrough in terms of its raw potential to put EDA on the map.

It was challenging to develop an effective sequence for the material in this book. At first, we wanted to lay out absolutely everything there was to tell about EDA, and then go into detail on SOA and the implementation of EDA. However, after some reflection, we decided for the sake of overall comprehension to define EDA first, then look at SOA, and then go back to more subtle issues of EDA. Having already outlined the basics of EDA and its essential components, including event producers, event listeners, event processors, and so on, in this chapter, we now look at SOA, the actual approach that can be used to design these components. Chapter 3, "Characteristics of EDA," explores the characteristics of EDA, and Chapter 4, "The Potential of EDA," returns to the topic of SOA and looks at how SOA makes EDA happen in pragmatic detail. If you are already an expert on SOA, you might want to skim this chapter.

Our basic premise is that there cannot be EDA—at least the kind we want—without SOA, as it becomes an industry standard for interoperation. Of course, there are plenty of differing opinions on this, but we are, at the very least, pragmatists about this. There are a number of ways to develop EDA that are better than the current technological trend known as SOA, but let's be realistic: Those approaches are not getting the attention and installed base that SOA is getting. For this reason, we are going to work with the assumption that the EDA of the future will be built using SOA.

SOA: The Big Picture

Years ago, everyone seems to have agreed that enterprise architecture should be flexible and cost effective to change and maintain. The exact approach to getting to this state was far from obvious, and a number of attempts were made, all of which failed. Then, around 2000, as tech companies and industry groups watched the rapid growth of the Web, which is a human-to-machine interface, people wondered, "Why can't we do that for machine-to-machine interoperation as well?" The result was a remarkable agreement among a number of competing vendors to standardize on Extensible Markup Language (XML; and Simple Object Access Protocol [SOAP] XML in particular) for application integration. These were known as the Web services standards, the enablers of a service-oriented architecture.

Ignoring the hype, and there is plenty of that, SOA does provide the flexible, low-cost capability that we want in our enterprises, the architecture upon which we can build EDAs. SOA is based on the premise of universal interoperability among software components, regardless of operating system, programming language, or network proximity. As we move forward in this chapter, we look at how standards enable this universal interoperability, and the ways in which the standards pave the way for the creation of EDA components. To start, we first define what we mean by *service*, a concept that is poorly understood.

Defining Service

The SOA field is plagued with suboptimal name tags for simple technologies. *Web service* sounds suspiciously like an Internet service provider or Web site development tool. Service-oriented architecture gets muddled up with the "service economy" and service providers and consultants. It's confusing enough without the ambiguous words. To help frame the subject of SOA, then, we want to go over two basic concepts before we get into the in-depth material. First, what do we mean by a *service*? And, what is the difference between service-orientation, which is an approach to development, and service-oriented architecture, which is a global paradigm for enterprises?

When we talk about services in SOA, we mean pieces of software functionality that will be used by other pieces of software when needed. Let's use a real-world example to clarify the concept: Imagine that you have a thermometer outside your window, so you can see what temperature it is at any time of day or night. It's your thermometer, and you enjoy it all by yourself. Then, let's say that your friends want to know what temperature it is. They call you, and you look outside and tell them what the thermometer says. You have now become a temperature service to your friends. They don't have to buy a thermometer because they can call you when they need to know the temperature.

In enterprise software, you might have financial accounting software that has a sales tax calculation function. The tax function returns the total sales tax amount when provided a dollar amount and zip code. However, you could make that sales tax calculator available to other pieces of software that need that functionality. For example, you might have an e-commerce application that needs to calculate sales tax. One approach to this requirement is to code, or buy, a sales tax calculator module right into the e-commerce application. Alternatively, you could enable the sales tax function to be requested as a service by the e-commerce application. In the same way that your neighbor might call you to find out the temperature so he doesn't have to buy his own thermometer, the e-commerce application can leverage the financial application's sales tax calculator service instead of its own sales tax calculator code.

In the simple example we have set up, the integration between the e-commerce application and the financial application is known as *service-orientation*, the rather simple act of exposing a service and allowing other applications to consume it. Service-orientation is often the first step toward the attainment of an SOA. However, the SOA is a much broader concept, one that posits that virtually all applications in an enterprise will take advantage of service-orientation for their functioning.

Connecting the idea of a service, and service-orientation through to the EDA, you should imagine that any component of an EDA could be a service. The event producer could be a service, as could the consumer, and so on. What's significant about that is the potential of a service to be dynamic and implicit—free of tight connections to the EDA elements with which it needs to communicate. We explore this concept more and more as we move ahead.

Service-Based Integration

Over the past few years, an increasing number of organizations have embraced the notion of service-based integration as a cheaper, non-product-specific alternative to the proprietary middleware suites of the past. For example, in Figure 2.1, which continues the phone company example from Chapter 1, "EDA: Opportunities and Obstacles," the billing system consumes a SOAP Web service called CheckMinutes on the line management system. By exposing data and functionality as services to systems and users (choosing interoperability over traditional integration techniques), IT groups can meet business needs quickly and relatively painlessly. As a stepping stone to a fully realized SOA, or as a placeholder for an anticipated enterprise integration strategy, this is an excellent approach.

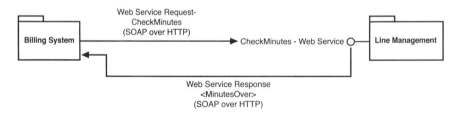

Figure 2.1   In service-based integration, a Web service consumer calls a Web service provider using a SOAP XML message over HTTP. The Web service processes the request and returns a SOAP response over HTTP.

There are drawbacks to this service-based integration because many such implementations are still point-to-point in nature, even if they are not case-specific. Federated management and governance of point-to-point services can be difficult to implement, and without a management mechanism, a service-based interoperability strategy will not scale with the needs of an enterprise. Unless you have a governance method in place, service-level objectives can slip (performance, reliability, scalability) without your knowledge, and your architecture can lose its agility.

Web Services

Web services, as described by the Web Services Interoperability Organization (WS-I, www.ws-i.org/), play a significant role in modern SOA implementations. Though SOAs do not require the use of Web services, and there are many viable alternatives, Web services have become the de facto standard technology for realizing SOA. When we refer to SOA and Web services in this book, we mean the three basic WS-I specifications standards: SOAP, Web Services Description Language (WSDL), and Universal Description, Discovery, and Integration (UDDI; including standards such as Web Ontology Language [OWL-S]). In a nutshell, Web services accept requests and send responses in SOAP format. Service characteristics are described by a WSDL document, and advertised using a registry services application programming interface (API) such as UDDI or other "registry, discovery, and dynamic invocation" standards like OWL-S. The following sections provide high-level descriptions of each specification, for your information. For the latest and most complete specification information, and for press releases related to emerging related specifications, refer to the WS-I Web site mentioned earlier.

It's important at this point to clarify the difference between a *service* and a *Web service*. Whereas a Web service uses Hypertext Transfer Protocol (HTTP) as a transport protocol and SOAP as a message formatting standard, both of these qualities are actually optional for the implementation of an SOA. Several technologies allow exposing services over Transmission Control Protocol/Internet Protocol (TCP/IP), Simple Mail Transfer Protocol (SMTP), or other transport protocols (e.g., Windows Communication Foundation). For the sake of simplicity in this book, we most often use the example of Web services.

Simple Object Access Protocol (SOAP)

At its core, a Web service is a means of processing and returning SOAP messages. SOAP defines a format for XML that includes a transport-independent enveloping mechanism. The SOAP envelope contains a body element and optional header and fault elements. The SOAP body holds the message itself and is distinguished from the header element by a namespace prefix. In general, a message sent to a remote component through the invocation of a Web service causes a method to run on the remote object. The response is the result of the method invocation, also formatted in a SOAP message. Such an implementation is called a remote procedure call (RPC) style of SOAP message. The SOAP specification also allows for the exchange of XML documents using what is called the Document Literal style of SOAP message. The `style` attribute of the SOAP protocol binding determines which style is in use and tells the client of the Web service whether to use RPC conventions.

(For further reading on Document Literal, see http://msdn2. microsoft.com/en-us/library/ms996466.aspx.)

RPC style services are not loosely coupled, so they pose serious interoperability concerns. This has caused many to push for removal of RPC from the WS-I Basic profile. In the interoperable spirit of this book, we do not recommend using RPC style Web services.

The SOAP header can hold security information (tokens, usernames, etc.), routing information, reliability indicators, conversation identifiers, and anything else you might find useful to embed in the header. Many emerging specifications define standard ways of using the SOAP header for these sorts of things. The great thing about putting information of interest in the SOAP header (as opposed to the transport message header) is that it can pass unchanged and unexamined through various layers of security, both physical and logical. Examples of these SOAP extensions include WS-Addressing (standards for specifying routes), WS-Security (standards for exchanging credentials and encryption), WS-Attachments (a standard way of attaching documents to the SOAP message), and the like. Figure 2.2 shows a schematic of a SOAP message.

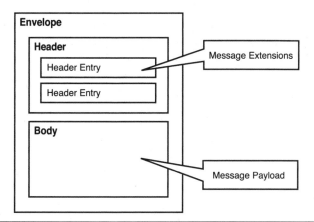

Figure 2.2 A SOAP message consists of an envelope, header, and body formatted in XML using the SOAP standard format.

The following is an example of a SOAP message. Note the envelope, header, and body sections. The SOAP envelope establishes the beginning and end of the SOAP message. The header contains message-level content, such as where the message came from. The body contains the payload of data or procedural instructions. Pay attention especially to the line of code in the body section that reads `<w:GetSecretIdentity xmlns:w="http://www.wrox.com/heroes/">`. This line is a procedure call that invokes a Web service called `GetSecretIdentity`, which is located at the URL www.wrox.com/heroes/. We point this out to show you how Web services put software functionality in reach of applications by publishing them to the Web, literally. `GetSecretIdentity` has its own URL, which can be coded into the Web service consumer. The SOAP specification can be viewed at the W3C site: www.w3c.org.

Throughout the book, lines of code that are too long to fit on one printed line have been manually broken and the continuation preceded with a code-continuation arrow (➥).

```
<SOAP-ENV:Envelope
  xmlns:SOAP-ENV="http://schemas.xmlsoap.org/soap/envelope/"
  SOAP-ENV:encodingStyle="http://schemas.xmlsoap.org/soap/
➥encoding/"/>
    <SOAP-ENV:Body>
```

```
<e:Book>
   <title>My Life and Work</title>
   <firstauthor href="#Person-1"/>
   <secondauthor href="#Person-2"/>
</e:Book>
<e:Person id="Person-1">
   <name>Henry Ford</name>
   <address xsi:type="m:Electronic-address">
      <email>mailto:henryford@hotmail.com</email>
      <web>http://www.henryford.com</web>
   </address>
</e:Person>
<e:Person id="Person-2">
   <name>Samuel Crowther</name>
   <address xsi:type="n:Street-address">
      <street>Martin Luther King Rd</street>
      <city>Raleigh</city>
      <state>North Carolina</state>
   </address>
</e:Person>
   </SOAP-ENV:Body>
</SOAP-ENV:Envelope>
```

Source: www.W3C.org XML Protocols (www.w3.org/2000/03/29-XML-protocol-matrix)

Note about the preceding example: The SOAP 1.2 specification recommends that all SOAP body child elements be namespace qualified. That is recommended for an EDA deployment.

It might be in the best interest of your organization or infrastructure to build policies around acceptable SOAP messages. For example, SOAP messages can be Document Literal or RPC encoded. Some organizations prohibit RPC-encoded SOAP messages because of interoperability concerns. This is the sort of policy that can be applied programmatically to the service description (WSDL; see the following section) at design time (predeployment) as part of your governance cycle. Industry- or company-specific SOAP conventions should be part of the research and definitions produced by your SOA-related initiatives.

Web Services Description Language (WSDL)

Consuming a Web service requires knowledge of what the service provides as well as the format of the data to be sent and received. A Web service is described by a WSDL ("wiz"-dul) document.

WSDL documents are XML documents. The elements in a WSDL document list the types of data available (**types**), the methods available for use (**messages** and **operations**), groupings of these methods (**port types**), specifications for accessing these method groupings (**binding**), and where the service is made available (**ports**). The types, messages, operations, port types, bindings, and ports are made available at the uniform resource identifier (URI) specified in the **service** element of the WSDL. The WSDL indicates whether the service is synchronous (request/response) or asynchronous (request/notify or one-way), specifies the transport protocol to be used, and the like.

The following example of a WSDL, taken from www.w3c.org, is a *WSDL 2.0 Document for the GreatH Web Service:*

```
<?xml version="1.0" encoding="utf-8" ?>
<description
    xmlns="http://www.w3.org/ns/wsdl"
    targetNamespace= "http://greath.example.com/2004/wsdl/
➥resSvc"
    xmlns:tns= "http://greath.example.com/2004/wsdl/resSvc"
    xmlns:ghns = "http://greath.example.com/2004/schemas/
➥resSvc"
    xmlns:wsoap= "http://www.w3.org/ns/wsdl/soap"
    xmlns:soap="http://www.w3.org/2003/05/soap-envelope"
    xmlns:wsdlx= "http://www.w3.org/ns/wsdl-extensions">

  <documentation>
    This document describes the GreatH Web service.
➥Additional
    application-level requirements for use of this service—
    beyond what WSDL 2.0 is able to describe—are available
    at http://greath.example.com/2004/reservation-
➥documentation.html
  </documentation>

  <types>
    <xs:schema
        xmlns:xs="http://www.w3.org/2001/XMLSchema"
```

```
        targetNamespace="http://greath.example.com/2004/
➥schemas/resSvc"
        xmlns="http://greath.example.com/2004/schemas/
➥resSvc">

    <xs:element name="checkAvailability" type=
➥"tCheckAvailability"/>
        <xs:complexType name="tCheckAvailability">
          <xs:sequence>
            <xs:element  name="checkInDate" type="xs:date"/>
            <xs:element  name="checkOutDate" type="xs:date"/>
            <xs:element  name="roomType" type="xs:string"/>
          </xs:sequence>
        </xs:complexType>

    <xs:element name="checkAvailabilityResponse" type=
➥"xs:double"/>

    <xs:element name="invalidDataError" type="xs:string"/>

  </xs:schema>
</types>

<interface  name = "reservationInterface" >

  <fault name = "invalidDataFault"
         element = "ghns:invalidDataError"/>

  <operation name="opCheckAvailability"
         pattern="http://www.w3.org/ns/wsdl/in-out"
         style="http://www.w3.org/ns/wsdl/style/iri"
         wsdlx:safe = "true">
      <input messageLabel="In"
          element="ghns:checkAvailability" />
      <output messageLabel="Out"
          element="ghns:checkAvailabilityResponse" />
      <outfault ref="tns:invalidDataFault" messageLabel=
➥"Out"/>
  </operation>

</interface>

<binding name="reservationSOAPBinding"
```

```
        interface="tns:reservationInterface"
        type="http://www.w3.org/ns/wsdl/soap"
        wsoap:protocol="http://www.w3.org/2003/05/soap/
➥bindings/HTTP/">

    <fault ref="tns:invalidDataFault"
      wsoap:code="soap:Sender"/>

    <operation ref="tns:opCheckAvailability"
        wsoap:mep="http://www.w3.org/2003/05/soap/mep/
➥soap-response"/>

    </binding>

    <service name="reservationService"
          interface="tns:reservationInterface">

      <endpoint name="reservationEndpoint"
                binding="tns:reservationSOAPBinding"
                address ="http://greath.example.com/2004/
➥reservation"/>

    </service>

</description>
```

The true benefit of describing a service with a WSDL is that consumers of a service can programmatically consume the WSDL document and generate the corresponding method calls at design time or at runtime. Furthermore, components of a WSDL can be mapped to registry entities, facilitating the exposure of service descriptions via dynamic lookup at runtime (a powerful component of a fully functional SOA).

Most mainstream Integrated Development Environments (IDEs), such as VisualStudio.NET WebSphere Studio Application Developer and WebLogic Workshop, can read WSDL documents and generate corresponding .NET class (proxy code) or Java skeleton code. Sun Microsystems provides Java APIs for reading or generating. So the benefit of exposing data and functionality as a Web service described by a WSDL is that consumers need not spend time familiarizing themselves with your service interface beyond using the WSDL consumption tools available to them in their development environments.

Universal Description, Discovery, and Integration (UDDI)

UDDI is a registry standard for referencing Web services against a published set of metadata. The UDDI specification facilitates the mapping of service providers and WSDLs to UDDI structures.

Initially, much of the hype associated with UDDI focused on the notion of enabling dynamic discovery of publicly exposed Web services. The obvious barriers to widespread adoption of this notion were the licensing and access constraints that most service providers want to place on consumption of their services. Consequently, UDDI failed to gain popularity, and its true power, that of providing runtime access to completely decoupled services in an SOA, is only now being widely leveraged.

Web service registries and the UDDI specification play an important role in the scope of an SOA. If a goal of your SOA implementation is to achieve true abstraction and loose coupling, you need to ensure that the consumers of services need not know the exact location (server), version, or policy status of the services. The only way to ensure this level of abstraction is to have the consumer query either the registry itself (or with an implicit query provided by an intermediary as part of a management application with an embedded registry) every time a service is requested. This allows the service to be fully abstracted from its consumer, protecting the consumer from failover activity, upgrades, support changes, and the like. It also allows you to get creative with how you discover services in the future—perhaps incorporating common logic into a management application that selects an appropriate service provider based on a set of common rules.

If your long-term SOA goals do not include that level of abstraction, you need to plan for some sort of asset management mechanism in which services can be referenced at design time. However, we recommend that you begin your SOA implementation using a "registry, discovery, and dynamic invocation" standard like UDDI or some of its newer variants. The benefits of doing this up front will be well received when enforcing standards and governing the proliferation of services. For more information about UDDI, visit www.uddi.org.

EDA and Web Services

If you accept the premise that EDA components such as event producers and event listeners will be services and be connected through service-orientation, the prevalence of Web services leads us to a basic conclusion: EDA components in the future will likely be Web services.

Although there are differing opinions on this—many of which are quite intelligent and valid—the sheer scale of the Web services and SOA paradigm shift dictates that any realistic attempt to build an EDA will involve using SOAP XML Web services as the EDA components. Furthermore, the use of Web services as EDA components will be accompanied by the use of WSDL to describe EDA component functionality and UDDI to publish the availability of EDA components throughout the EDA.

What Is SOA?

SOA is a flexible method of structuring and managing component-based systems. Components in an SOA-based environment might be software or hardware based, might perform a generic business function (transfer funds, for example) or an enterprise function (security, policy application, routing, or logging, for example), or might be an application-specific function. Components in an SOA might also include frameworks for interactive applications (portals) or event management systems (pub/sub, event correlation). All of these units of work are services in an SOA and must be managed and monitored in a uniform way. We often refer to the whole as a service network.

In an SOA, services (typically Web services) are the preferred unit of work. We talk about services being loosely coupled and featuring standard interfaces with messages sharing common identifiers, formats, and protocols. The formats are network-ready; the protocols are concern-based and composeable.

Services can be combined in various ways to create multiple applications.

The diagram in Figure 2.3 illustrates how a full-featured SOA might be constructed. Note that this diagram has logical representations of components that in reality could be distributed physically. Figure 2.3 also illustrates the use of intermediaries to execute the functionality of shared cross-cutting concerns. One of the most significant characteristics of an SOA is the abstraction of nonfunctional concerns from business functions or applications. This means that the remedies for reliability, security, transactionality, adaptability, synchrony, and all of the other *ilities are refactored out of business services and into the service network as service intermediaries. Many runtime governance frameworks provide support for intermediaries and their configuration with declarative policy assertions.

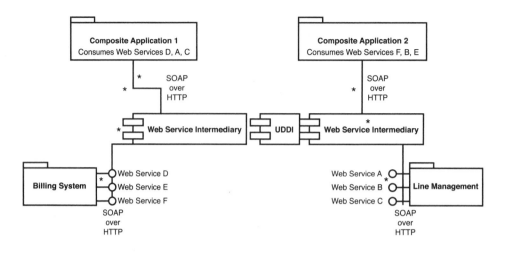

Figure 2.3   In this service-oriented architecture phone company example, there are six Web services exposed on two systems. Through intermediaries, two separate composite applications can be developed that use the functionality of the Web services without requiring any new coding to achieve the functionality that they deliver.

Loose Coupling in the SOA

As we have discussed, EDAs work best when there is a low level of constraint on EDA components to communicate. If there are tight restrictions on how the event listeners can communicate with the event producers, the EDA will be inflexible and limited in scope. To put this idea in SOA terms, we now discuss the concept of *coupling*.

Beyond the simple exposure of data and functionality as services, SOA reinforces the notion of loosely coupled, component-based, distributed systems. The very existence of an EDA requires an SOA to be loosely coupled. Loose coupling of components means that each component need not—and should not—know anything about its counterparts or about its environment in general. In the situation used in Figure 2.1, the line management system that provides a minutes balance in response to a request from the billing system should not have any awareness of the line management system. That is, for the coupling between the two systems to be "loose," the less specific information about the line management system that the billing system needs to have to process the request for the minutes balance, the better. The more information it needs, the more "tight" the coupling. The coupling is directly tied to the amount of preconceived information required to engage another software component. As you decrease the coupling (preconception), you increase the ability to evolve and change unencumbered. This is the true essence of SOA.

One of the reasons SOAs are achievable today is the remarkable cooperation of the major enterprise technology vendors and their participation in the Web Services Interoperability (WS-I) group. The vendors in this group coordinate their usage of versions of the applicable standards in the latest versions of their software. That acceptance by the vendors has created a cohesive standard for integration never before accomplished. The broad acceptance has allowed loose coupling to exist where it would have been difficult before. Indeed, SOA is omnipresent in the IT landscape. Every major player has their version of it. Microsoft's SOA is based on their .NET framework, BEA has Aqualogic, IBM has the WebSphere SOA Stack, Oracle has Fusion Middleware, SAP has NetWeaver, and so on.

Chapter Summary

- Service-oriented architecture (SOA) is a breakthrough in integration and interoperability among heterogeneous software. As such, it provides the optimal, or at least the most pragmatic and extant, basis for developing dynamic, implicit, and complex EDAs. Based on a remarkable agreement between competing IT giants to use one standard form of XML for interfacing software components, SOA has the potential to simplify, quicken, and cheapen the burdensome task of integrating applications. At the same time, SOA introduces a number of new governance challenges, including security and management, that must be addressed to deploy a successful SOA.

- The core ingredient of an SOA is a *service*, a piece of software functionality that can be invoked on demand by other pieces of software when needed. The value of the service is in its ability to eliminate the need for creating a new piece of code with the identical functionality elsewhere. Services lead to reuse of software assets, which can reduce IT costs.

- Though there are several different, valid approaches to attaining an SOA, the one that we use throughout the book, and the one generally accepted by the industry, is that of Web services as defined by the WS-I standards. These include Simple Object Access Protocol (SOAP), a form of XML used for messaging, Web Services Description Language (WSDL), a standardized XML-based document format for describing the functionality of a Web service, and Universal Description, Discovery, and Integration (UDDI), a standard for a registry of Web services available for use.

- Web services enable data exchange and procedure calls between any number of applications, regardless of the software language they are written in, the operating system they run on, their physical or logical location, or their network. For this reason, Web services can deliver nearly universal interoperability—a boon to integration and agility.

- An enterprise architecture composed of Web services, which utilizes service integration to achieve the creation of new *composite* applications, which are composed of Web service components rather than new code, is a service-oriented architecture.

- SOA and Web services will form the building blocks of the new EDA. Though there are alternative approaches, many of them quite valid, the scale and scope of the SOA trend is such that any practical plan to develop an EDA will be based on SOA standards, particularly SOAP XML Web services.

- In our view, the event producers in an EDA will be built using Web services. They will be discoverable through UDDIs and described through WSDL.

CHAPTER 3

Characteristics of EDA

Firing Up the Corporate Neurons

Getting to a complete understanding of event-driven architecture (EDA) takes us on a step-by-step process of learning. First, we discussed the enterprise nervous system and the way EDAs are formed by connecting event listeners with event consumers and event processors, and so on. Then, to explain how these EDA components will likely be realized in today's enterprise architecture, we learned about Web services and service-oriented architecture (SOA). To get the full picture, though, we now need to get into depth on the characteristics and qualities of EDA components.

If the EDA components are like the neurons in the enterprise nervous system, then we need to understand how their "synapses" and neural message pathways work if we want to form a complete picture of EDA. We need to know how they actually can or should work together to realize the desired functionality of an EDA. In this context, we go more deeply into the concept of *loose coupling* and also explore in depth the ways that an EDA needs to handle messaging between its components. With the key concepts defined, we then lay out a thorough definition of EDA, using an idealized EDA as an example.

Revisiting the Enterprise Nervous System

Returning to our cat scenario, if your cat steps on your toe, how do you know it? How do you know it's a cat, and not a lion? You might want to pet the cat, but shoot the lion. And, perhaps most important, how can you be sure that your body and mind learn how to distinguish between the cat and the lion in the first place? How do you keep learning to process sensory experiences? The world is constantly changing, so our nervous systems, and our EDAs, must be flexible, adaptable, and fast learners. We want our EDAs to be as sensitive, responsive, and teachable as our own nervous systems. To get there, we need to endow our EDA components with nervous system–like capabilities.

When the cat's paw presses against your toe, the nerve cells in your toe fire off a signal to your brain saying, "Hey, something stepped on my toe." In this way, the neurons in your toe are like event producers. The neural pathways that the messages follow as they travel up your spine to the brain are like the messaging backbone of the EDA. Your brain is at once an event listener and an event processor. If you pet the cat, your hand and the nerves that tell your hand to move are event reactors. Figure 3.1 compares the EDA with your nervous system.

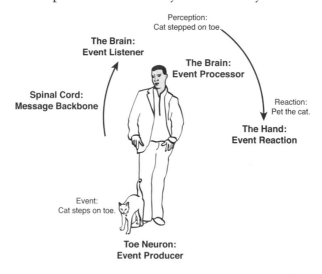

Figure 3.1 The human nervous system compared with an EDA.

The nervous system analogy is helpful for getting the idea of EDA on a number of levels. In addition to being a useful model of the EDA components in terms that we can understand (and perhaps, more important, that you can use to explain to other less-sophisticated people), we can learn a lot about how an EDA works by understanding how the nerves and brain communicate and share information. As a first step in mapping from nervous system to EDA in terms of its characteristics, we look at event-driven programming, a technology that is comparable to an EDA and quite familiar, as well as informative.

Event-Driven Programming: EDA's Kissing Cousin

We all use a close cousin of EDA on a daily basis, one whose simplicity can help us gain a better understanding of EDA, perhaps without even realizing it. It's called event-driven programming (EDP) and it's common in most runtime platforms. It's also found in CPU architectures, operating systems, GUI interfaces, and network monitoring. EDP consists of event dispatchers and event handlers (sometimes called event listeners). Event handlers are snippets of code that are only interested in receiving particular events in the system. The event handler subscribes to a particular event by registering itself with the dispatcher. The event dispatcher keeps track of all registered listeners then, when the event occurs, notifies each listener through a system call passing the event data.

For example, you might have a piece of code that executes if the user moves the mouse. Let's call this a mouse event listener. As shown in Figure 3.2, the mouse event listener registers itself with the dispatcher—in this case, the operating system. The operating system records a callback reference to the mouse event listener. Every time the user moves the mouse, the dispatcher invokes each listener passing the mouse movement event. The mouse movement event signals a change in the mouse or cursor position, hence a change in the system's state. Other examples of event-driven programming can be found in computer hardware interrupts, software operating system interrupts, and other user interface events, such as mouse movements, key clicks, text entry, and so on.

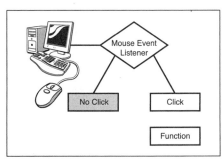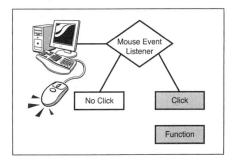

Figure 3.2   The PC's instruction to listen for mouse clicks is an example of event-driven programming (EDP), a close cousin of EDA. When the mouse is clicked, the mouse click event listener in the PC's operating system is triggered, which, in turn, activates whatever function is meant to be invoked by the mouse click. When the mouse is not clicked, the event listener waits.

Wikipedia describes event-driven programming as, "Unlike traditional programs, which follow their own control flow pattern, only sometimes changing course at branch points, the control flow of event-driven programs [is] largely driven by external events."[1] The definition points out that there is no central controller of the flow of data, which is counterintuitive to the way most of us were taught to program.

The reason we bring this up is to emphasize a key distinction between EDP and conventional software: a lack of a central controller. This distinction is critical to understanding how EDA works. When you first enter the programming world, you're taught how to write a "Hello World" program. You might learn that a program has a main method body from which flow control is transferred to other methods. The main method is treated like a controller (see Figure 3.3).

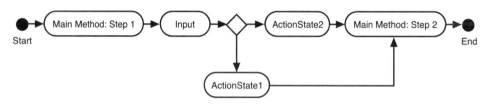

Figure 3.3   In a conventional programming design, a controller method controls the flow of data and process steps.

In contrast, in event-driven programming, there are no central controllers dictating the sequence flow. As shown in Figure 3.4, each component listening for events acts independently from the others and often has no idea of its coexistence. When an event occurs, the event data is relayed to each event listener. The event listener is then free to react to that information however it chooses, perhaps activating a process specifically intended for that particular event trigger. The event information is relayed asynchronously to the event listeners so multiple listeners react to the event data at the same time, increasing performance but also creating an unpredictable order of execution.

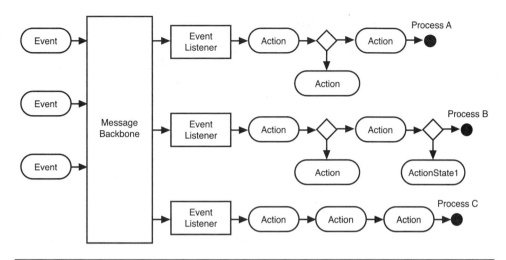

Figure 3.4 In event-driven programming (EDP), event listeners receive state change data (events) and pass them along to event dispatchers, which then activate processes that depend on the nature of the triggering events.

As shown in Figure 3.4, the listeners execute concurrently. This is quite different from the typical program that controls the flow of data. In a typical program, the controller method calls out to each subcomponent, passes relevant data, waits for control to return, then continues to the next one—a very predictable behavior. Of course, the controller method could take an asynchronous approach, but the point is that one has a predefined flow of data whereas the other does not.

When waiting for events, event listeners are typically in a quiescent state, though occasionally you'll see a simulated event-driven model where event listeners cyclically poll for information. They sleep for a predefined period then awaken to poll the system for new events. The sleep time is usually so small that the process is near real time.

Similar to EDP-based systems, EDA relies on dynamic binding of components through message-driven communication. This provides the loose coupling and asynchrony foundation for EDA. EDA components connect to a common transport medium and subscribe to interested event types. Most EDA components also publish events—meaning they are typically publishers *and* subscribers, depending on context. The biggest difference between EDA and EDP is that EDP event listeners are colocated and interested in low system-level events like mouse clicks, whereas EDA event consumers are likely to be distributed and interested in high-level business actions such as "purchase order fulfilled."

More on Loose Coupling

Let's go deeper on loose coupling, a core enabling characteristic of EDA. You can't have EDA without loose coupling. So, as far as we EDA believers are concerned, the looser the better. However, getting to an effective and workable definition of loose coupling can prove challenging. If you ask nine developers to define loose coupling, you'll likely get nine different answers. The term is loosely used, loosely defined, and loosely understood. The reason is that the meaning of *loose coupling* is context sensitive. For EDA purposes, loose coupling is the measurement of two fundamentals:

- Preconception
- Maintainability (Changeability)

Preconception: The amount of knowledge, prejudice, or fixed idea that a piece of software has about another piece of software

Preconception is a quality of software that reflects the amount of knowledge, prejudice, or fixed idea that one piece of code has about another piece of code. The more preconception that an application (or a piece of an application) has in relation to another application with which it must interoperate, the tighter the coupling between the two. The less preconception, the looser the coupling. We've all seen tight coupling that stems from high levels of preconceptions. Think of systems where every configuration attribute and every piece of mutable text is hard-coded in the system. It can take days just to correct a simple spelling mistake. During design, these systems all made a single, yet enormous, configuration preconception—they assumed that the configuration would be set at compile time and never need to be changed. You will never get to the flexibility of configuration that you need to build an EDA with this kind of tight coupling.

Ultimately, to move toward EDA and SOA, you should strive for software that makes as few presumptions as possible. To use a common, real-world example of tight coupling, consider a point-of-sale (POS) program calling a credit card debit (CCD) program and passing it a credit card (CC) number. As shown in Figure 3.5, the POS program has a preconceived notion that it will always be calling the CCD program and always be passing it a CC number, hence the two systems are now tightly coupled.

Maintainability: The level of rework required by all participants when one integrated component changes

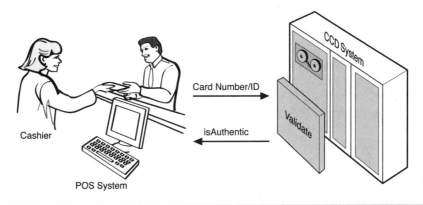

Figure 3.5 In this classic example of tight coupling, a POS system sends a credit card number to a CCD program and requests a validation, which is indicated by a returned value of `isAuthentic`. The two systems are so tightly bound together they can almost be viewed as one single system.

Maintainability, the other EDA-enabling component of loose coupling, refers to the level of rework required by all participants when one integrated component changes. When a piece of software changes, how much change does that introduce to other dependent software pieces? Best practices dictate that we should strive for software that embraces and facilitates change, not software that resists it. As a rule, the looser the coupling between components or systems, the easier it is to make software changes without impacting related components or systems.

Consider the hard-coded POS system described previously. A simple configuration change requires a source code change, compilation, regression testing, scheduled system downtime, downtime notifications, promotion to production, and the like. A system that resists change is considered a tightly coupled system.

What Your CFO Is Thinking

Imagine that you are the owner of this tightly coupled POS system, and your CFO tells you that, as of some very rapidly approaching date, she expects the POS systems to accept coupons as a form of payment in addition to credit cards. Unlike the credit cards, which have a 16-digit identifying number and a matching expiration date, the coupons have a 10-character identifier composed of letters and numbers. When you tell your CFO that it might take you three months to make this change, she is not going to be too interested in the issues of maintainability and preconception involved in the POS software, but you know that these two tight coupling demons are to blame. The coupons might actually provide you with a good pretext to start discussing an EDA/SOA approach to POS. You can tell the CFO that you can make future coupon transitions faster if you loosen up the coupling in the POS systems.

Now let's suppose we begin to alleviate our headaches by removing some of the system's preconceived ideas. As a start, let's assume we make the following two changes:

- First, we remove the hard-coded instructions from our system code, and instead let behavior be driven by accessing values stored in a configuration file (presumably read into memory at instantiation).

- Second, we enable our system to be dynamically reconfigured (meaning our system would have a mechanism for reloading new versions of the configuration file while still active).

In this case, making a simple change to our configuration file, such as indicating that an entry in coupon format is a valid form of payment or even correcting a spelling mistake, only requires a regression test and a signal sent to the production system to reload its configuration. The system is *maintainable*—we updated the system while it stayed in production, and we did so without compiling a lick of code.

We have also successfully decreased the coupling between our system and its configuration. The system is now loosely coupled with respect to this context but it might still be tightly coupled in other areas. We have only increased its loosely coupled index. We have increased its changeability and decreased its preconception with respect to configuration, but how does it interact with other modules or components? It might be tightly coupled with other software.

This is where the meaning of loose coupling is context sensitive. We can say the system is loosely coupled if that statement is made within the context of the configuration file. We can also say it is not loosely coupled if the statement is made referring to its integration techniques.

This example oversimplifies the situation because hard-coded systems are often very difficult to modify into configuration-driven systems, and even harder to modify to dynamically configuration-driven systems, but the points are valid. We did decrease the tight coupling and ease our headache. Moreover, we can see that significant rework time would have been saved had the system designers taken this approach from the beginning.

To illustrate our point, we have just used an example where we increased the degree of loose coupling of the system by loosely coupling configuration attributes. However, the term is typically used to reference integration constraints. Two or more systems are tightly coupled when their integration is difficult to change because of each system's preconceptions.

Our previous point-of-sale (POS) scenario is an example of two tightly coupled systems. Changes in either system are very likely to necessitate changes in the other. At the extreme (though not uncommon) end of this spectrum, the overall design might be so tightly integrated that the two systems might be considered one atomic unit.

The POS system has preconceived notions about how to interact with the CCD system. For example, the POS system calls a specific method in the CCD system, named `validate`, passing it the CC number. Now suppose the CCD system changes the method name to `isAuthentic`. This might happen if a third party purchased the CCD system, for example.

What we want to do is isolate those changes so that we do not have to change our POS system with every vendor's whim. To loosen up the architecture, let's exercise a design pattern called the **adapter** pattern. We will add an intermediate (adapter) component between the POS and CCD systems. The sole purpose of this component is to isolate the preconceived knowledge of the CCD system. This allows the vendor to make changes without adversely affecting the POS system.

Now vendor changes in the CCD system are isolated and can be bridged using the intermediate component. As the diagram in Figure 3.6 illustrates, the vendor can change the method name and only the adapter component needs to change.

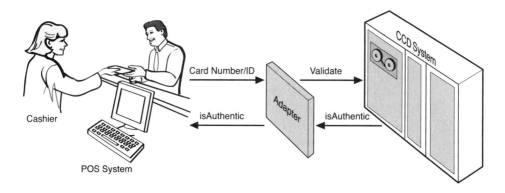

Figure 3.6   The insertion of an adapter between the POS and CCD systems loosens the coupling. Changes to the CCD system are isolated and can be bridged using the adapter.

This reduces the POS system's preconception about the CCD giving the systems greater changeability. In essence, we now have greater business flexibility because we now have the freedom to switch vendors if we choose. We can swap out the Credit Card Debit (CCD) product for another just by changing the adapter component.

The true benefits of the design shown in Figure 3.6 are radically evident when we talk about multicomponent integration, which is shown in Figure 3.7. Here, the benefits are multiplied by each participating component. This is also where the return on investment shows through reuse. Understand that the up-front time spent on building the adapter is now saving more money with each use. The more you use it, the more you'll save.

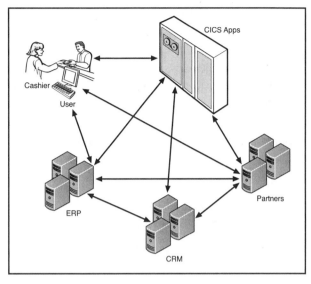

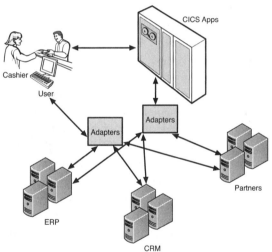

Figure 3.7 Use of adapters in multicomponent integration.

The argument can be made that we have now only shifted the tight coupling to our adapter, which is true, though we have added a layer of abstraction that does, in fact, increase maintainability of the system. We'll demonstrate how to fully decouple these systems when we talk about event-driven architecture later in this chapter.

There will always be a degree of coupling. Even fully decoupled components have some degree of coupling. The desire is to remove as much as possible but it is naïve to think the systems will ever be truly decoupled. For example, service components need data to do their job, and as such will always be coupled to the required input data. Even a component that returns a time stamp is tightly coupled with the system call used to retrieve the current time. As we strive for loose coupling, we should remember that the best we can achieve is a high "degree of looseness."

More about Messages

Coupling, loose or tight, is all about messages. For all practical purposes, it is only possible to have loose coupling and EDA, with a messaging design that decouples the message sending and receiving parties and allows for redirection if needed. To see why this is the case, let's look at two core aspects of messaging: harmonization and delivery. Harmonization is how the components interact to ensure message delivery. Delivery is the messaging method used to transfer data.

Message harmonization is how the components interact to ensure message delivery.

Harmonization can be synchronous or asynchronous. Synchronous messaging is like a procedure call shown in Figure 3.8. The producer communicates with the consumer and waits for a response before continuing. The consumer has to be present for the communication to complete and all processing waits until the transfer of data concludes. For example, most POS systems and ATMs sit in a waiting state until transaction approval is granted. Then, they spring back into life and complete the process that stalled as the procedure call was completed. Comparable examples of synchronous messaging in real life include instant messaging, phone conversations, and live business meetings.

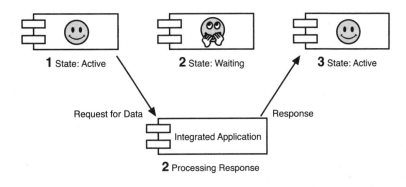

Figure 3.8 Example of synchronous messaging, a process where the requesting entity waits for a response until resuming action.

In contrast, asynchronous messaging does not block processing or wait for a response. As Figure 3.9 illustrates, the message consumer in an asynchronous messaging setup need not be present at the time of transmit. This is the most common form of communication in distributed systems because of the inherent unreliability of the network. In asynchronous messaging, messages are sent to a mediator that stores the message for retrieval by the consumer. This allows for message delivery whether the consumer is reachable or not. The producer can continue processing and the consumer can connect at will and retrieve the awaiting messages. Examples include e-mail (the consumer does not need to be present to complete delivery), placing a telephone call and leaving a voice mail message (versus a world without voice mail), and discussion forums.

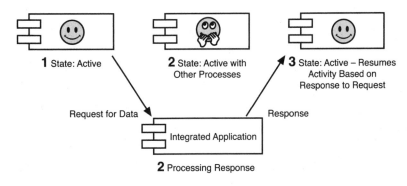

Figure 3.9 Example of simple, point-to-point asynchronous messaging.

There are multiple ways to execute message delivery whether synchronously or asynchronously. Synchronous messaging includes request/reply applications like remote procedure calls and conversational messaging like many of the older modem protocols. Our focus here is on asynchronous messaging. Asynchronous messaging comes in two flavors: point-to-point or publish/subscribe.

Message delivery is the messaging method used to transfer data.

Point-to-point messaging, shown in Figure 3.9, is used when many-to-one messaging is required (meaning one or more producers need to relay messages to one consumer). This is orchestrated using a queue. Messages from producers are stored in a queue. There can be multiple consumers connected to the queue but only one consumer processes each message. After the message is processed, it is removed from the queue. If there are multiple consumers, they're typically duplicates of the same component and they process messages identically. This multiplicity is to facilitate load balancing more than multidimensional processing.

Publish/subscribe messaging, shown in Figure 3.10, is used when many applications need to receive the same message. This wide dissemination of event data makes it ideal for event-driven architectures. Messages from producers are stored in a repository called a topic. Table 3.1 summarizes the differences between the two modes of message flow. Unlike point-to-point messaging, pub/sub messages remain in the topic after processing until expiration or purging. Consumers subscribe to the topic and specify their interest in currently stored messages. Interested consumers are sent the current topic contents followed by any new messages. For others, communication begins with the arrival of a new message.

Topics provide the advantage of exposing business events that can be leveraged in an EDA. One consideration is the transaction complete indeterminism, and we will soon explore ways to handle this.

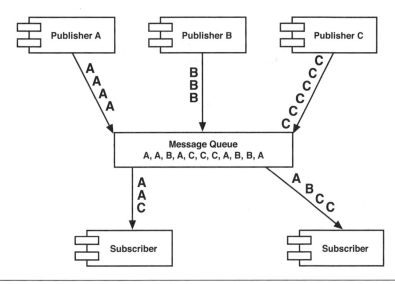

Figure 3.10 Example of publish/subscribe (pub/sub) asynchronous messaging using a message queue.

Asynchronous messaging requires a message mediator, or adapter. This can be achieved using a database, native language constructs like Java Channels, or the most common provider of this functionality, message-oriented-middleware (MOM). MOM software is a class of applications specifically for managing the reliable transport of messages. This includes applications like IBM's WebSphere MQ (formally MQSeries), Microsoft Message Queuing (MSMQ), BEA's Tuxedo, Tibco's Rendezvous, others based on Sun's Java Messaging Specification (JMS), and a multitude of others.

JMS is the most prominent vendor-agnostic standard for message-oriented-middleware. Before its creation, messaging-based architectures were locked in to a particular vendor. Now, most MOM applications support the standard, making it the primary choice for implementation teams concerned with vendor-agnostic portability.

Table 3.1   Point-to-Point Versus Publish/Subscribe

Point-to-Point Queues	Publish/Subscribe Topics
Single consumer	Multiple consumers
Preconceived consumer	Anonymous consumers
Medium decoupling	High decoupling
Messages are consumed	Messages remain until purged or expiration

The Ideal EDA

Having taken our deep dive into the key characteristics of EDA, we can now examine a workable, if idealistic definition of EDA. With the usual caveat that no architecture will, in all likelihood, ever embody EDA in 100% of its functionality, we can define EDA as an enterprise architecture that works in the following ways:

EDA: What It Is

- An EDA is loosely coupled or entirely decoupled.
- An EDA uses asynchronous messaging, typically pub/sub.
- An EDA is granular at the event level.
- EDAs have event listeners, event producers, event processors, and event reactors—ideally based on Simple Object Access Protocol (SOAP) Web services and compatible application components.
- An EDA uses a commonly accessible messaging backbone, such as an enterprise service bus (ESB) as well as adapters or intermediaries to transport messages.
- An EDA does not rely on a central controller.

EDA: What It Does and What It Enables

- An EDA enables agility in operational change management.
- An EDA enables correlation of data for analytics and business process modeling, management, and governance.

- An EDA enables agility in realizing business analytics and dynamically changing analytic models.

- An EDA enables dynamic determinism—EDA enables the enterprise to react to events in accordance with a dynamically changing set of business rules, for example, learning how to avoid shooting the cat and petting the lion (in contrast to controller-based architectures that can be too rigid to be dynamic, for example, shooting the cat, not being aware of the lion).

- An EDA brings greater consciousness of events to the enterprise nervous system.

Though we delve more deeply into the ways that SOAP Web services enable EDA later in the book, we want to go through a basic explanation at this point because our described use of Web services as event producers might appear confusing to some readers. Much has been written about Web services in recent years, and, indeed, many of you likely already work with them. It might seem incorrect to characterize a Web service as a "producer" of SOAP Extensible Markup Language (XML) event state messages when Web services, to be accurate, actually respond to invocation, perhaps sending off SOAP XML if instructed to do so. This is, of course, correct. A SOAP Web service does not transmit a SOAP message without being triggered to do so. Thus, when we talk about Web services functioning as event producers, we are describing Web services that are specifically programmed to send event data to the message backbone. These event Web services could be triggered by activities occurring inside an application or by other Web services. The reason we suggest that event producers should be configured in this way—as Web services that transmit event state data upon invocation—is that there is a high level of utility in transmitting the event data in the portable, universally readable SOAP XML format.

Figure 3.11 revisits our phone company example and shows a high-level model of how its systems would function and interoperate in an ideal EDA. Let's make a few basic observations about how the company's EDA works. With an EDA, in contrast with the traditional enterprise application integration (EAI) approach, the company's three system groups all send event data through adapters and message listeners to a service bus, or equivalent EDA hub that manages a number of pub/sub message queues for all systems that need that event data to carry out their tasks.

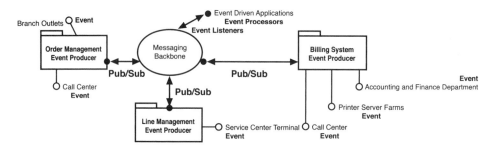

Figure 3.11   A high-level overview of an event-driven architecture at a phone company. Each system group is loosely coupled with one another using standards-based pub/sub asynchronous messaging.

As shown in Figure 3.12, using a dynamic determinism model, the order management system can now listen for overages in minutes and unpaid bills that occur in billing and line management system events and respond to them according to the business rules. Thus, if "John Q" exceeds his allowance of wireless minutes and fails to pay for the overage, the business rules contained in the order management system will deny him the right to add new services to his account.

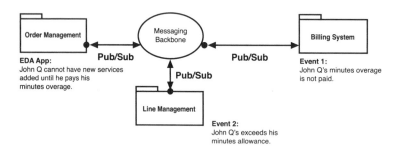

Figure 3.12   In the phone company EDA example, separate events in two systems—an overage in wireless minutes and an unpaid balance in the billing system—are correlated by an application that then denies the order management system the ability to grant the customer a new service request.

The order management system does not have to have the kind of preconception about the line management system that it needed to have to provide this function under the EAI model. The two systems are decoupled but still interoperating through the EDA. The billing system is the event producer and the order management system is the event consumer.

Figure 3.13 shows how event listeners detect the two separate events—the unpaid overage charge and the overage in minutes itself. The EDA-based application that authorizes or declines the new service request subscribes to the event publishing done by the line management and billing systems. The combination of events—unpaid balance and overage of minutes—combines to change the state of John Q's account. The change in state is itself an event. John Q's status goes from "eligible" to "ineligible" for new services. If John Q requests new services, the order management system looks to the EDA application to determine if John Q's status is eligible.

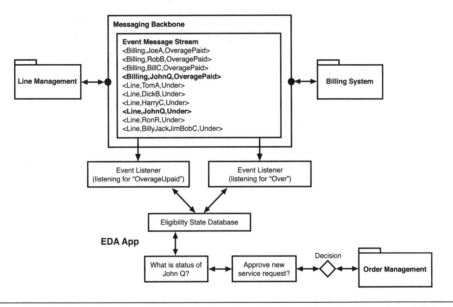

Figure 3.13   The EDA-based application subscribes to event data that is published and consumed by event listeners on separate systems. This gives the EDA-based application the ability to have awareness of changes in state related to John Q without tightly coupling any of the applications involved in the query.

EDA opens new worlds of possibility for IT's ability to serve its business purpose. Think of all the business events a system could leverage if events were exposed—examples include events such as order processing complete, inventory low, new critical order placed, payment received, connection down, and so on. Today, it's a struggle to expose the needed events because they're hidden away within legacy systems. It's common to resort to database triggers or polling to expose these critical actions, but imagine the supportable agility if the systems exposed those actions natively.

Exposing system actions is the root of most integration complexities. "Upon completion of processing at System A, send result to system B," and so on. Most legacy systems were not designed with unanticipated use in mind. They assumed they would be the only system needing the information and thus didn't expose key event data for easy access. If you're lucky, the system will provide an application programming interface (API) to retrieve data, but rarely will it facilitate publishing an event or provide any event retrieval mechanism. Because events are typically not exposed, the first thing you have to do is create an algorithm to determine an event occurred. Often, legacy system events have to be interpreted by correlating multiple database fields (e.g., "If both of these two fields change state, then the order has been shipped..."). Imagine how much easier integration would be if such event actions were natively exposed.

Event-driven architectures are driven by system extensibility (not controllability) and are powered by business events. As shown in Figure 3.13, event handlers listen to low-level system events while EDA agents respond to coarser-grained business events. Some agents might only respond to aggregate business events, creating an even coarser system response.

EDAs are based on dynamic determinism. Dynamic determinism relates to unanticipated use of applications and information assets. Events might trigger other services that might be unknown to the event publisher. Any component can subscribe to receive a particular event unbeknown to the producer. Because of this dynamic processing, the state of the transaction is managed by the events themselves, not by a management mechanism.

EDA embraces these concepts, which facilitate flexibility and extensibility, ultimately increasing a system's ability to evolve. This is accomplished through calculated use of three concepts—loose coupling, asynchrony, and stateless (modeless) service providers—though it doesn't come free. EDA brings inherently decentralized control and a degree of indeterminism to the system.

One of the main benefits of EDA is that it facilitates unanticipated use through its message-driven communication. It releases information previously trapped within monolithic systems. When designing EDA components, you should design for unanticipated use by producing events that can provide future value whether a consumer is waiting or not. Your EDA components should be business-event-intuitive, publishing actions that are valued at a business level.

Imagine an EDA billing component. After it has finished billing a customer, it should announce the fact even if there is no current need. What if all financial actions were being sent via events? Recognizing that there was no immediate need for these events when the systems were originally built, look at how beneficial it would be today. Imagine how easy that would have made your company's Sarbanes-Oxley compliance efforts. Of course, it takes a degree of common sense in determining what might be of value in the future, but it's safe to say that most concrete business state changes will be valued. The caution to note here, though, is that it is possible to create an event publishing overload that overwhelms system and network capacity.

EDA components should also be as stateless as possible. The system state should be carried *in the event*, not stored within a component variable. In some situations, persistence is unavoidable, especially if the component needs to aggregate, resequence, or monitor specific events. However EDA components should do their job and pass on the data then return to process or wait for the next event. This gives the system ultrahigh reuse potential and flexibility. The flexibility of an EDA is leading to emerging concepts that leverage events at a business process level.

Consciousness

EDA brings consciousness to the enterprise nervous system. Without event-driven architecture (EDA), enterprises operate as if they're on life support. They're comatose (brain dead), meaning they are unaware of their surroundings. They cannot independently act on conditions without brokered instruction or the aid of human approval. Service-oriented architectures (SOAs) define the enterprise nervous system, while EDA brings awareness. With the right mix of smart processing and rules, EDA enables the enterprise nervous system to consciously react to internal and external conditions that affect the business within a real-time context.

Consciously reacting means the architecture acts on events independently without being managed by a central controller. Underlying components react to business events in a dynamic decoupled fashion. This is in contrast to the central controller commonly seen in SOAs.

Imagine the analogy of our consciousness with a cluster of functional components. Sections of consciousness process certain information, just like each component has an area of expertise. Components wait for pertinent information, process, and fire an output event. The output might be destined to another component or to an external client. Our consciousness works in the same manner, processing information and sending output to either other synaptic nodes or externally, perhaps through vocal communication. In both of these cases, the messages were not sent to a central controller to decide where to route or what to do. The behavior is inherent in the design.

This is in direct contradiction to the way we teach and learn to program. Schools and universities teach us to start every project with a central controller. In Java, this would be the *main* method, where the sequence of control and the flow of information are controlled. This type of system is tightly coupled with the controller and is difficult to make distributed. Today's architectures need to be looser coupled and more agile than we've been taught.

Today's systems need true dynamic processing. Systems are classified as dynamic or static, but, in reality, most systems are static; they have a finite number of possible flows. If a system has a central controller, it's definitely static even if control branches are based on runtime information. This makes testing easier because of the degree of predetermination but does not provide the agility of a dynamic system.

A central controller with a limited number of possibilities decreases agility. When the system needs to change outside of those possibilities, new rules and branches are added, increasing the tight coupling and complicating the architecture. Over time, the branching rules become so complex that it's nearly impossible to manage and the system turns legacy.

EDA is about removing the rigidity created by central control and injecting real-time context into the business process.

We need to be clear about one thing here: When we talk about removing central control, we are not suggesting that you can be effective in an EDA by removing all control from the application. An uncontrolled application would quickly degenerate into chaos and lock itself up in inaction, or in inappropriate action. Real-world autonomic systems see this: Three moisture-ridden sensors in a B-2 bomber sent bad data to the aircraft's computer, causing it to fly itself into the ground. Another example is the human body's response to significant blood loss: If the body loses a large volume of blood, the brain detects the fact that it's not getting enough oxygen (decreased blood) and automatically dilates the vascular system and increases the heart rate. If the blood loss is due to an open wound, this serves only to lose blood faster! So when we talk about EDA's lack of reliance on central control, we mean that the control is distributed in the form of business rules—and distributed rules must be configured to trigger appropriate actions. The event components contain business rules that are implemented as each event component is activated. The result is an application, or set of applications, that operates under control, but not with a central controller.

Event-driven architectures insert context into the process, which is missing in the central controller model. This is where the potential for a truly dynamic system emerges. Processing information has a contextual element often only available outside of the central controller's view. Even if that contextual change is small, it can still have bearing on the way data should flow.

One contextual stimulus is the Internet. The Internet has opened up businesses to a new undressing. Business-to-business transactions, blogs, outsourcing, trading partner networks, and user communities have all cracked open the hard exterior of corporations. They provide an easily accessible glimpse into a corporation's inner workings that wasn't present before. This glimpse inside will only get larger with time making the inner workings public knowledge and making media-spin-doctoring of unethical practices more evident.

Don Tapscott in *The Naked Corporation*[2] talks about how the Internet will bring moral values to the forefront as unethical practices become more difficult to cover and financial ramifications increase. Businesses will be valued on their financial standing along with reputation, reliability, and integrity. This means businesses will have to change their process flow based on external conditions such as worldly events and do so efficiently.

Information is being aggregated in different ways. Business processes are changing and being combined in real time with external data such as current worldly events. Because of the increased exposure through the Internet, questionable businesses practices are being uncovered. Sometimes, these practices are unknown to the core business, hence businesses want to react quickly to the publicity. Imagine a news investigation that uncovers a major firm is outsourcing labor to a company involved in child slavery. For example, company X is exposed for buying from a cocoa farm in West Africa's Ivory Coast that uses child slavery. The business would immediately want to stop their business transactions with that company and reroute them to a reputable supplier before the damage becomes too great.

For ethical reasons, eBay continually blocks auctions that attempt to profit from horrific catastrophes like major hurricanes, a space shuttle accident, or even a terrorist attack like 9-11. Imagine the public impression of eBay if this was not practiced and they profited from these events.

Now imagine having a system that's worldly aware enough to circumvent business processes if these cases should occur. Suppose this system had an autonomous component that compares news metadata with business process metadata and curtails the process at the first sign of concern. The huge benefits definitely outweigh the calculated risks. Simply rerouting a purchase order to another supplier with comparable service levels definitely has a big upside. If the autonomous deduction was correct, it might have saved the company millions in bad press while maintaining their social responsibility. If it was wrong, then no real harm was done because the alternate company will still deliver on time.

A similar scenario could support eBay's ethics. An autonomous component that compares news metadata with auction metadata could withhold auctions based on real-time news events. If correct, it could save the company from public embarrassment. If wrong, little harm was done other than to delay an auction start time.

EDA can provide this dynamic monitoring, curtailing, and self-healing. Event-driven architecture facilitates bringing these external contexts into the business process. The idea is that the separation between concrete business process and day-to-day reality is blurring. Businesses might be required to change their process based on unexpected external events. This is much different from the days where an end-to-end business process happened within a company's boundary (and control). Combining this need with the traditional business need for rapid change means flexible architecture design is paramount. One way to ensure this flexibility is through the SOA/EDA way—by reducing central control and adding context to the business process.

BAM—A Related Concept

Business Activity Monitoring (BAM) is related to EDA, but different enough that we discuss it in brief. Our goal is to help you differentiate between BAM and EDA, as the two ideas are often used interchangeably in IT discussions. We do not think they are interchangeable.

BAM is the idea that business decisions would be better and more timely if they were based on timely information extracted through business activities that are exposed near real time. Too often, decisions are made based on warehoused data that is stale or misrepresented because of the available gathering technique. Event-driven architectures make it easier to tap into key business activities. BAM components monitor these activities, aggregate the information, watch for anomalies, send warnings, and represent the data graphically.

Historically, most of the activity in this area was achieved with in-house built dashboards. Now we're seeing more vendor products in the space. BAM is most useful in situations where quick critical decisions are important. Interesting applications of this concept include illustrating Key Performance Indicators (KPI), watching for homeland security anomalies, monitoring supply chain activities, and discovering business-to-business (B2B) exchange patterns. Implementing a BAM solution within your EDA is almost always a good idea.

Chapter Summary

- In this chapter, we move forward with our metaphor of EDA as the enterprise nervous system and match the EDA components—event producers, listeners, processors, and reactors—to their equivalent in the nervous system. Event producers and consumers are likened to the sensory nerve endings that pick up and relay information about our senses to our brain, which is like an event processor. Reactions, such as physical movements, are like the event reactors. For additional context and framework, we look at event-driven programming, a core technology of most PCs, as a comparable example of events, event listening, and event processing on a lower level of functioning than an EDA.

- To complete our understanding of how EDA works, we then carry this enterprise nervous system idea further and take an in-depth look at the characteristics of EDAs and their components. Again, our focus is on the EDA of the future: an implicit, complex, and dynamic EDA, one that can adapt easily to changes and continually expand its reach of event detection and event reaction.

- EDA components must be loosely coupled to function dynamically. Loose coupling requires that EDA components have low levels of preconception about each other and maintainability. An EDA works best if each component functions independently, with little need to know about the other components it is communicating with, and few ramifications if one component is modified.

- EDAs, unlike conventional applications, do not rely on central controllers.

- Events (state change notifications) are central to an EDA. An event can take the form of a message and an EDA is a message-based idea. To work, an EDA's loosely coupled components must be able to produce and consume messages. The messages could be related to event listening, processing, or reactions. The more easily the messages can flow across the EDA (which might span multiple enterprises), the better the EDA will work.

- Asynchronous, or publish/subscribe (pub/sub) messaging, is one of the best foundations for an EDA. As the EDA components communicate with one another, they feed messages (events) into an event bus. Event listeners receive the events, and then EDA components process the event data as required by the EDA's designed purpose. Pub/sub is ideal for EDAs because it removes a lot of message flow dependencies from individual components. It is simpler, for example, to connect event listeners using pub/sub than to tightly couple them together, where changes in configuration are costly and slow to accomplish.

- To achieve loose coupling and asynchronous messaging, an EDA relies on message intermediaries. In some cases, these are known as service buses.

- The ideal EDA, therefore, is a loosely coupled, pub/sub-based architecture, with low levels of preconception and high degrees of maintainability among the components.

Endnotes

[1] Wikipedia. Event-Driven Programming. August 2004. http://en.wikipedia.org/wiki/Event-driven_programming.

[2] Tapscott, Don. *The Naked Corporation*. New York: Free Press, 2003.

CHAPTER 4

The Potential of EDA

Introduction

According to rock-and-roll legend, Johnny Rotten once said, "I don't know what I want but I know how to get it." He didn't realize it, but he was predicting the current state of event-driven architecture (EDA). The uses of EDA are many, and the range of misunderstanding about them is just as impressive. Before we plunge into the practical issues involved in implementing EDA, we thought it would make sense to catch our breath for a moment and look in more depth at why EDA is a good idea for some (but not all!) enterprise computing scenarios.

EDA has the potential to transform IT and computing on many levels. The paradigm can improve existing modes of IT, as well as introduce wholly new ways of doing things. Although there are many places where these improvements can be realized, we would like to focus on four primary areas. EDA is poised to make sweeping changes in enterprise computing, particularly in cost reduction through outsourcing and better system management. EDA has the potential to render great advances in agility and analytics. EDA will also be a boon to computing in the general societal level, including government and academia. Finally, EDA has the potential to improve compliance, a high-pressure area for many in the IT field.

EDA's Potential in Enterprise Computing

Many discussions of EDA focus on how the paradigm can benefit businesses or organizations through improved analytics or responsiveness to events. However, EDA also has great potential to improve the way IT itself is conducted, so we want to highlight several areas where EDA can benefit the IT organization on its own turf. The opportunities for EDA in IT systems management fall into three basic categories, which we call "old dog, new tricks," "new dog, new tricks," and "new dog, no tricks." The last category covers innovations from EDA that don't quite exist, although some people think they do.

The Old Dog, with New EDA Tricks

System monitoring is an existing area of IT that EDA has the potential to transform. As IT infrastructure grows in both scale and complexity, EDA can help system monitoring software work smarter. For example, if we consider data about server load levels to be events, we can set up event listeners to track server load levels. An EDA-based system monitor can intelligently process the server load event data and respond accordingly. To some extent, system monitoring software already works this way, but the standards-based pub/sub design, and the inherently dynamic characters of an EDA, can enable a higher level of system monitoring responsiveness to changing server usage patterns. The interesting point here is that the system monitor can learn from the causality of problems and then send future alerts warning of potential problems before they happen. If fact, many of the infrastructure monitoring suites are beginning to add this functionality now.

Security monitoring is another area where EDA can bring about positive change. A relative of system monitoring, security monitoring is a collection of activities that involve the generation, audit, and interpretation of any number of security-related system logs. For example, a large enterprise might simultaneously generate logs of system use, logins, firewall access attempts, intrusion detection warnings, and so on. Figure 4.1 shows a network that has multiple security logs for its routers, firewalls, servers, and so on. Analyzing these logs can be difficult, or even impossible. Certainly no human being can look over a thousand log records an hour and put them into any kind of order. Storing and outsourcing of log interpretation is a costly necessity for many organizations. Interpreting security events across multiple logs can be highly challenging, and that is where EDA can come to the rescue.

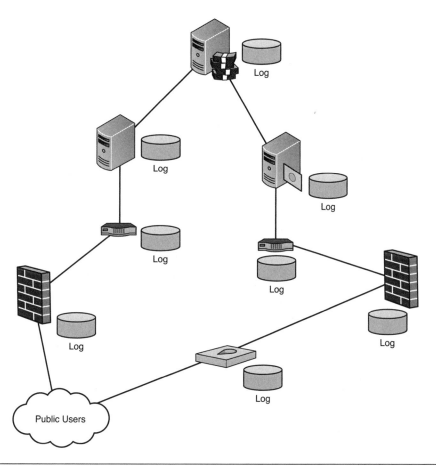

Figure 4.1   A network with multiple security logs, including firewalls, routers, certification servers, and biometric devices.

A security monitoring EDA can establish event generators to analyze the event stream of log entries, looking for patterns, and producing events based on analytical criteria. The event processors can then correlate actions across security logs and produce security alerts in real time for consumption by system administrators and security personnel. An EDA-based security monitoring application is represented in Figure 4.2. By analyzing the security logs in parallel, and in real time, the EDA security monitor can catch patterns of events that might elude the individual analysis of security logs. With today's hacker attacks growing more sophisticated, this kind of real-time multilevel security analysis can make the difference in detecting an attack before it begins.

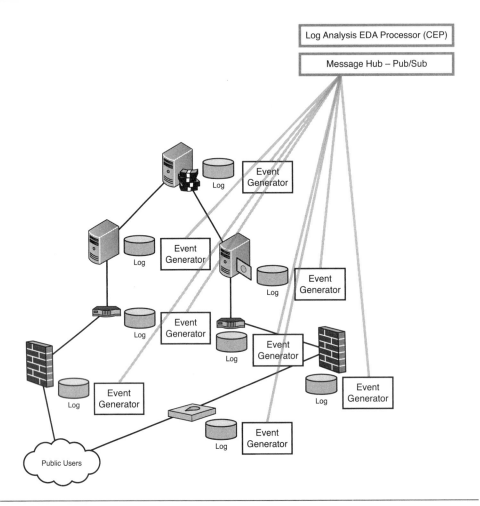

Figure 4.2   Placing event listeners by each security log, the security monitoring EDA can examine security event data in parallel and in real time, potentially recognizing and reacting to patterns that might not be apparent from the analysis of separate logs individually.

Of course, you could set up multiple streams of monitoring through conventional application integration techniques, and to some extent, security monitoring already works this way. However, the breakthrough of an EDA approach is in the dynamic processing and loose binding used. If connecting a security log to a security monitoring and analytics system requires too much time and money, it either won't get done at all or the integration project will be scheduled for when time permits. If connecting, disconnecting, or reconfiguring a security log's integration with a security monitoring system is relatively simple, fast, and inexpensive, as it could be with an EDA, then that security monitoring system will have a lot more ability to be on top of security data in real time.

The flexibility of the EDA approach also allows for new monitoring to be added quicker. As new hack approaches emerge, it's much easier to add additional event processors to monitor and mitigate the risk. These new forms of attack could even come from external sources, meaning companies could share the attack approach upon initial detection, hence thwarting subsequent attacks on other companies. This demonstrates the wide awareness concept of EDAs.

The other existing area of IT where EDA can bring change, mostly in the form of savings in time and money, is software integration. Most modern commercial software packages offer application programming interfaces (APIs) to enable integration with other applications. However, integrating through proprietary APIs can require extensive reengineering. Service-oriented architecture (SOA) and Web services can both improve application integration speed and budget through the use of standards. However, EDA can do even better because of the way that EDA revamps the whole approach to application logic. Let's assume that the conventional, proprietary middleware approach to enterprise application integration (EAI) is the slowest and most costly. SOA/Web services introduce a degree of speed and cost improvement, but in most cases the application logic would remain the same. That is, the applications being integrated would still process data on their own and share it with other applications through the Web services API. In contrast, an EDA approach would pull apart the tiers of application logic and move certain logical operations into distinct event processors loosely coupled together to provide the desired result.

As an example, look at Figure 4.3, which depicts a simple application integration scenario. In the phone company case, the line management system needs to update the billing system regarding which accounts have an overage in their minutes. In the baseline case, shown at the top, the company sets up proprietary middleware EAI, which sends a `MinuteOverage` message from the line management to the billing system, and then ferries back a confirmation message. As we know, although there is nothing wrong with this approach, it can be costly and slow to change. Modifications to either system might necessitate changes to the middleware, and so on.

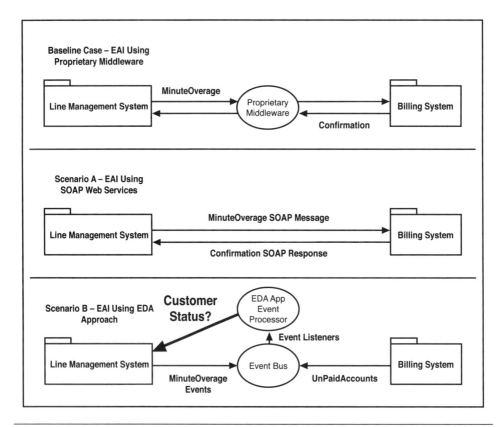

Figure 4.3   Contrasting three modes of application integration: conventional proprietary middleware, SOAP Web services, and EDA.

In Scenario A, the company uses a basic Simple Object Access Protocol (SOAP) Web service to achieve the same application integration. In Scenario A, the line management system exposes a Web service that can send MinuteOverage messages upon invocation by its own system rules. The MinuteOverage SOAP message triggers a SOAP response of confirmation from the billing system that travels back to the line management system. This approach saves the company the expense and complexity required to maintain the proprietary middleware. However, it is still a point-to-point solution, and might in fact be fairly fragile if the systems are changed. Overall, it is still simpler and less expensive to maintain and change than the proprietary middleware, but there is a better way.

Scenario B, shown at the bottom of Figure 4.3, illustrates an EDA approach to this kind of application integration. Though EDA is not an application integration technology, per se, EDA can result in a very agile integration approach. Imagine that there are two event streams at work here: a series of `MinuteOverages` and a series of `UnPaidAccount` updates, which flow into a message hub. Event listeners can review the event streams and pick out correlated pairs of `MinuteOverages` and `UnPaidAccounts`. The event processor can then respond to customer status requests from the order management system.

This approach, while perhaps time consuming to implement and costly to initially set up, enables very fast changes in application integration moving forward. With an event bus as the enterprise's core of application integration, and each application set up to listen for and process event data using standards, application integration becomes a matter of plugging and unplugging to the event bus and modifying application logic in discrete locations. If the EDA has been established with a low level of maintainability and preconception among the components, this is possible.

Overall, EDA has the potential to improve the speed and cost characteristics of a number of existing IT activities. Although these activities, such as system monitoring, security monitoring, or application integration, are not new at all, the EDA can make them different and expand the range of possibilities that can be achieved in IT through these existing activities.

New Dog, with New EDA Tricks

EDA offers several new functions to enterprise IT. Or, at the very least, these functions are so highly innovative as to be considered new versions of existing practices and functions. These include new application models, agility of architecture, and adaptability and reuse of system components.

Reuse of IT assets is a potentially beneficial quality of EDA and SOA. By breaking applications into universally accessible components, or services, the event exposure of EDA enables reuse of those services across multiple composite applications. For example, an event listener that detects stock market fluctuations could be used by a trading application, a stock market research application, a mobile market reporting application, and so on, without any modification to its basic design or communication interfaces. In the EDA context, the potential for reuse spans beyond that of Web services in the context of an EDA. They are so isolated from one another, in terms of preconception and maintainability, that they can be reused with a high degree of efficiency. Just to be clear, we are not saying that reuse is always justified or even desirable. There are certain situations where software reuse is a great way to be agile and economical, but others where it is not worth the extra effort involved. And, governing reuse and managing load levels can be challenging, but that is a topic we take up later on in this book.

The value of code reuse emerges in composite applications. EDA, like SOA, enables the development of composite applications, software that functions using a collection of software modules, most likely SOAP using Web services, that function in concert to accomplish the requirements of the program.

Though not exactly new, the standards-based approach of SOA and EDA to composite application design changes the way that IT manages software assets. In contrast to conventional software deployment, where an application is typically installed on a server, or group of servers as a stand-alone functional entity, the composite application resides on many servers, including ones that might be outside of the enterprise itself. There are many benefits to this approach in terms of cost flexibility and management. At the same time, the increase in flexibility can increase complexity and must be managed accordingly.

Figure 4.4 shows an example of event services being reused in more than one composite application. In this case, we have a consumer portal that offers an auto loan referral service, which is a lead generator for the auto loan finance companies, as well as banner ads from car companies. The consumer portal uses an EDA-based application to correlate the event streams of loan referrals and car ad clicks to generate lists of highly qualified leads for specific cars. If a site visitor requests information on an auto loan and also clicks on an ad for Ford Mustang, for example, then the EDA application identifies that person as strongly interested in a Ford Mustang. The potential for reuse and composite application development comes from the many add-on applications that can be created out of these existing modules. The event streams coming from these two modules—the auto loan referral and ad server—can be reused to create consumer analytics applications, credit repair referral services, and follow-on ad server functions.

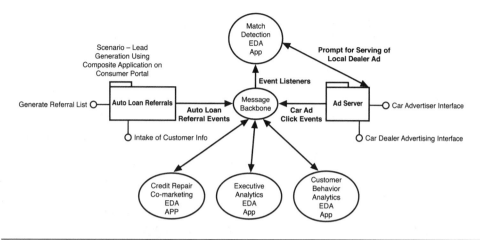

Figure 4.4   After a message backbone carries event data in a pub/sub manner, it becomes possible to repurpose the event stream for use in a number of composite applications with relatively little effort, compared with conventional application integration for each derived application.

Overall, though, the EDA and SOA approaches to application design result in an increased agility for enterprise architecture. As it becomes simpler to unplug, move, and reconnect EDA components dynamically with the help of standards, the IT change process will begin to speed up. EDA also enables enterprise architecture to be more adaptable to changes in its required use than conventional architecture.

New Dog, No EDA Tricks

Like all new paradigms, EDA has generated some dubious potential capabilities. Whether they are the product of misunderstandings by early adopters or vendor excitement, these faux innovations of EDA can be confusing to the rest of us. We want to focus on a couple of IT functions for which EDA does not provide much in the way of innovation.

Service virtualization, for example, is an IT trend that is largely separate from EDA. A virtual server replicates the functions of one server on any number of other machines, a process that increases the efficiency of data-center asset utilization. Although EDA system types can help manage virtualization by monitoring virtual machine usage and activity levels, the EDA itself does not create the virtual machine.

Similarly, grid computing (sometimes known as *utility computing*) is an IT model that can use EDA for management and systemic self-awareness, but the EDA is not essential to its design.

EDA and Enterprise Agility

We've already said that EDA leads to greater agility in business, but now that we know more about the workings of EDA, we can take a much more in-depth look at why this is the case. In the Preface, we described agility as a process that involves a cycle of activities, shown in Figure 4.5. To be agile, an organization must be able to perceive circumstances in a way that indicates that an agile move might be required. Based on the information received, and the logic used to assess this information, the organization might elect to make a move, or not. Either decision—yes or no—could be the hallmark of an agile organization. The better the assessment logic, the better the agility will be. If the organization makes a move, it must execute on the decision, a process that typically involves information systems on multiple levels. Then, the organization must assess whether its agile move was a good idea or not, and repeat the process once again, with fresh, postexecution data feeding into the "perception" step of the agility cycle.

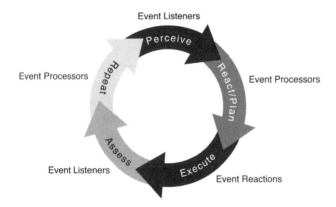

Figure 4.5   The agility cycle, which requires perception and reaction to information about a business's operating or strategic environment, as well as execution and assessment of the reaction, is enhanced by EDA. Each phase of the agility cycle corresponds, in loose terms, to an EDA component.

Strategic agility refers to an organization's capacity to change its strategic plan or business model in a rapid enough cycle to match changing business conditions. Operational agility, the ability of an organization to modify how it operates in response to changing conditions, is the flip side of strategic agility. Typically, a strategic shift necessitates a reworking of operations, with a concomitant shift in IT. Functional agility is a measure of how well a company can change its ongoing business processes in response to business conditions.

EDA has the potential to improve all three types of agility. As the best possible "nervous system" for the enterprise, EDA is ideally suited to serve the needs of perception, reaction, execution, and assessment that form the core of agility. Best of all, the "react and plan" function is really reacting and planning, not simply following a sequence tree of predefined logical condition matching. In strategic terms, an EDA can provide high-quality data about business conditions that relate to strategic decision making. EDAs have the capacity to deliver real-time (or near real-time) data about business conditions. Although some strategic decisions need to be made too slowly to benefit from real-time data, most strategic thinking is influenced by the latest information about a particular business situation. Certainly, the more accurate and timely data that strategic decision makers have, the better off they will be. EDAs also give strategists the ability to correlate data from diverse sources and observe hidden trends over long periods of time. This is an advantage that EDA delivers to strategic decision making.

Operationally, the EDA's flexibility and IT asset reuse enables the kind of fast operational changes that a strategic agile move might require. In particular, a well-designed EDA can speed the kinds of business transitions that occur in mergers or reengineering projects that are so often associated with agile decisions. The loosely coupled nature of EDA components makes them relatively quick and inexpensive to move around and reconfigure, so business transformation with EDA can be faster than those done using conventional middleware approaches to EAI. There are a number of challenges to this simple idea, and we explore them in depth as we continue in the book.

In the functional area, the EDA's flexibility and ability to sense real-time or nearly real-time changes in business conditions can result in a high degree of agility. EDA can be a key enabler of what the industry calls *real-time analytics,* systems that feed information to decision makers rapidly through management dashboards and reports. The event listeners and processors can look for specific patterns of events and report them to decision makers. Moreover, the monitoring of events lends itself to learning, through event pattern recognition, allowing business alerts to be issued even before human detection.

EDA also has great potential to enable the use of business process modeling tools, or BPM. BPM is a set of technologies and business practices that breaks down a business process, such as sending out an invoice, into a discrete process step, for example, "Look up customer address" and "Seal envelope" and correlates it to underlying IT systems where appropriate. BPM is useful for mapping business management's requirements to IT capabilities and systems. And, while BPM can be used with many different enterprise architectural paradigms, the loosely coupled quality of EDA has the potential to render BPM the most effective and agile.

Looking forward, the EDA will actually make BPM tools of today obsolete. In EDA, it's the events that drive the flow and transition of state, not a BPM controller. In an EDA, the BPM tool simply provides insight to the listeners, how they're linked, and who is processing what. The linkage representation (matching events to listeners) is an important part because this is all done in real time. The EDA BPM becomes a looking glass into the processing of information instead of the traditional controller model.

However, when we talk about EDA being the paradigm that has the potential for the greatest levels of agility, we are assuming here that the EDAs have been designed adequately for the tasks of perceiving changes in the business environment, and that they are sufficiently standards-based and decoupled to ensure the kind of flexibility that is needed for all types of business agility. There is nothing inherently agile about an EDA, especially if it has not been designed to help assist management in making agile decisions.

EDA and Society's Computing Needs

The power of EDA reaches far beyond the boundaries of corporate IT. Computers and software play a major role in virtually every aspect of society and public life, from health care to government, education at all levels, and the sciences. EDA, with its real-time responsiveness to changes in conditions and its rapid change cycle, has the potential to alter, and in some cases improve, the way that society uses computing.

EDA and the Government

The old saying, "Figures don't lie but liars always figure..." is often used to refer to politicians and the policy "wonks" who feed them information about the state of the world and what ought be done about it. Where does all this information come from? Much of it comes from databases, public and private, that store information about diverse but related areas of interest to policymakers. For example, a policymaker might say that obesity in America is connected to the rise in the use of corn syrup in processed foods. Whether this is actually true or not is open to debate, and it not our intention to get in the middle of any contentious issues. However, what we want to point out is that a public policy discussion that links obesity with corn syrup consumption is one that connects two wholly separate sets of data and places them into the same argument.

There is data about obesity and there is data about corn syrup. There is a correlation between the two trends: Obesity is on the rise, and so is corn syrup consumption. However, that does not necessarily mean that there is a cause-and-effect relationship between the two trends. Perhaps there are other factors that influence obesity as well, such as excessive television viewing, lack of exercise, obesity-producing hormone additives in meat, and so on. How do those factors contribute to obesity? Or, perhaps, one or more do not figure in? An EDA approach to researching obesity could give policymakers more accurate data about the true nature of a trend and what needs to be done about it.

Now, you might think, "Do you need an EDA to compare trends in different data sets? Can't you do that with Microsoft Excel or any number of other techniques?" Yes, of course you can, but an EDA gives you several capabilities that can be quite tricky to pull off using standard techniques. For example, you can observe trends in multiple data sets in real time, and continually add data sets for comparison or modify the way they interact in real time. EDA gives you a high level of control and flexibility over dynamic data analysis.

Taking a look at a more urgent and practical example of EDA's potential in the government sector involves what is going on (and not going on) in sharing information about terrorists among the multiple agencies of the Department of Homeland Security. To keep it simple, let's hypothesize that there are two databases of suspected terrorists in the U.S. Government. One is at the CIA and the other is at the FBI. (Just to be clear, we are working up this example on a purely theoretical basis to illustrate a point using a situation that most of us can appreciate. The true nature of these types of databases is beyond our specific knowledge.) As we have read in the news, there were historically some problems in coordinating the sharing of information about terrorist suspects between these two organizations.

Although some of the problems might be organizational, a good measure of the issue is technological in nature. The two sets of data stores are likely to be running on different platforms, written in different languages, and utilizing incompatible labeling methods. For example, the FBI might categorize terrorist risk profiles on a scale of 1 to 5, whereas the CIA might categorize them using letters A, B, and C. The two agencies might want to exchange data, but the technological and data labeling challenges make it complex and costly to do so. On top of that, there are great security concerns about who can see the data on each side, and so on.

Now, at the risk of repeating ourselves, we know that it is possible to integrate these two systems so they exchange data using proprietary middleware. However, it is going to be too costly and slow to really work. Using an EDA approach based on SOAP Web services, we could establish some *event services* (more on this in Chapter 5, "The SOA-EDA Connection") that produce events whenever a terrorist profile is updated or created in each system. Without preconception or maintainability issues between them, the two event services (event producers) at the FBI and CIA, respectively, could feed valuable data into a central message hub for use in any number of EDA processors.

Adding to this setup, let's say that the Transportation Safety Administration (TSA) wants to be able to plug in the names, or some other unique identifier, of airline passengers and match them against known aliases of high-profile terrorists. The inquiries from the TSA consist of a stream of events that asks "Name_match?" for each passenger name. The EDA processor can pull together these inquiries with the streams of events, and patterns of past events, from the FBI and CIA databases in real time. This setup is shown in Figure 4.6.

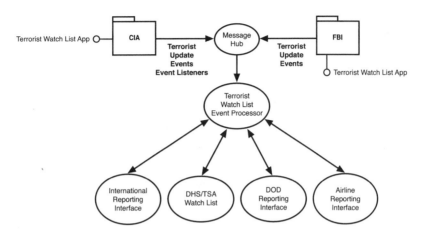

Figure 4.6   Using a message hub to create a pub/sub stream of terrorist watch list updates gives the CIA and FBI the opportunity to collaborate without a major EAI effort, and also create a number of derivative event processor applications that can serve terrorist watch list needs at other agencies.

Furthering the example, we might also want to correlate if any of these passengers who have names that match known terrorist aliases have paid for the tickets with a debit card, or are flying one way, and so on. To accomplish these follow-on objectives, we could set up a complex event processing application that listened to events from a number of separate entities, including the banking system, the NSA, and so on. As shown in Figure 4.7, the event processor could be programmed to look for the matches, and flag them as suspicious passengers. The whole key to this working is the ability of the EDA to view multiple event streams in real time. This is only possible to do with any kind of efficiency or economic justification using EDA.

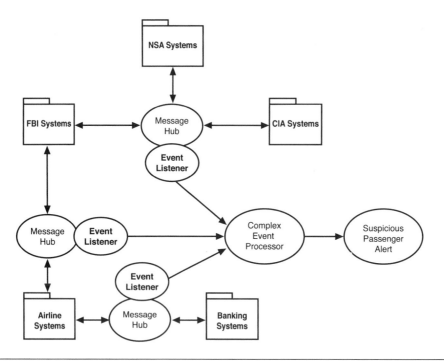

Figure 4.7   Event listeners can integrate numerous systems that might be entirely separate from one another, forwarding event data to a complex event processor. In this example, event data from five different agencies and private entities is examined for patterns that would indicate a suspicious airline passenger.

EDA and Health Care

The ability to synchronize the analysis of multiple data streams in real time is a great potential boon to health-care researchers and providers. Whether it involves correlating cancer treatments with genotypes worldwide or figuring out which brand of bedpan breaks the most, research of health-care practices is an urgent task for a large number of stakeholders. The health-care industry typically wants to provide good care at an ever decreasing cost. Insurance companies, drug companies, doctors, patients, labor unions, private employers, the government, and the academic world all have a stake—and a say—in how health care is managed and paid for. EDA-based approaches to IT offer value on many fronts in this regard.

If we convert the complex EDA approach we used for the government in Figure 4.7 and applied it to the health-care field, it might look like Figure 4.8. If the integrations between the players in the health-care industry are achieved through a message bus pub/sub approach, event listeners can be deployed to examine the event streams that occur within the conduct of daily business among the players. Without any dedicated integration, then, a complex EDA can look for patterns that are relevant to specific lines of inquiry. For example, from the EDA, it could be possible to detect abuse of prescriptions, the success of treatment protocols, or prescribing patterns of specific doctors.

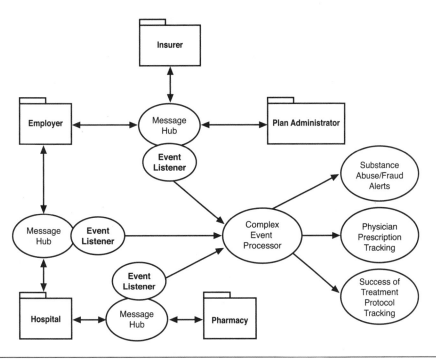

Figure 4.8   Taking the complex EDA to the health-care industry, there is the potential to use event listeners to enable multiple analytical systems based on event streams occurring among hospitals, insurers, pharmacies, and so on.

EDA and Compliance

Compliance is the other area where EDA has the potential to make a positive impact. This is a vast subject, one on which an entire book could be written. However, for our purposes, the EDA-related benefit to concentrate on with compliance is the paradigm's ability to enable continuous monitoring of separate activities, which is often the key to compliance. Simple compliance, the requirement that a single set of activities, such as financial accounting controls, be monitored and verified, is itself a complex IT challenge. Multithreaded compliance, which requires that multiple independent systems or even multiple companies and government organizations all provide visibility for audit and control, can be so complex as to render it cost prohibitive.

For example, a global corporation must comply with a host of separate financial disclosure laws, environmental laws, and privacy laws worldwide. The simple act of exporting an employee's personal address from a European data center to an American one could trigger a criminal charge for violation of the EU's strict privacy laws. How can a company be sure that it is not violating such laws? Add to this the distributed and independent nature of certain corporations worldwide and you can see the enormity of the challenge.

With an EDA approach, it is possible to set up event listeners that can examine event data relating to multithreaded compliance activities and alert auditors. In our employee privacy example, the data export activity of the employee databases in the EU can be monitored for events that signal that an improper data export has been initiated, or requested. The event processor can then issue a warning to the administrator or the user that the data export violates both company policy and the law. Or, the event processor could be programmed to block the export itself. In this way, EDA provides a dynamic, cost-effective, and flexible way to achieve the monitoring necessary for global multithreaded compliance.

Chapter Summary

In this chapter, we looked at several of the areas in business and society where EDA has the potential for positive impact. The following are places where EDA has a strong potential for positive change:

- Within enterprise computing itself, at the infrastructure and data-center operations level, EDA has the power to enable improvements in real-time system monitoring and security monitoring, two areas where conventional integration techniques can be slow to set up and modify, and costly to maintain.

- EDA has the potential to bring about changes in application integration, beyond even the benefits wrought by Web services and SOA. The level of flexibility potentially enabled can have an impact on the way that data centers support application infrastructure.

- The capacity to enable complex composite applications is both an innovation of EDA and also a challenge to data-center operations. As applications become increasingly detached from specific servers and distributed across multiple boxes, data centers, and even organizations, the IT team must understand and respond by modifying their support, testing, and deployment processes.

- Overall, EDA results in enterprise agility. The paradigm helps make real-time data more readily available, which has the ability to guide decision makers in strategic planning. Operationally, EDA's inherent flexibility makes possible the kind of rapidly cycling changes in business that strategic agility demands.

- In the broader societal context, EDA has the potential to change the way that government and the sciences use computing to accomplish their missions. For example, antiterrorism programs can be greatly aided by the rapid, simultaneous visibility into multiple criminal and commercial databases worldwide.

- In terms of compliance, a major stress for large companies, EDA enables cost-effective and dynamic continuous monitoring of separate systems. This is a boon to auditors who need to set a level of assurance that multiple threads of global legal requirements are being followed.

The SOA-EDA Connection

Getting Real

The time has come to get real. Having familiarized ourselves with the definition of event-driven architecture (EDA), the characteristics of its components, its potential, and the essential makeup of Web services, the likely building blocks of EDA, we are finally ready to delve into the "how-to" of EDA. For the purpose of this book, we focus on building an EDA using a service-oriented architecture (SOA) as the foundation. Although there are many other ways to create an EDA, keeping the focus on SOA gives you insight into a real-world approach to EDA that is being practiced today. In fact, building an EDA in this fashion could be viewed as a specialized, mature form of SOA because many of the building parts and concepts are shared between the two concepts.

This chapter establishes the SOA-EDA connection and lays out the specific ways in which SOA powers the EDA. Although simple in concept, the realities of bending the raw Simple Object Access Protocol (SOAP) Web services into a functioning EDA are quite challenging and complex. In particular, we look at the ways in which Web services can serve as event producers, event listeners, and event processors. We examine the ways in which SOA messaging constructs, such as the enterprise service bus (ESB), enable EDA.

Event Services

From now on, when we talk about events, we mean SOAP-encoded data. To be precise, an event is a piece of SOAP XML that carries some data about the event that has occurred. The event data can then be relayed to a Web service that acts as an event listener or other EDA component. Let's call this type of EDA Web service an *event service*. An event service can be created in two ways: organic development or adaptation of an existing event data source. In the organic development mode, a developer uses a software development tool, such as Visual Studio, to create a SOAP Web service that transmits and receives SOAP XML to indicate that an event has occurred. For example, you might develop a Web service that generates a one-way SOAP message every time someone logs in to a Web site. Each login would trigger the event service that, in turn, sends out the SOAP XML message saying—hypothetically—the time and date of the login. Such a Web service might be developed to sit on the Web server that manages the Web site. This event service is an event producer that transmits the event data to the event bus for receipt by the event listeners. In reality, this kind of wholly new event service might function as both the event producer and the event listener. It produces the event data and publishes it at the same time. However, the discrete functionality of generating the data and publishing it might be separate methods within the single event service.

An adaptation approach to creating an event service involves using a SOAP Web service development tool to transform data that originates in another application into SOAP XML and publishes it directly to the event bus. For example, there are extensive arrays of legacy applications that manage the trading in the stock market. These applications generate all kinds of data about stocks and the overall market. You could create an event service that functions as a generator of an event stream of stock data. This Web service would be an event producer, adapting the data it receives from the stock trading systems. It converts the stream of data in the legacy format into SOAP XML, which it can then publish for event consumption. Figure 5.1 diagrams what this kind of Web service EDA would look like.

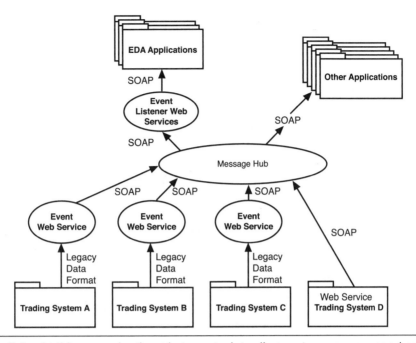

Figure 5.1 In this example, three legacy stock trading systems are exposed as event Web services, while the fourth one is a native Web service already. The four event Web services feed event data into the event bus, where it is consumed by Web services acting as event listeners.

As Figure 5.1 shows, the event listeners can also be Web services that communicate with the messaging hub and the event processors using SOAP. Keeping with our premise that the EDA of the future will consist of Web service and SOA components, every piece of the EDA shown in Figure 5.1 is based on Web services standards, including the message hub.

For practical purposes, the message hub that we refer to is an enterprise service bus (ESB), though there are, of course, alternatives in use. To keep things simple, though, let's stay focused on ESB. The ESB is a messaging technology that enables Web service consumers and providers to connect. The ESB is the hub of the SOA and the EDA as well. Event Web services publish event data to the ESB. Event listeners subscribe to event services (event producers) through the ESB, and forward event data to event processors. The ESB (or groups of ESBs) is the message bone that facilitates the pub/sub structure of the EDA. Other applications, beyond the scope of the EDA, also tap into the ESB to connect with the underlying Web services, which expose the functionality of the trading applications as SOAP XML.

The technology used to implement an EDA bus varies widely, from vendor products to native language constructs. You can do the following:

- Leverage an enterprise-class vendor product from Microsoft, IBM, Oracle, SOA Software, or the like.
- Wrap IBM's WebSphereMQ with the Java Messaging Standard (JMS) for an enterprise-class reliable transport.
- Use a lightweight and inexpensive enterprise service bus (ESB).
- Use a lightweight JMS provider or the JMS service provided by a J2EE server.
- Grow your own backbone using MDBs, JINI, JVM Channels, or .NET functionality.
- Leverage an XML-based network appliance either as a lightweight ESB or as a gateway to a heavier-weight ESB (potentially eliminating some XML transformation, security, and schema validation that are much more expensive in general-purpose hardware, where a traditional ESB runs).

Any of these would be fine technologies for the main EDA service bus. Your selection will depend upon a number of inputs, as always: constraints of budget, capability, or time, scope of the implementation and long-term road map, and so on. Generally speaking, moving away from a mainstream vendor solution should be done with some caution—particularly as the vendor solutions mature and become more interoperable.

The Service Network

Figure 5.1 provides the high-level view of the EDA's fit with an SOA. Let's look closer at the implementation of an SOA, which is the first practical step toward building the EDA. To get started on the subject of SOA adoption, we would like to introduce a way of viewing the SOA that can help cut through the complexity and keep you focused on the pragmatic reality of what is going on. Meet the *service network*.

A service network is a specific form of SOA that includes Web service providers, Web service consumers, service intermediaries, and ESBs all working in concert in a unified network. Figure 5.2 presents a very simplistic service network that contains these core elements. In the service network view of SOA, any application can be both a consumer and provider of Web services. In reality, this means that the applications that connect to the service network have separate Web service consumers and Web service providers. In Figure 5.2, we show just one or two of each for the applications, though in real life there might be thousands of Web service providers and Web service consumers.

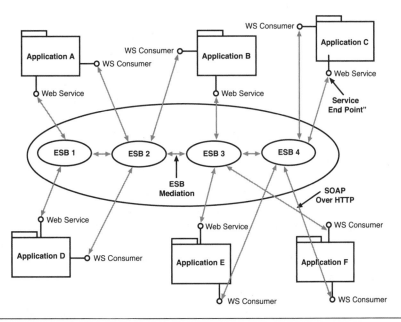

Figure 5.2   The service network, shown here, consists of applications that both consume and provide Web services. The service network's core is a group of ESBs that provide the message hubs necessary for connecting all the service endpoints.

The service network connects Web service consumers with Web service providers, which are also known as *service endpoints*. Though this might be a little confusing, we use this terminology to reinforce the notion that the Web service itself is at the endpoint of a chain of messaging that originates with the Web service consumer and terminates with the Web service itself, or at the very least, with a proxy for that Web service. For this reason, we sometimes refer to Web services as endpoints.

The Web services, or endpoints, themselves might represent a variety of processing functions. They might be event Web services (or event services) that feed event data to event listeners and event processors. Or, the Web services might be *business services* that handle business-specific logical processing.

In the service network, there might be more than one ESB implementation. The ESBs, and related intermediaries, route the SOAP messages from consumer to endpoint, handling routing, transformation, and so on. In fact, one of the great challenges of designing and implementing a service network is working through the mediation necessary to get multiple ESBs to operate together simply. In a service network, some of the Web services themselves might be deployed to help the service network with its own functioning. Such Web services are not involved in business processes, but rather in the management and administration of the service network itself. These are known as *enterprise services*.

Implementing the SOA and Service Network

Thinking of your SOA service network in terms of network design and management is an appropriate first step in understanding the undertaking of SOA adoption. In network management and design, network devices provide specific functions. Some functions are case specific and some are generic. Some nodes handle routing, some handle security, some serve only certain types of traffic, some are interactive in nature, and some are self-healing in that they adjust their behavior and alliances based on events or on the state of the network. All can be managed and monitored using a single tool or suite of tools. Design of a network includes many considerations—performance requirements, service-level requirements, organizational structure and support models, and even funding models. As you think about your SOA, you must consider the same. In network architecture, devices (nodes) and their scope are typically vendor-produced and well defined. In SOA design, service identification, scoping, and granularity are defined by you, and in most cases, services are built by you. SOA definition requires a level of sophistication typically underestimated by most corporate IT shops today. Take, as an example, the capacity planning discipline required to implement and maintain an SOA environment. The shared service nature of an SOA coupled with being oriented entirely around agility means that capacity planning is critical. These concerns are only amplified by the computational complexity of XML parsing because it has to happen for every message. Thinking about an SOA as a service network can accelerate understanding of SOA concerns, and the following paragraphs outline many of the characteristics of a service network.

Service networks provide several common capabilities, an important one being service-oriented legacy enablement. When we talk about SOA, we often concentrate on the notion of composing applications from a variety of services like the ones mentioned earlier in this chapter (business services, enterprise services, intermediaries, etc.). This might lead you to believe that SOA only works with new applications built with new components. It's true that if we consider all noncomposite applications as black box, all existing applications are legacy applications. Service networks actually allow for the incorporation of legacy (black-box) applications just as they allow for the incorporation of brand-new, vendor-produced commodity applications that we might bring into our infrastructure. In some cases, bringing a legacy or black-box application into the service network is as simple as providing service wrappers into the application. In other cases, this approach is inappropriate, and classic integration mechanisms must be employed. In the case studies outlined later in this book, we see examples of both.

Service networks allow for event-driven composition and business-level integration. This is the big promise—the future (and in some cases the present) of SOA. Because elements in a service network present their capabilities through virtualized service abstractions, they promote distributed creation, execution, and evolution—facilitated by federated governance. In plain English: Because the functions provided by the "nodes" in your service network are being described in a uniform way, and the descriptions should be made available in a uniform way, services can be consumed dynamically by evolving composite applications, and services can be maintained, versioned, and retired without impact.

Disparities in service granularity and interface semantics can be significant barriers to interoperability and reuse, so in addition to common interface description and availability of service registries, enterprises need to be careful of variations in granularity and semantics.

The elements of a service network focus on specialization. Servers host services and specialize in specific areas of computing, such as routing, persistence, formatting, authenticating, orchestrating, and so on. These services often leverage each other in a symbiotic way, thereby providing a consistent underlying computing fabric. In essence, our old monolithic applications are being broken into smaller components that can be easily recombined via a linked model. By doing this, we facilitate reuse and enable a rapid development/rapid change model.

The last decade has taught us that change is continuous and evolution must be tolerant across time and space. System faults must be assumed. SOA is about creating a network application platform where manageability and programmability scale economically—operationally and organizationally—to unprecedented levels.

This style of software solution enables cost-effective business and IT alignment through protocol-based interoperability and composeability of shared cross-cutting concerns. So what to consider as you build out your service network? First, identify the types of services/components/nodes. This should include vendor-provided black-box systems, legacy or core systems, data sources, frameworks, enterprise services, business services, externally hosted functions or services, data or network feeds from external sources, and integration infrastructure and event services infrastructure. SOA specific items should include service registries and repositories and runtime governance mechanisms (typically in support of intermediaries). These last items are described later in this chapter, and sample usage is provided in the case study section of this book. The design of your SOA includes these service network components; how the components are structured, managed, and monitored; how traffic and transactions across the environment are managed; what policies are enforced at design time and runtime; and the nature of the enforcement, and these should be optimized for your case. Considerations include not only the technical landscape of your product or enterprise, but also your organizational structure and funding model. We get more into these items later in the book.

The Evolving SOA

Service-oriented architectures can evolve over time; one seductive characteristic of this type of architecture is that it can be built incrementally without a large initial investment. For example, a common approach is to start by exposing existing components as Web services before entering them in a registry or building in a management platform.

Although there is some value in supporting a uniform way to consume functions/services in your network, there is a *major* drawback associated with simply service-enabling existing components without registry services or runtime governance. First, you are propagating a point-to-point integration approach. This means that you will have versioning and compatibility issues as services explicitly invoked by the consuming application change. It also means that you will have little or no visibility into transactions that rely on multiple serial service requests, making troubleshooting very costly.

That being said, if you choose to take any incremental approach, it's important that you define your long-term strategy and best practices up front, so that the design of your Web services is in line with your long-term goals. If multiple application teams will be developing these early Web service interfaces, keeping an eye on the long-term will require immediate process changes to include, at a minimum, a review of the proposed services.

This point is important enough to reiterate: A successful SOA requires a long-term strategy to be in place before incremental work begins. Ensure that your long-term architectural plans are in line with your strategic business objectives, and be prepared to make a case to your senior management. Understand how you will show your SOA to be profitable, and show how you will calculate your return on investment (ROI). The case studies in this book illustrate useful methods for these tasks.

In a Perfect World

Ideally, you will have the opportunity to build your SOA from the top down. To do this, you should have an enterprise-level architecture team in place. This team should be made up of highly skilled architects—technologists and strategists with an overarching view of your enterprise, including a deep understanding of the existing technological landscape and an appreciation of the strategic business goals of your organization.

The ideal size of the architecture team depends on the size of your organization and the scale and complexity of the service implementation at hand; in some cases, two or three members will suffice, and in some cases, two dozen members could be necessary. The size is not important so much as the skill set and authority levels of the members.

The success of your SOA will hinge on the work of your architecture team. The responsibilities of this team should include the following:

- Define your long-term SOA strategy such that it is aligned with your organization's long-term business goals.
- Incorporate a plan for meeting short-term business goals as part of your SOA strategy.
- Define best practices and policies for Web services, deployment, governance, and so on.
- Identify common services or components to be leveraged cross-functionally and deployed early in the process.
- Communicate the SOA road map to management, development, and support teams.
- Adjust the existing software development and deployment process to fit your new architectural requirements—this should include governance activities such as reviews, advertising available services, and so on—and be prepared to constantly reevaluate and adjust this process.
- Create a collaboration vehicle for the constant review of service implementations and priority levels.
- Select and incorporate the technology required for brokering and managing services, including service discovery through registries or service invocation through brokers.
- Select and incorporate the technology necessary to meet requirements for monitoring, auditing, change control, and so on.
- Calculate profitability of the architecture and show ROI to senior management.

Is that all? Probably not—but the preceding list gives you some idea of what it means to define an SOA strategy or road map. All of these items must be defined at some point, and some of it must be complete before even an incremental approach to SOA development can be undertaken with a reasonable hope of long-term success.

In a Less-than-Perfect World

Unfortunately for many of us, we might not have a strong enterprise-level architecture team in place, nor can we spare the resources with the appropriate skills to create one. So if the tasks in the preceding list must be completed as part of an SOA definition, what's next?

Step One: Create a project. Get a project manager, or project management body (PMO), to take ownership of tracking the deliverables associated with defining an SOA. Start with what we call Phase 1 tasks. These tasks on your plan should include the identification of short-term and long-term goals, followed by tasks associated with the definition of a road map.

Step Two: Staff the project with existing resources currently assigned elsewhere—ask for one day per week, or 20% of their time, to dedicate to your SOA initiative. If you are lucky enough to have received funding for your project, allow these resources to charge their time to it. Alternatively, identifying an existing project as a "strategic initiative" and creating a subteam associated with that project to address SOA-related concerns is often a good way to organize around the build-out of the first increment of your service network.

Step Three: Socialize the findings of your ad hoc or subteam—presumably, your team was made up of cross-functional representatives, domain experts, senior technologists, and senior strategists. The credibility of your team will lend credibility to its findings, and these findings and recommendations can be taken back to your funding committee for what we call Phase 2 of the SOA project. Perhaps, in addition to a blessing, you'll receive funding and even full-time resources for Phase 2.

Step Four: Begin Phase 2, and start defining best practices and policies. Perhaps the organization and funding of common services or components can begin, either as part of your team's deliverables or as part of another ongoing project. Your team should start working with all implementation teams (assuming an incremental approach to SOA implementation) and socializing best practices and the road map. Perhaps you have achieved some organizational authority by Phase 2 and can start using your proposed governance model and reference architecture.

No need to walk through the many potential iterations and tasking combinations therein. Suffice it to say that by placing the tasks associated with building an SOA into buckets, or iterations, and reconciling yourself to working within resource and time constraints of your organization, you will have a better chance of success than if you walked in to your senior management with a proposal for significant investment in what might be perceived to be either unproven technology or ivory tower architecture. Taking into consideration our natural aversion to change, not to mention the backlash IT departments have experienced as a result of enthusiastic adoption of any new technology in the "boom" years, we must be willing to prove that an SOA can be profitable for our organizations. The proof might only be achievable through multiple iterations, as described previously, and that's something to consider as you start to sketch out your road map.

That being said, many organizations, both enterprise IT organizations and product development groups, have fully embraced SOA as it is defined by the industry today. A quick Web search will produce no shortage of case studies to be used as anecdotal evidence and planning aids for successful SOA implementation. Some of the case studies outlined in this book are based on many such successful implementations in the real world, and our hope is that you will benefit from seeing the approach taken and lessons learned.

Before going through the aforementioned cases, you should understand the technology on which modern service-oriented architecture is based. This technology includes Web services, registries, service buses, message brokers, management platforms, and the like. First, let us consider Web services.

How to Design an SOA

Now that we understand the scope of a service-oriented architecture, the steps associated with creating an SOA, and a bit about the building blocks of an SOA, let's talk about design.

Designing for the Future

The most common driver for SOA development (and a key component of ROI calculation) is the immediate and future interoperability advantage it presents. Designing for the future, so to speak, has a number of obvious implications: You must define and embrace new development practices and standards, you must define and implement a governance model, you must be able to track and recalculate your profitability or ROI, and so on. Let's talk about each one of these concerns.

Service Design and Development

Your design practices for services must adapt to provide the greatest potential for service reuse. When we talk about service design as it relates to interoperability and reuse, the internal implementation details of a service are not generally of interest. The part we care about is the interface exposed by the service and the messages it sends and to which it responds.

In Chapter 3, "Characteristics of EDA," where we talked about loose coupling, we learned that protecting service consumers from knowing anything about the implementation specifics of a service promotes long-term flexibility and interoperability. In the case diagramed in Figure 5.2, we could substitute another service for this one, and as long as the same requests can be answered, the consumer does not need to know about the change. Because Web services are truly autonomous in nature, they perform tasks in response to messages. As long as the requests can be honored, the underlying data or objects are not of interest to the consumer.

A number of patterns can be used to achieve this sort of abstraction, including the Façade, the Mediator, or even the Delegation pattern. The consumption of the service can be further abstracted through the use of a proxy or agent.

A more sophisticated loose coupling of services would allow for the dynamic consumption of services through the explicit or implicit querying of a service registry (Universal Description, Discovery, and Integration [UDDI]). This would allow for almost a complete decoupling of services in that the consumer queries for the type of service required rather than explicitly invoking a service.

Many people believe that in order for services to be loosely coupled, they must be stateless. There is some truth to that; however, it is not always necessary for services to be completely decoupled. We are typically concerned with degrees of coupling and striving for as loose as possible to achieve maximum reuse potential. In the case where your service must participate in a conversation with its consumers, you are more likely to be bound to your consumers than otherwise.

Creating services with reuse in mind means not only allowing for generic coupling, but also means exposing both fine- and coarse-grained services. The **granularity** of a service refers to its scope of functionality. A fine-grained service could return a single value in response to a request for data, for example, whereas a coarse-grained service would expose the result of a business process, typically composed of multiple functions and objects, abstracted by a service. There are many shades of granularity, of course, but the coarser grained your services are, the more business value they can offer, supporting reuse. Coarsely grained services are of great use in building composite applications (a major benefit of an SOA).

Business value should be a major factor when designing your services. Ideally, services in an SOA should be understandable to the business community in your organization so that they can be used in the definition of new processes, and eventually in the creation of composite applications. To this end, your published service interface should include not only technical particulars for consuming the service, but also some description of the business functions they perform.

In some large organizations, enterprise business services are divided in two segments: finely grained business services and coarsely grained business services. The latter are used by composite applications and are themselves composites of the former. The former, finely grained business services, might not be Web services at all, but rather native constructs (such as Enterprise Java Beans [EJBs], and so on).

Publishing meaningful descriptions of your services is essential to create a robust SOA environment. A **contract** is consumable programmatically (machine-readable) and should include the messages your service sends and receives, any policies to be enforced (security, requirements, etc.), and a description of the business functions they perform.

A contract or description of a Web service is in the form of a Web Services Description Language (WSDL) document, as mentioned in Chapter 2, "SOA: The Building Blocks of EDA." Many mainstream development tools expect to have access to a service's WSDL at development time, and can generate code that corresponds to the functionality of the service (the bindings are generated). Management tools use the WSDL to govern adherence to policies and best practices, and to monitor the operation of the service in production. Of course, if your WSDL is available in a registry, a requesting application can create a binding to your service at runtime, presumably after ascertaining your service provides the optimal functionality for a particular case.

Many Integrated Development Environments (IDEs; Visual Studio .NET, WebLogic Workshop, etc.) allow you to wrap a procedure in a Web service with the click of a button, and the associated service description (WSDL) is generated by the IDE. There are some pitfalls associated with WSDL generation—one of them being that the default type of SOAP message is typically RPC-encoded, potentially leading to interoperability issues (and potentially failing the design-time, policy-based assertion application that might be part of your governance process).

The **messages** sent and received as part of your Web service are described in the WSDL. One design issue introduced by SOAP messages is the notion of applying different characteristics to different parts of a message. So in a single message, some aspects might be visible to all consumers while other parts are encrypted and visible only to a trusted group of consumers. Still other parts of the same message might be signed. The SOAP specification and the corresponding WS-* specifications provide the rules for this sort of adaptability.

ESBs and Fabrics

The term enterprise service bus (ESB) is one of the more confusing parts of an SOA definition, primarily because of the disparate definitions of ESBs provided by the vendor community at large. Thus far in this book, we have not explicitly mentioned the need for an enterprise service bus. We *have* said that we need a uniform way to support discovery of services, routing of messages, monitoring of services, policy application to messages/services, and other nonfunctional concerns such as transformation, logging, and so on. The industry adopted the use of the term ESB to describe a mechanism for providing service access and management as described previously, *before* the notion of a service network or fabric was propagated by the SOA industry leaders of today. The two terms are not inherently in conflict, but many ESB offerings look more like old-school enterprise application integration (EAI) stacks than the sophisticated management fabrics discussed by industry thought-leaders today.

One reason for this is that leading EAI vendors, like IBM and BEA, have packaged their integration offerings as ESBs. This means that their products can be used to provide access to data and functionality hosted by systems plugged into the bus, and nonfunctional concerns like the ones mentioned previously will be remedied by the functions provided by their product stack. This is a fine approach to SOA support and management as long as your enterprise feels comfortable with your vendor of choice and doesn't mind the potentially enormous costs associated with scaling the product stack out to support all of the traffic in your enterprise. Think about the costs associated with your EAI platform today— then imagine that all traffic between all components in your service network flows through the platform. The combinatorial consequence is significant. Many popular J2EE-based integration platforms require that the entire stack be deployed everywhere any part of it is to be leveraged, and many rely heavily on compiled code versus declarative artifacts (as supported by some SOA vendors). The ESB model defines a distributed solution with what amounts to a container deployed in the environments of interest (hence the "lightweight" characterization of ESBs and management fabrics). That being said, there is value in having a single-vendor platform for interoperability and integration, and if you can stand the price tag and vendor dependence, it might be the safest way to go, given the complexity of designing an SOA.

Other vendors produced products not part of an EAI stack that provide similar capability, and they are also billed as ESBs. These ESBs provide a number of container-based mechanisms, abstracting things like life cycle management and thread pooling from an application implementation. Such a mechanism would remove the need for service consumers to be aware of a service location, although as mentioned previously it's typically a good idea for routing decisions to occur at distributed nodes as opposed to a centralized hub. It supports rule-based routing, data transformation, and business process orchestration.

For the purpose of this chapter, let us refer to the runtime governance of services as a management fabric. A management fabric might be billed as an ESB implementation or not. Runtime governance of services can be managed by a single, standards-based solution (from a vendor or perhaps from the open source community), or it can be a composition of utilities of your choice. The management fabric should be available across an enterprise environment, regardless of organizational silos or technical disparity of systems, but can be leveraged for narrow, localized integration solutions as well.

A management fabric, like traditional heavyweight integration products, may support J2EE-based technology like JCA (J2EE Connector Architecture) or JMS (Java Message Service) to interact with an application, or it could use traditional application programming interfaces (APIs), or SOAP-based Web services. Fabrics can provide data transformation capabilities (leveraging XSLT, XQuery, and the like), and may support routing of requests to appropriate services at runtime. This is often implemented in the form of a message broker, where messages are routed based on a set of rules applied at runtime, may be event-driven, and may be exchanged using a publish/subscribe model. Facilities for transaction management and security services should be handled by the management fabric.

A quick note of caution: Do not think of an SOA management fabric (or ESB) as a standard heavyweight integration platform, even though many of the popular integration platform vendors purport to provide ESBs in their products. Although it should provide enterprise-class stability, your service infrastructure, by nature, should be lightweight—it should have a small footprint, is typically distributed, and must be inexpensive to deploy. Some use JMS (Java Message Service) or Jini MQ, a JMX (Java Management Extensions) backbone, JNDI (Java Naming and Directory Interface) directory, and one of the open source cluster frameworks (like those used in JBoss, JoNaS, and others). Although it's not necessary that a runtime governance fabric or ESB implementation be based on Java technology, it often works out that way.

Another important point of clarification is that a fabric (as its name implies) should not feature a hub-and-spoke architecture (many **integration brokers** are hub-and-spoke). It should support deployment of distributed components (**containers** or **intermediaries**) that support the capabilities necessary for each case. Ideally, the components will have a configurable footprint, and will be managed remotely and independently from other components.

These characteristics also differentiate a fabric from a **message bus**. A message bus can provide access to multiple disparate systems, and it's certainly lightweight, but management functions are typically centralized, not distributed, and it does not support the nonfunctional concerns (the *ilities) typically supported by a management fabric.

Designing an SOA around an industry-leading management fabric in support of your long-term SOA strategy is the most straightforward way to go. Leveraging a management fabric allows you to build your SOA incrementally, as is often preferable. This means that you can introduce a management fabric into a local architecture and leverage it to integrate globally later; the pitfall of such an approach is that it might be tempting to solve the local problem without an eye to the global architecture. As with any SOA definition, keep the greater goals in mind at all times.

Your Service Infrastructure, Fabrics, and SOA

By now, we have learned that a management fabric is an integral part of your service infrastructure and fills a major role in an SOA. It can act as a distributed broker for synchronous or asynchronous Web services, with all consumers invoking services through the management fabric, with dynamic routing at runtime. It facilitates abstraction of services, dynamic discovery, centralized management of utilities, decentralized runtime control of services, and the like.

The CFO Conversation, Part I

"Doesn't one vendor do all this?" your CFO might ask. "Why am I being asked to sign licensing agreements with multiple SOA providers? I thought SOA did away with all this IT vendor nonsense." "Well… maybe yes, maybe no," you could respond. Although SOA does have the potential to reduce costs and streamline system development, the challenges of governance and security are still quite serious, and might need to be addressed through more than one SOA solution.

Because management fabrics support the complete decoupling of a service from other applications or services in your environment, its structure is particularly important when your SOA becomes event-driven. As mentioned earlier, an *event-driven architecture (EDA)* is an extension of the SOA model. In an EDA, business processes can be kicked off and managed in response to a particular event. A request to a service could be received, acknowledged, split into multiple corresponding requests, and finally answered with multiple responses according to the process in work.

Your management fabric should support (or work in conjunction with) event service and correlation. This allows for complex business process flow management; of course, its sophistication depends upon its support for orchestration language standards (Business Process Execution Language/BPEL or Business Process Execution Language for Web Services/BPEL4WS). Business process orchestration standards typically define a variety of process flow constructs that can be used to abstract the process flow from the logical or physical infrastructure of participating applications. We talk more about business process modeling and management later in this book.

Service Brokers

If you are taking an incremental approach to building out the service infrastructure of your SOA, you might find yourself relying on a (typically homegrown) *service broker*. In some cases, for one reason or another, the advantages offered by a management fabric are considered not worth the cost of the effort to implement in the early stages of an SOA build-out (this is akin to selecting against using J2EE containers for a Java application, by the way, so be careful when adopting this approach). As shown in Figure 5.3, a service broker is simply an abstraction layer between Web service endpoints. Implementing a service broker gets you part of the way toward achieving the loose coupling that is so important in any SOA implementation, and provides a single layer to use for simple monitoring and routing of Web services at a local level.

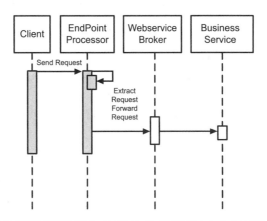

Figure 5.3   Diagram of service broker, both flow and logical, which is part of the J2EE core patterns.

(Source: CoreJ2EEPatterns.com)

Management Concerns

Let's say that you have designed an SOA with multiple, geographically distributed, technically disparate applications. You are planning to support dynamic discovery and routing of services, and you have decided to build (or assemble) a management fabric (or ESB) as a backbone. Now ask yourself: How are you going to manage security, deployment, and operational activities? Let's say that you are prepared to expect the components (services, containers, etc.) of your SOA to provide Java Managed Extensions Managed Beans (JMX MBeans) or Simple Network Management Protocol Management Information Bases (SNMP MIBs). Will this put you a step closer to a management solution? Perhaps. How will you handle business process management (BPM)?

Ideally, your management solution will have become evident during the design process of your SOA. In the case of an incrementally built SOA where design was solidified over multiple iterations, you might be trying to retrofit a management solution with much of your SOA already in place.

Your options for SOA management are as follows (good, bad, and ugly, in no particular order):

- Provide no SOA management and let each application rely on its own monitoring tools and be managed, deployed, and secured individually.
- Create a "patchwork quilt" of existing management solutions with homegrown management functionality sewn in based on emerging standards.
- Leverage the centralized management offered by a heavyweight integration platform.
- Select a vendor-based SOA management solution.

Let's talk about each option. The first option is the default—if you don't have an SOA management solution, each application or component must rely on its native management tools for security, deployment, versioning, monitoring, and the like. The problems with this option are manyfold: no end-to-end security, no business process modeling, no automated versioning, no uniform management tie-in with the development cycle for each component, no centralized monitoring of areas of interest in an SOA, no centralized measurement tools for monitoring service-level objectives, and so on. Long-running transactions that span multiple services will not be managed as a single transaction, but as multiple hops across decoupled services.

The second option is not pretty—you could layer multiple management solutions that are not SOA-specific to meet your immediate management requirements. For example, you could use an existing application monitoring product that leverages agents to report basic health information back to a central server, host a separate business process management or workflow tool, and implement a homegrown deployment and versioning scheme for your SOA. You could even use your knowledge of emerging management specifications like Web Services Distributed Management (WSDM) to build Web-service-based communication between your management applications, manage the relationships between the components and underlying resources supporting your SOA, and even monitor end-to-end business process flow if based on Business Process Execution Language (BPEL). Of course, WSDM is still an emerging specification from the Organization for the Advancement of Structured Information Standards (OASIS), but in theory, it could be used in conjunction with existing management tools to grow your own SOA management solution. That being said, the justification for constructing such a solution would have to be the belief that a homegrown solution would offer some sort of competitive differentiation (typically not the case for infrastructure management solutions). More often, logs from multiple management solutions would be consolidated and parsed for meaningful notations in this patchwork-quilt style of management.

The third option is to leverage the management functionality that comes with a large, heavyweight integration server. To do this, you must have decided to use the server in question, of course. The advantages of adopting an integration platform are significant. BEA's offering as well as IBM's offer so-called ESB functions: asynchronous messaging backbone, data transformation, content-based routing, connectivity to multiple technologies and platforms, and full support for Web services and many WS-* standards. Full-blown EAI (enterprise application integration) platforms also offer many of the EAI functions you'd expect, including BPM, integrated development tools, adapters to major enterprise applications, and the like. They offer robust, centralized management mechanisms that can meet needs you didn't know you had.

Why is this option suboptimal? Depending on your case, it might not be. We do know it breaks a couple of key ideals of a management fabric: First, it's an integration broker—everything related to integration is centralized in a proprietary stack. One of the neat things about a management fabric (in fact, its distinguishing characteristic) is that you can rely on configurable, distributed components for many of the functions an integration broker would provide centrally. For example, data transformation services can be deployed as part of the service network, allowing messages to be converted in-flight from one format to another. Specialized monitoring functions can also be deployed as part of the service network, as would security functions and other nonfunctional remedies. As long as these functions are deployed as services, you can essentially "plug and play" these integration tools anywhere management fabric can reach. This allows for very precise scaling and tuning and versioning, despite the distributed nature of the services. Alternatively, an EAI platform centralizes the integration services as part of its server functionality. It's a different, heavier, and significantly more expensive model. Is an

SOA based on an EAI product really an SOA? Of course—you're just betting the farm on a vendor product, service levels, pricing, and on your ability to pay to play as you need to scale up.

The fourth option is to leverage one of the specialized SOA management platforms on the market today. Before we talk about what these management platforms offer, it's important to understand the nature of the market and what drives each flavor of SOA management implementation. Simply stated, the Web service management tool market is overloaded. Each management platform vendor is taking a different approach to distinguish itself from the rest. Some are competing in ease-of-use and reporting, others are offering adaptive monitoring of service levels, and many have incorporated WSDM-based functions into their platforms.

In an SOA or Web services management platform, you can typically expect to see some or all of the following key features:

- Built-in registry solution for publishing and discovering services, as well as the ability to plug in to any compliant registry solution
- Policy definition and enforcement
- Service mediation and routing
- Metadata transformation
- Dashboard-style interface
- Logging, auditing, and monitoring (and billing options)
- Security options and enforcement (often through application of policies)
- Service discovery, provisioning, configuration, versioning

If the management platform offers a fabric, many of the preceding features would be distributed and configurable across the network. Management platforms (either heavy- or lightweight offerings) will provide the data for calculating return on investment (ROI). As you evaluate your management platform options, keep in mind your goals for your chosen method for ROI tracking.

Figure 5.4 shows a possible reference architecture for an SOA that embodies a complete infrastructure for governance and management.

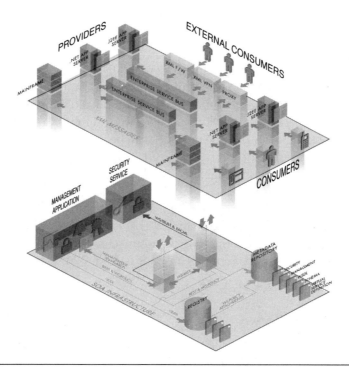

Figure 5.4   SOA Infrastructure Reference Architecture, including a management application, service intermediaries, registry (UDDI), and metadata repository.

(Source: SOA Software, Inc.)

Web service management and governance platform vendors in the market today include AmberPoint, WebLayers, Actional (+WestBridge), SOA Software, Oracle, and Infravio, to name a few. Many of the Web service management functions provided by these vendors today are compatible with generic application management platforms. We know that existing application management approaches are insufficient for full-scale management of an SOA, but when paired with an SOA-specific management toolset, mainstream management platforms can still offer a unified vision into your system.

The Real "Bottom Line"

Estimating the return on investment (ROI) or profitability of your architecture is one of the more esoteric tasks associated with our work. Estimating the ROI for an SOA implementation and building the associated business case is no less difficult—but we can follow some basic rules for estimating how profitable our SOA can be.

In any sort of enterprise ROI calculation, you must have some knowledge of your anticipated total cost of ownership (TCO). This is a figure not measured on a yearly basis—this is a single figure corresponding to the total cost of owning a service infrastructure. Then you must consider three inputs: anticipated cost savings (this requires an understanding of your existing cost structure), opportunity costs, and anticipated revenue (this requires an understanding of your business and the benefits of agility).

Cost Savings

Cost savings can be calculated by starting with the advantages of supporting common components. In this case, your implementation costs associated with building common business logic into every application or product is replaced with the anticipated costs of simply consuming a business service. The difference is the first part of the savings (difference * estimated reuse opportunities = projected savings). Support costs for common components versus multiple implementations are similar enough to leave out of our calculations. This calculation assumes you have an understanding of how much it costs to build and support blocks of business logic today.

Cost savings associated with common components include reduced interface development costs. Having common interfaces is estimated in general to reduce interface development costs by 60%–70%. Think of the costs associated with not only development, but also testing, SLA negotiation between endpoint owners, and the like. The interface development that is still required is streamlined through a common practice for development, testing, monitoring, service exposure, and governance. Take a look at your last project that exposed a function to multiple consumers. This will give you some idea how much savings is available to you in building out a service network with common business services.

There is cost savings associated with the management and governance of a service network (or network architecture), but it is not as simple to calculate. There is quantifiable value in providing a uniform method of addressing nonfunctional concerns and enterprise policies (rather than having every application figure out how to implement security, transformations, etc.). Management of system resources, visibility into long-running transactions, and governance of activity is all streamlined through the use of common mechanisms across the service network. The savings model is similar to that of the common components, described previously, in that the savings is realized through the sharing of common mechanisms and standardized approaches (development, testing, monitoring, support) as well as the reduced number of implementations. Again, calculating the savings requires an understanding of the cost structure for your existing enterprise support model. Because many large organizations distribute responsibility for these items organizationally, this might be more difficult to accurately quantify.

Maintenance costs can also be reduced in an SOA environment. An SOA framework allows you to target maintenance-related items for outsourcing, for example, and this can reduce your costs significantly, particularly if you are already planning to go to an outsourced model.

If regulatory compliance is an issue in your organization, the service network nature of an SOA offers the uniformity in system management and governance that simplifies monitoring and logging efforts for auditing purposes. An SOA offers a uniform implementation of data access methods, and corresponding rules and logging mechanisms support data integrity (lineage) and reporting. Given the planned costs associated with your regulatory compliance efforts, and depending on your existing infrastructure, this can be a significant savings category for you (of course, fear is often the motivator for regulatory compliance efforts, not costs).

Opportunities

The value of *agility* can be calculated if you understand your business growth mode. High growth organizations require extreme responsiveness from an IT department, and a typical problem in such organizations is the proliferation of disparate, suboptimal implementations developed without regard to the environmental strategy. Most large organizations have pockets of high growth and stagnation, leading to a generally constrained product management organization. In such organizations, most business owners have calculated the benefit of being first to market with a new product or service, as well as the costs of being second, third, or last. These figures can help you quantify the revenue opportunities associated with providing an SOA.

Consider the cost of your SOA implementation over some time period. Then subtract the savings calculated for common components and the like over the same period of time, then subtract the average gain associated with agility (time to market) multiplied by the planned number of product offerings over the same time period, and you will have some notion of the costs/savings associated with an SOA approach. You might also want to factor in the cost savings associated with reduced rework for retrofitting suboptimal solutions that were delivered fast at the expense of quality.

To better understand lost opportunity costs, you can invite your business community members to talk about the following in the context of an SOA: customer relationship, information, and access management. Imagine a single approach for case-specific security application across multiple customer repositories and rule sets and events triggered based on changes in customer status, completely decoupled from the application layer. Depending on your current solution state, this might be another potential win.

An SOA contributes to competitive advantage directly in support of business process management. Business processes can be defined and managed at the enterprise layer—this allows you to eliminate redundant, conflicting, or overlapping business process definitions across the enterprise. The underlying business components would be commonly support, consumed, and monitored as part of the service network.

Your Business Case

A business case for SOA might include the following: **current cost of managing enterprise infrastructure** (HW/SW and projected growth based on replicated business processes and case-specific implementations, management tools associated with multiple environments, security infrastructure, cost of maintaining and monitoring interfaces across the enterprise, etc.), **current cost of application development** (costs to build business components under the current model, average number and cost of new interfaces required per application, costs associated with supporting multiple redundant applications, maintenance costs, etc.), **anticipated cost savings** (common components, common interfaces, management and governance savings, regulatory compliance, business process management, etc.), and **anticipated revenue opportunities** (speed to market, customer information and activity monitoring value, etc.).

The CFO Conversation, Part II

True ROI requires recognition of TCO at the organizational level, not broken into lines of business, products, markets, divisions, or along other artificial boundaries.

You might also want to consider the potential cost savings of streamlining your organizational structure and dependencies based on the SOA-based development, management, and governance model, both inside and outside of IT. You will want to consider automation opportunities and associated cost savings in your governance process. You will need to keep an eye on the point at which this model is unsupportable (for whatever reason) within an acceptable cost model, and the points at which this model is most likely to fail in your organization.

All that being said, if your goal is to simply estimate how long it will take you to recover your investment, your task might be fairly straightforward.

Chapter Summary

Although there are many different, equally valid approaches to creating an EDA, from this point on in the book we work under the assumption that SOA and the use of SOAP XML Web services will be the building blocks of the EDA.

- Events are produced by event Web services and listened for, and processed by, Web services. Like all Web services, event services can be created from scratch using a development tool or they can be exposed from existing applications using specialized tools.

- We work under the assumption that the message backbone for the EDA will be an enterprise service bus (ESB). Event Web services publish event data to the ESB, and event listening Web services subscribe to event data through the ESB.

- The event Web services, the ESB(s) used to connect them, and all the other moving parts in the EDA can be described as a service network that provides connectivity for any set of event Web services, listeners, and processors through the ESB(s). Creating a service network requires a high level of governance and mediation among all the separate components to function securely and effectively.

- EDA exists on top of SOA, so to have an EDA, you should ideally first have developed a good SOA infrastructure. Before starting the EDA process, you should have established the business rationale for the SOA, allocated the personnel and resources to its development, standardized on a security and governance framework for the SOA, and deployed the core messaging infrastructure, such as ESBs, to make it all work properly.

EDA in Practice

CHAPTER 6

Thinking EDA

A Novel Mind-Set

Event-driven architecture (EDA) requires a quite novel mind-set when it comes to application design and IT architecture. The goal of this chapter is to get you started on "thinking EDA" as you approach your architectural and application development work. Luckily for you, some of the groundwork for thinking in EDA terms has already been covered with the advent of object-oriented programming and the Web. However, old habits die hard, and thinking in EDA terms typically means erasing a lot of conventional software architecture concepts from your mind. When you think EDA, you want to reduce central control of application flow. You need to enable autonomous behavior in application components and allow for asynchronous parallel execution. You must design for unanticipated use whenever possible. And, in what might be the greatest challenge to conventional thinking, you must enable the event itself to carry its own state information. At the end of this chapter, we look at some situations where EDA is not the answer, and show how thinking EDA sometimes means not doing EDA at all. We also take a look at an example of an existing commercial EDA suite and show how thinking EDA is now being baked into standard industrial offerings.

Reducing Central Control

If you've watched TV in the last 40 years, you might understand that CONTROL is trying to save the world from KAOS (aka "Chaos"). So it is in IT as well, and we all need to "get smart" to combat chaos, although we might need less control than we thought. Unlike Agents 86 and 99 in the classic TV show, as aspiring EDA professionals, we should aspire to less control. However, even as we release the brakes on control, we will never yield to chaos.

The key to thinking EDA is to reduce your reliance on central control of applications. Reducing central control is as much a change in your state of mind about application design and architecture as it is a change in the way that you design and architect applications in practical terms. To get to the point where you have reduced central control enough to realize a functioning EDA, you must take several steps. First, you have to reduce the presence of actual controllers themselves and replace them with trusted executors that function as elements of an EDA. These EDA elements must then be able to function autonomously and operate asynchronously in parallel. They must be designed for unanticipated use (to the greatest extent possible) and deployed with minimal dependencies on one another. Each of these factors is highly relevant to putting together a real EDA. Let's take a look at each one and improve our understanding of how to make it all happen.

Controllers Versus Trusted Executors

Controllers are software elements that maintain state and control process flow. They can be discrete applications, a part of a larger application, or even the enterprise application integration (EAI) suite controlling multiple system interactions. What is significant about controllers is their assigned duty of imposing control over a sequence of programming activities.

For example, suppose you have an order entry process that contains four business process steps, as shown in Figure 6.1. If you were developing an application to manage this order entry process, your first thought might be to create a controller that manages the sequential flow. The controller would receive the new order, verify the data, and then call out to the shipping system to calculate shipping charges. Upon completion, it would call the warehouse system to pack the order and then call the financial system to bill the customer.

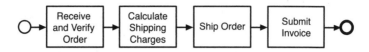

Figure 6.1   Process flow for "New Order."

The conventional, controller-based approach to executing the New Order business process, as shown in Figure 6.2, is fine, but also contains a number of execution constraints. Changes in the application functions that affect order entry might require changes in the controller, and vice versa. The execution of the functional steps in order entry is reliant on the controller.

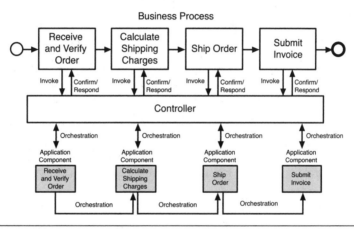

Figure 6.2   Execution of the New Order business process using a conventional, controller-based application.

Let's try to think EDA in this order entry process. Thinking EDA, shown in Figure 6.3, helps us envision that each step in the process can be carried out through trusted executors. The application function corresponding to each business process step could act upon detection of an event trigger. Each function would have an event producer, event listener, and event processor. Each application component listens for their particular event. The New Order component receives the `new_order_received` event, verifies the information, changes the event type to `order_verified`, and pushes it to the bus. The shipping component receives the event, processes it, adds the shipping charges to the event data, changes the event type to `order_charges_calculated`, and pushes it to the bus. The warehouse system receives the event, processes it, changes the event type to `order_shipped`, and pushes it to the bus. Finally, the financial system receives the event, processes it, changes the event type to `order_billed`, and pushes it to the bus.

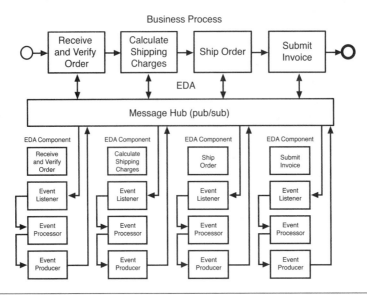

Figure 6.3   Applying the "think EDA" ideal to the business process of New Order removes the central controller in favor of the event-driven EDA model.

The simple scenario shows how the EDA approach exposed key data that was buried in the controller model. To be clear, although this approach might require additional work to set up the first time around, thinking EDA should confer a number of architectural benefits right away and down the line as well. For example, modifying the business process for order entry becomes simpler in the EDA approach. Analysis and monitoring of the process can also happen without disrupting the design. Parallel processing becomes easier. For simplicity's sake, we did not execute multiple steps in parallel though we could have easily executed the tasks to calculate the shipping cost and the ship order in parallel.

Let's take this EDA example and demonstrate how modifying the process has become easier. In Figure 6.4, we have added the `Notify_Shipper` component. The `Notify_Shipper` component will take advantage of the exposed state change event `order_charges_calculated`, process the data, and then notify the shipper with an advanced notice of the demand. Adding the new functionality was as simple as adding a new component. The addition of the new component didn't disrupt the remaining components nor the flow. We can also turn off the new functionality just as easily without impacting the flow. In contrast, adding this new functionality within the central controller model would have been tough and would have required downstream regression testing, downtime, deployment coordination, and the like.

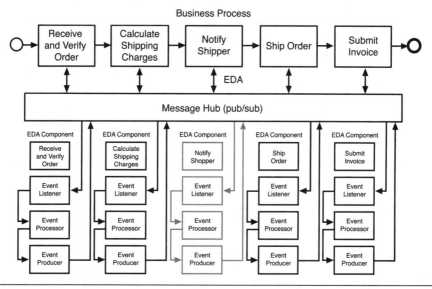

Figure 6.4 In the EDA model, the addition of a process step, Notify Shipper, can be simpler and faster to implement than in a centrally controlled approach. The Notify Shipper component would run in parallel with Ship Order.

Thinking EDA by reducing your dependency on a central controller requires that you also maintain state and process information within the events themselves. In EDA, state is not centrally maintained but is carried throughout the system by the events. EDA components are inherently stateless because they carry state in their messaging. We realize this sounds like a contradiction—how could something carry state but be stateless at the same time? Yet, that is just it: By carrying state, the EDA component does not rely on the central controller for its state. This is the essence of getting an EDA to work in real life. The events must carry their own state information to break free of the central controller.

Right now you might be thinking, "Hold on a second—without the controller, nothing ensures successful order processing." EDA architectures work heavily through trust but that does not mean monitoring isn't implemented. You actually have more ways to ensure the process executed than before. Each new order event can trigger a watcher component to monitor for the `order_billed` event. The sole purpose of this component could be to wait for the `order_billed` event and change the event to `order_complete`. If it doesn't receive the event after a predetermined time, the watcher can send an alert. The alert might flow to an event listener that flags the time lag and forwards it to an event processor for correction or a person who can intervene. Also monitoring tools can be used to watch for stale events on the bus, monitor event volumes, or look out for component faults.

This decoupling might actually undo a secondary benefit of a central controller. Because the decoupling of components eliminates preconception, it also makes it more difficult (in the absence of very good documentation) to understand exactly how a process functions. The presence of a central controller obfuscates siloed process steps. This isn't a technology problem as much as it is a process/organizational/business problem—but it's a good idea to be aware of the potential issues.

In keeping with our heavy reliance on caveats, though, we need to temper our enthusiasm for thinking EDA slightly at this point. We do need to point out that shifting of the central control model can introduce some complexity to the design of the EDA components. The components must carry event state. And, the components might need to be configured to listen for new event triggers when new process steps and components have been added to the process flow. In our example, if you need to insert a new event processor in parallel to the old one (for example, if you need to have Notify Shipper *before* Shipping Order), you must either change Shipping Order to respond to a different event (Notification Sent) or block it from executing until Notification is sent. These kinds of requirements might make moving to EDA unappealing, depending on the nature of your process flows and the way your application developers like to work.

It is also possible, today, to get some of the same benefits of decoupled business process components using workflow orchestration engines, such as Microsoft BizTalk or Oracle BPEL, as flexible controllers that allow easy plug in of stateless application components. This is an overlap between the EDA approach and the emerging service-oriented architecture (SOA)-based business process modeling approach that is gaining in popularity. We note this overlap because we believe that non-EDA approaches are often preferable to EDA based on many specific requirements in a particular situation. We never think that EDA is always the best way to go. The good news is that you have a growing number of choices in today's market.

Carrying State inside the Event

Events carry current state data. Perhaps the best way to understand this is to contrast it with the alternative, which is to preserve state in the central controller. In our shipping example, under the centrally controlled approach, the controller would contain the state of the transaction. For instance, the controller would know that Customer X needs shipping for Order Y to Address Z and pass this information along to the application components it needed to process the order. In this example, the controller might send a procedure call to `ShipOrder` that contains Customer X, Order Y, and Address Z. Upon shipment, the `ShipOrder` component would send an acknowledgement back to the controller that said, simply, "Order Y, Shipped." The controller would then send a procedure call to `SubmitInvoice` that asked for Customer X to be invoiced for Order Y.

In contrast, when thinking EDA, you store process information in the event. Process flow information can be removed from the controller and stored in the event. This allows EDA components to change the flow if the context changes midstream. In the EDA approach, each component would carry the full event state in its messaging. Each component would know that it was Customer X, Order Y, and Address Z. To contrast with the central controller model, for example, instead of the `ShipOrder` component sending an acknowledgement to the controller that said, "Order Y, Shipped," it would send an Extensible Markup Language (XML) message to the enterprise service bus (ESB) that said, "Customer X, Order Y, Shipped to Address Z." This might seem like a lot of extra work, but there is a very good reason for the event components to carry this kind of state information. Doing so helps decouple them and lets them operate autonomously. That way, when you add a new component, like `NotifyShipper`, it can operate fully without reliance on a central controller because it picks up all the needed event state information from the `CalculateShippingCharges` component, and it can forward the shipping information to the `ShipOrder` component without any need for central control. The result is an increase in flexibility in modifying the application.

Enabling Autonomous Behavior

EDA is autonomous behavior. When thinking EDA, strive to produce stateless, autonomous components. Think about breaking down sequential steps into multiple parallel executions. In many situations, these actions must be joined to continue processing. These cases might require a composite event processing component or a complex event processing agent. Either component will have to maintain a state while waiting for both actions to complete. The component should then combine the events and return to a stateless condition.

Designing for Unanticipated Use

The most important aspect of thinking EDA is designing for unanticipated use. Key data should be appropriately exposed. As seen in our previous example, the best way to do this is to break down the business processing into discrete components. Central controllers tend to hide the relevant state change information that future components might find helpful. The process should be broken down into similar areas of concern and delegated. Event data then travels between these components exposing key business data.

In the previous example, the `Notify_Shipper` component took advantage of the exposed state change event `order_charges_calculated`. In that same vein, we could introduce an event wiretap component to analyze the `order_charges_calculated` events and produce a daily report of which shipper was used the most, was the cheapest, was the highest priced, and so forth. Both of these examples demonstrate the concept of unanticipated use.

Thinking about EDA Implementation

To gain a feel for some of the in-depth work you will need to do in realizing an EDA, you need some detail about recommended practices for EDA implementation. As part of this exercise, we introduce you to the term *agent,* which is sometimes used in the industry as an alternative to describe event listeners, producers, and processors. Although this might be confusing at first, it will hopefully give you some preparation to deal with conversations that use this term.

Agents are responsible for receiving events, filtering, processing, forwarding, and transmitting new events. They are constructed to be self-contained and as self-sufficient as possible, allowing business event processing without outside intervention. They do not directly interact with other agents. However, they might interact with other systems, components, or services. This approach gives the agent collective an extremely agile architecture.

The parallel nature of EDA increases architectural agility by easing refactoring and component deprecation. With EDA, new functionally equivalent components can be plugged into the architecture and executed in unison. An audit of the new agent's output compared with the deprecated agent will confirm their functional equivalence. And all of this can be done without interference to the enterprise system. We didn't have to recompile any flow controller or register our new agent's location. We simply had to attach new Web service components to the desired enterprise service bus.

Of course, there are drawbacks to the parallel paradigm. The three main constraints are lack of flow control (statelessness), indeterminate event processing sequences, and debugging difficulty. In the next section, we see how to counteract these disadvantages by interjecting some SOA into the architecture. However, for now we discuss the larger aspects of the inherent difficulties in managing event-driven architectures.

To facilitate EDA manageability, you should follow two best practices:

- Event management
- Agent typing

Event management is made up of two practices: mandatory event metadata and event dictionaries. Predefining some elemental mandatory event metadata pays for itself tenfold when it comes to debugging the system. Mandatory event data is data that must be present for all events on the bus. For example, event metadata should contain event type, sender, time stamp, causality, unique ID, trace data, and payload. Depending on design requirements, metadata might also require delivery, process, and security attributes. If using Java Message Service

(JMS), this metadata can reside in name value pairs at the message header level, which increases performance.

Agents attach to the bus using subject-based subscriptions to filter unwanted events. This requires an enterprisewide homogeneous event namespace to ensure unique names. Event names should use hierarchical uniform resource identifier (URI) notation. This can be as simple as `Control.Category.Event_Type.Event_Name` (or, in this example, `Production.WarehouseManagment.RFID.PackagReceived`). The `Control` attribute allows similar messages to be released in the same environment without interfering. A control attribute could be set to "Beta" or "Deprecated" and used in conjunction with other systems with minimal impact. The other attributes further define the event. Agents can also use the * wildcard to subscribe to whole categories of events, for example `Production.WarehouseManagment.RFID.*`

An event dictionary should be constructed containing an organized view of all business events. Predefine your business event types based on your business process models and store these interface specifications in the event dictionary. The dictionary should contain the interface definition, pertinent service-level agreement information, time to live, auditing, and cross-references. Predetermined semantics are needed— otherwise, the dictionary could grow with similar event definitions that are vastly different implementations.

Making the event dictionary accessible and editable by everyone involved is important. One dictionary format is a hierarchical wiki Web page. This creates a living document allowing designers to update the dictionary as new business processes are defined. As new events are defined, corresponding new agents will be deployed to handle the processing.

EDA Agent Types

EDA architectures employ many different types of agents. Take some time during design to define your project's agents and their types. An agent's type will characterize the expected behavior, increasing reusability while decreasing unpredictability. You'll find that most agents can be classified as simple, infrastructure, or domain specific:

Simple agents: The most reusable agents will be simple agents. These agents receive events, process the information, and output an event. The most common simple agents are *transformation agents, augmenting agents*, and *persistent agents*.

Infrastructure agents: These agents are used to manage, control, and monitor the EDA environment. This includes agents such as the following:

Monitor agents: Agents wait on the bus for particular situations to happen. They might wait for an event to occur, watch for events not to occur, or watch for exceptions. They can contain a limited time to live (timeouts) and have alerting capabilities.

Prevention agents: These agents receive events and block the triggering of other events or other processing.

Complex event agents or aggregation agents: Aggregation agents collect multiple events then process the cumulative payload. These events typically output a new event type, signifying a complex event has occurred.

Domain agents: These agents provide domain-specific implementations like Fulfill FDA Audit, Send Inventory Count, and so on. They mostly consist of the other agent types but are customized versions to suit a specific domain or vertical market.

Specialty agents: Agents that are customized for a particular situation are called specialty agents. Specialty agents are rarely reusable. They are constructed to execute a temporary job or play favoritism to a particular client or event.

All agents will rest on a message backbone. The bus itself is a logic term meaning there could be multiple physical message backbones that can be bridged together. Events travel on the bus through channels or topics. Ideally, you want as few topics as possible, but for logical and performance reasons, separate topics make perfect sense. You might have a separate channel for auditing and logging or a separate channel for high-priority events. It's common for agents to listen to more than one channel and even send output to multiple channels.

When EDA Is Not the Answer

Part of thinking EDA involves the necessary thinking *not* EDA, which we occasionally recommend when circumstances dictate. You might be thinking, now wait a minute! EDA is *not* always the answer? Yes, there are situations, many in fact, when EDA is not the optimal way to approach enterprise architecture or application design. In this IT version of "When Good Pets Go Bad," we look at some of the factors that diminish the benefit or feasibility of EDA. These include application logic constraints, system performance constraints, governance and security barriers to EDA, organizational challenges, and cost-benefit misalignments.

The most basic reason not to do an EDA is if there is no inherent purpose for one in the application requirements nor any future benefit that anyone can discern from reuse down the line. This might sound obvious, but there is an unfortunate tendency in the IT field to get hyped up by trends and want to make every system you are building play by the new rules. Remember "Web enabling" a few years back? EDA might hold the same Svengali sway over even the most hard-minded of us.

As a rule, the higher up the application stack a process is, the better a candidate for EDA it will be. Lower-level processes, such as database mirroring, database access by applications, or packet routing, are not good candidates for EDA. The reason is that these deep processes are often highly reliant on fixed, fast-performing, proprietary protocols, but with no ill effect on integration or agility.

Performance can be a huge issue in migrating toward an EDA or SOA. XML and Web services, the base units of EDA, tend to be inefficient compared with other interfaces. They tend to create "chatter" on networks when they require authentication and they are generally difficult to accelerate. For these reasons, systems that require a high level of performance might be poor candidates for EDA. For example, the waiting time experienced by an ATM user might affect the customer's opinion of the bank. If the ATM is excessively and consistently slow, the bank's business might suffer. As a result, a slower functioning but more agile EDA might be exactly the wrong choice for an ATM network.

EDAs also have the potential to generate unpredictable and possibly disruptive amounts of traffic on networks. Because EDAs are dynamic in design, and patterns of message exchange are harder to predict in an EDA than in a conventional architecture, EDAs can strain networks. When combined with the fact that EDAs can span multiple networks, under no one entity's direct control, the network management aspects of EDA can become daunting. If network performance and utilization is not a major issue, then network problems should not stand in the way of an EDA. However, if network utilization and performance is critical, or network performance could affect overall system performance, then the network could be a barrier to EDA that makes other options look more appealing.

Ultimately, all of these issues relate to the EDA's cost and benefit calculation. It is possible to overcome virtually any challenge to EDA, but it might not be worth the cost. Any EDA component can be secured, at a cost. Any network performance issue can be overcome, at a cost. However, the EDA has to deliver a value in excess of those costs to be worthwhile. The costs might not be financial, and the same goes for value. For example, there might be a compelling national security value developing an EDA for counterterrorism, although the cost might be quite high in dollars. Yet, it could be worth it. In contrast, it might be costly to convert a set of well-designed and properly functioning legacy systems to EDA, but if the value realized is not high, the project is probably not worth undertaking.

The solution to the challenge of cost versus benefit is to evaluate where in a chain of processing steps EDA really adds value and where it is a "nice-to-have" feature. As you examine the total flow of business process steps and underlying systems that your architecture supports, you will likely see areas that are ripe for EDA and service-orientation, and other places where a migration to EDA can take place later. The important learning in this vein is to see where reuse and extensibility of EDA components can add value to the enterprise and focus your efforts and resources on those places first.

An EDA Product Examined

It turns out we are not the only ones thinking EDA. Some of the major IT suppliers are also beginning to roll out their versions of EDA. That's a good thing. It would be a shame to do all this great thinking and find out we were the only true geniuses in the world and no one cared what we thought.

We thought it would be helpful to look at an example of an actual EDA package that is on the market today. So, let's explore one of the big vendor EDA suites and see how it compares with our ideal EDA, for better or worse. We are very gratified that so many large vendors have embraced EDA to the point where they are willing to stake engineering and marketing dollars on the paradigm.

Sample EDA Suite Features

The datasheet for our sample EDA suite contains the following statement:

> ...enables customers to monitor, analyze, and respond to business events in real time. Organizations need to analyze increasingly large volumes of information and more rapidly respond to business events by adapting their applications and IT systems to become event driven. However, current infrastructures for processing and managing events are limited and require complex and expensive code development....EDA Suite complements the service-interaction model of SOA, providing infrastructure to manage event-based interactions and complex event analysis in real time.[1]

As you can see from this description, the folks at our selected vendor totally get what EDA is all about. They have tried to put together a solution offering that enables users to monitor, analyze, and respond to business events in real time. To make this work, they assembled a suite of software products. The suite contains an enterprise service bus (ESB), an event listener, and an event producer. The event listener/producer can connect with Radio Frequency Identification (RFID) sensors as well as temperature gauges and other devices that translate physical events into EDA-ready data. The EDA suite comes with JMS and a J2EE developer kit. With these elements, a user of this suite can develop event processors and specialized event listeners and producers. Event-based reactions can be programmed in J2EE as well.

Our sample suite's datasheet describes a feature set that includes Business Activity Monitoring (BAM), real-time analytics, data enrichment, content-based routing, content filtering, asynchronous messaging, business rules, and a rules software development kit. Some of these terms refer to concepts that we have already covered, but with different names. For example, *data enrichment* describes a type of event processing that modifies data detected in an event so it can be acted upon correctly by the event processor.

Content filtering is equivalent to event stream processing. *Content-based routing* is a type of event processing that moves event data messages from one place to another, depending on rules that respond to the content of the event data. For example, let's say that the EDA suite is detecting temperatures and needs to respond one way to high temperatures (over

75 degrees) and another way to low temperatures (under 75 degrees). Content-based routing provides a way for the EDA to make its different responses to the two temperature choices. Structurally, in this case, an event Web service would transmit temperature information to an event listener, which would route high or low temperature data to an event processor. You can accomplish this goal of content-based routing in two ways, and the pragmatic issues of performance and cost in an EDA make it worth the time to delve into them.

One approach to content-based routing in the temperature-detecting EDA is to have the event listener parse the entire body of the Simple Object Access Protocol (SOAP) message containing the temperature event data, and use a rule to determine if the temperature is high or low. In the situation, there would be an event Web service that transmits raw temperature data to the event listener, which analyzes the SOAP body and reads the temperatures. The advantage of this approach is that the event listener can essentially wiretap an existing temperature reporting Web service that wasn't necessarily designed to function as an event producer. The disadvantage of this approach is that it is cumbersome and slow to have an event listener parsing the entire SOAP body to determine if the temperature is high or low.

A more efficient approach, from a performance perspective, is to build the content-routing into the event Web service itself. In this case, the Web service that reported the temperature would send one of two messages, called either `HighTemp` or `LowTemp`, depending on the temperature, and the name of the message, contained in the message header, would make life a lot easier for the event listener, which would not have to parse the entire SOAP message and apply an involved business rule. Performance-wise this approach is much better. Depending on your circumstances, the latter approach might be preferable because of cost considerations.

Our sample suite uses BAM to "define and monitor events and event patterns that occur throughout an organization." The suite's Business rules engine captures, automates, and enables change to business policy. The interesting point here is that the vendor provides a specific toolset to help the developer design an event processor. Of course, you could develop a wholly new event processor using the suite's J2EE kit, but the suite makes it possible to establish and enforce business policies, or rules, that process event data. For example, let's say you were using this suite to create an EDA for a property management company. You could define a business rule that said, "If the temperature goes above

90 degrees, then switch on the air conditioner, keep track of the time that the air is on, and invoice the tenant for the air conditioning service used." The Business rules engine streamlines the process of putting that event processing logic into action.

Our sample EDA suite contains a "multi-protocol Enterprise Service Bus (ESB) to connect applications and route messages…[the] ESB provides multi-protocol messaging, routing, and transformation capabilities to distribute event messages and integrate services." The ESB also comes with adapters, which provide "standards based access to virtually any data source." To get specific, this ESB supports JMS, SOAP, JCA, WSIF, JDBC, HTTP, and FTP messaging protocols. It provides configurable JMS qualities of service with different types of persistence stores including database, file, and in-memory. The combination of the adapters and the multiprotocol capabilities are very powerful in EDA terms. They show that the EDA suite has the capability, at least in theory, to connect event processors, listeners, and producers at virtually any point in an enterprise.

Gaps in the Commercial EDA Solutions

Commercial EDA offerings are not without gaps, however. One gap in most of these solutions is their reliance on the developer and architect to be able to think EDA to deliver the kind of truly dynamic, complex, and implicit functioning that we want from an event-driven architecture. If the developers do not have a far-reaching understanding of thinking EDA, with its emphasis on decoupling of application components at the design stage and reducing dependencies, then the EDA that is developed through the product suite (or its analogs from other vendors) runs the risk of becoming a tightly coupled EDA. A tightly coupled EDA has lost a majority of its potential for dynamic, complex use.

That being said, there are few shortcuts to EDA. As with so many other endeavors in IT, there is an advantage to the user-friendly, wizard-based approach in that it enables fast deployment and shares advanced technologies with relatively untrained users. However, there is also no substitute for true expertise. (And if you're reading this book, we congratulate you on your drive to learn the real stuff!) The challenge with deploying a packaged EDA solution like this suite is to know enough about event-driven architecture to bring out all of the suite's best EDA qualities but not let any of its embedded logic throw you off track on the way to complex, implicit, and dynamic EDA.

One of the other potentially major gaps in most of the commerical EDA suites that we see is the risk of becoming dependent on proprietary elements of the suite. For example, though it is standards based, there are some subtle aspects of the many vendor-packaged ESBs that can lock the developer into the vendor stack. Once locked in, there is a potential risk that it will become costly or difficult to extend the EDA to non-vendor-based event components. Or, at the very least, such extensibility might require the purchase of proprietary adapters, and so on, which limit the essence of the EDA's functioning.

Albeit, this kind of lock-in would occur with virtually any vendor solution. With an open source solution, the lock-in might occur with the architects and developers who built the components. Using any proprietary knowledge involves risking holding one hostage waiting for maintenance and extensions to the framework. There are no easy answers to this problem.

One possible mitigation to the vendor lock-in dilemma is to build an EDA component mediation into the EDA itself at the design stage. There are several solutions on the market today that offer the capability to mediate the XML and SOAP message traffic between multiple ESBs and Web service consumers, providers, and other network elements that make up a truly broad, complex, and implicit EDA. With a mediation solution, you can develop an EDA with the confidence that an event component, such as an event service, will be able to communicate with event listeners that are based on any ESB in any enterprise, regardless of platform, transport protocol, or SOAP version in use.

Chapter Summary

This chapter starts us on the path to practical use of EDA theory by getting us to "think EDA" as an approach to application design and enterprise architecture. In particular, to think EDA, we need to keep the following distinctive EDA factors in mind:

- **Reducing central control**—The essence of EDA is the reduction or elimination of central control from the application design. In an EDA, each event component functions autonomously. Of course, there is a flow of event processing steps, but the flow is not reliant on a central controller or main method for its functioning.

- **Carrying state inside the event**—To operate without central control, event components must carry event state. In the example used in this chapter, an event component that notifies shippers of shipment status needs to send and receive the full order detail as its state information. This carriage of event state enables the event component to operate autonomously and makes possible more flexible modifications to the application.

- **Designing for unanticipated use**—EDA components should be designed for unanticipated use. If you can design an EDA component that can serve multiple uses, it is easier to assemble and reassemble them into event-driven composite applications.

- Understanding that the term agents is an alternative to the phrasing of event listeners, processors, and producers. Recommended best practices for EDA implementation include agent typing and the mandatory carriage of event metadata by EDA agents.

- In this chapter, we considered some situations where EDA is not the answer. Many factors could make an EDA a poor option, including high cost that cannot be justified by business outcomes of EDA, performance issues, and organizational readiness.

- Finally, in this chapter, we looked at a sample commercial EDA offering to see what is available on the market today. We chose a high-end EDA suite, which includes an ESB, adapters, rules engine, and RFID server. It appears to be a robust solution, with many positive attributes, though any package of this type carries the risk of vendor lock-in and a reduction in the practical EDA skills of the development staff, who might rely on the prebuilt product to think EDA for them.

Endnotes

[1.] Oracle product datasheet

CHAPTER 7

Case Study: Airline Flight Control

In the classic movie, *Airplane*, the director of the airport orders his men to "dump all the lights you have on the runway" as an ailing plane prepares to make an emergency landing. In the next shot, a large dump truck unloads hundreds of table lamps, sending them crashing to the runway pavement. Though surely not produced with EDA in mind (who asked Shirley, anyway?), this scene illustrates one of the great vulnerabilities of airline flight control. Though airline flight control involves a lot of complex, logistical matters, it relies to a great degree on human-to-human voice communication or dead-ended and circumscribed views of disconnected information systems.

Of course, much of the system is automated, but there is significant room for improvement. In this case study, we look at how an EDA approach can solve one of the major deficits of existing airline flight control systems, which is their inability to provide comprehensive updates in real time to all stakeholders who experience the "ripple effect" of a serious service disruption.

Air traffic flow management is a fantastically complex subject, and a lot of very smart people are thinking about how to improve it as part of their daily work. Our goal in this chapter, therefore, is not to solve the whole problem, but rather to highlight how an EDA approach can help yield desired results in this challenging situation. We refer to existing expert research and discussion of the subject throughout.

Learning Objectives

- Understanding how EDA can offer a unique solution to a complex, multiplayer problem in the real world
- Getting a basic sense of the life cycle for a large EDA project
- Understanding the flow of work from concept through deployment in a large EDA project
- Understanding the governance issues inherent in a complex, multistakeholder EDA

Business Context: Airline Crunch Time

Airline Flight Control is a high-stakes matter. In the United States alone, commercial air travel was a $163 billion business in 2006,[1] and overall, it's not an industry in particularly good health. Several of the largest carriers are either operating in bankruptcy or have just recently emerged from bankruptcy. The industry has been less than profitable in the years since the 9/11 attacks, and while things have picked up for the airlines in 2006 and 2007, the industry is still struggling and savagely competitive.

The numbers involved are staggering. In the 12 months ending in February 2007, U.S. airlines embarked on 10,576,953 flights, flying over 7 billion route miles and logging 17,804, 595 hours in the air.[2] And, as we know, service could be better. In the same period, between 22% and 32% of all those flights were late.[3]

Although many factors contribute to low profitability and poor on-time records for airlines, one of the biggest culprits identified in the industry dialogues is the core set of systems and processes that governs the flow of airline traffic around the country. Expert after expert suggests that improvements in the Air Traffic Control System Command Center, and its various systems, subsystems, and territorial centers, could lead to increased efficiencies in air traffic flow and improved industry on-time performance and financial results. The airline industry, hurting as it is, could certainly use such an improvement. Besides, the volume of flights keeps increasing every year, so the matter is as urgent as ever.

The ATCSCC and Related Systems

As we discuss inefficiencies and potential improvements in the air traffic management problem, we do not want to do a disservice to the existing systems. Indeed, there is an impressive array of information gathering and distribution technologies at work keeping 45,000 flights safely in the air every day in the United States! However, as with any large-scale work in progress, there is always room to make things better.

Figure 7.1 shows a screen capture of one aspect of the FAA's Air Traffic Control System Command Center (ATCSCC) software. The ATCSCC, which is a bundle of related and connected systems from across the country, tracks all the flights in the air and on the ground, serving up information about flight status and flight volume to air traffic control managers and other stakeholders. Many operational decisions at airports, airlines, and support providers, such as refueling services, are based on information provided minute by minute during the day from the ATCSCC.

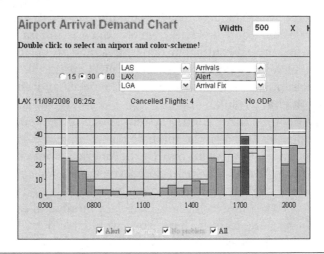

Figure 7.1 A display from the FAA's ATCSCC system showing the flow of inbound flights headed toward Los Angeles International Airport, graphed against the airport's capacity (the horizontal white line).

In this case, the application is showing a graphic display of the capacity of Los Angeles International Airport to handle the expected flow of incoming flights over a period of hours. The thin, white horizontal line indicates the maximum flight-handling capacity of the airport. As we can see, the day looks like smooth flow until 1700 hours, when the number of inbound flights will exceed the airport's capacity. The red bar shows this alert. The result of this overflow will be a delay to some flights. The graphical display gives airport personnel and the airlines opportunity to work around the impending overflow and try to mitigate its impact on the schedule. The yellow bars show time slots where there is a risk of going over capacity and causing delays.

The Playbook

When most of us think of flight control systems, we picture airplanes and control towers. The planes, though, are only one part of a large, complex system with many moving parts and separate participants, each of which plays an integral role in keeping the planes moving on time. There are airports, with their limited gate capacity and ground support services, including fueling and maintenance. There are personnel such as pilots and flight crews. There is the air traffic control network itself, which tracks the whereabouts of each plane and guides its path. There is the schedule and route network, which contains thousands of multistop flights and arrival-contingent departures, and so on. For example, if a plane is late, it might throw subsequent flights in the day off schedule and disrupt the utilization of support services and airport capacity in other cities as a result.

The airline flight control system is one of numerous and intricate dependencies between the multiple parties involved. And, it is a global system, even if our focus is only North America. For example, if JFK Airport in New York City were to close, even for a couple of hours, flights all around the world would be affected. New York–bound flights would not be able to take off, which would cause any number of cascading backups elsewhere. Flights from New York would be delayed, which would aggravate schedules in yet another collection of cities. In each place, airlines would have to scramble to find alternatives, such as flying to Newark, canceling flights, waiting to fly to JFK, and possibly taxing ground services and crews, and so on.

At present, the airline flight control system is pretty responsive to service disruptions, but its performance is not reliable nor is it particularly efficient. Figure 7.2 shows the "playbook," one factor in the system's responsiveness to disruptions. In the event of a major weather pattern, the playbook suggests a rerouting pattern for flights. Here is where the system works well but also has some major deficiencies. Much airline flight scheduling and airport traffic control is automated, based on integration with the FAA's systems and its response to playbook rerouting.

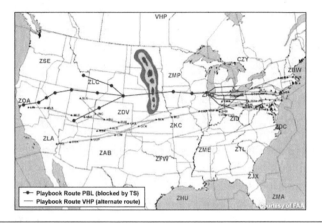

Figure 7.2   An example of the FAA playbook for rerouting flights around a major weather pattern.

However, other aspects of the system are automated but not con-nected to related operational areas. For example, the flight refueling service at an airport might have a computerized schedule, but changes to the schedule based on flight delays might be manual, or rely on manual or verbal overrides. Notifications about major disruptions in service are almost completely manual, or highly reliant on human interpretation of automated system data and transposition of system data to verbal dis-semination. In some respects, this is a good aspect of the system. Some of the stakes involved, such as safety, are quite high, and it is probably for the best that people are the key conveyers of information. Human involvement ensures a level of control over the situation, and allows a degree of flexibility that averts potentially disastrous results. However, the distributed and haphazard nature of the airline flight control systems leads to less-than-optimal results in terms of overall airline performance. This is what airline managers call the *ripple effect*.

The Ripple Effect

The ripple effect is the set of consequences that arise when there is a major disruption, such as the closing of an airport due to bad weather. As we saw with the example of JFK closing, the ripples can flow worldwide. The issue for us is this: How bad will those ripples be, what level of service disruption will result, and how can it be avoided? The problem is that the closure of an airport is bad enough, but sluggish responses to the closure can compound the ripples of disruption because of the network of dependencies that exists in the system. For example, if JFK is closed for one hour, let's say, due to a security alarm, but the word goes out that the airport is closed indefinitely, then an excessive number of flights will be diverted or canceled, a move that might overtax services at the diversion destinations and back the whole system up for a day or more.

In quantitative terms, the backlog in flights resulting from an outage resembles a buildup in work in process inventory on a factory floor when a key manufacturing process goes offline. The result is a bottleneck, with the slowest cycle setting the pace for the whole operation. Table 7.1 shows a simplified model of air traffic, with flights going in sequence from Airport A, to B, to C. Each airport can handle 10 flights per hour, and has 10 flights per hour traveling in and out. The result is stasis, with zero delay for any flight. In the second hour, Airport C is blocked. Over the next few hours, flights start to pile up at Airport B and then A as the chain of dependent connections is blocked. The delay would, in fact, be permanent if the rush of oncoming flights didn't slow down in the later hours. We're not making this up. A good recent example of the day-to-day realities of this problem could be found in the May 22, 2007, announcement that United Airlines was shifting a number of its morning flights to 5:30 AM to ease congestion at O'Hare airport. The 6 to 7 slot was so packed that the flights inevitably got delayed because the airport's capacity was maxed out at the later hour.

Table 7.1 The Closure of an Airport That Is in a Traffic Flow Creates a Backlog That Delays Flights in Feeder Airports

		Airport A	Airport B	Airport C
Hour 1	In	10	10	10
	Out	10	10	10
	Wait	0	0	0
Hour 2	In	10	10	0
	Out	10	0	0
	Wait	0	10	0
Hour 3	In	10	10	0
	Out	10	0	0
	Wait	0	20	0
Hour 4	In	10	10	10
	Out	10	10	10
	Wait	0	20	0
Hour 5	In	10	10	10
	Out	10	10	10
	Wait	0	20	0
Hour 6	In	5	5	10
	Out	5	10	5
	Wait	0	15	5
Hour 7	In	5	5	10
	Out	5	10	5
	Wait	0	10	10
Hour 8	In	5	5	10
	Out	5	10	10
	Wait	0	5	10
Hour 9	In	5	5	10
	Out	5	10	10
	Wait	0	0	10

Though the airlines, the FAA, airports, and service providers work hard on solving the ripple effect, the volume of information that must be managed in a tight time frame leads to inevitable inefficiencies and sub-optimal solutions to incidents that slow down air traffic. For example, although the FAA provides very good data, the airlines are not always completely able to integrate delay and playbook type of information into their flight scheduling. Certainly, most of the support providers lack tight integration with the FAA and airline scheduling systems. As a result, the flow of flights in an airport outage or slowdown might cause a severe overloading of an alternate landing site's capacity, a problem which then creates its own downstream delays.

The financial stakes are high. The hard-dollar costs of late flights can be significant, especially in an industry that is struggling to be profitable. For example, an Airbus 320 airliner sitting on the runway with its engines idling burns $400 of fuel an hour. A delayed airliner waiting to land or diverted to an alternative site burns fuel at an even higher rate. Add to that figure crew overtime, passenger refunds, and the cost of a $50,000,000 jet being underutilized, and multiply by thousands of flights per year. Throw in high-value intangibles such as customer attitude and airline reputation, and you're talking about a multibillion dollar problem.

The incentive to fix the ripple effect is very clear and strong, and the players are eager to find solutions. Indeed, there are many solutions being pursued or partially in place at this time. However, what's missing in the airline flight control system is a way for all the participants in the dance of coordinating flights to have access to reliable real-time information about the flight factors that affect their particular aspect of the system. To date, most attempts to solve the ripple effect have suffered from high costs of integrating systems, as well as the organizational complexity and inhibitions regarding integrating with third parties and competitors. For these reasons, EDA emerges as a workable solution approach to tie together the highly distributed, multiple parties involved in air traffic and the ripple effect.

The Ideal Airline Flight Control EDA

To a limited extent, the air traffic control systems already use an EDA, albeit one that relies extensively on human interactions to reach its full extent. As data flows out of the FAA systems, a series of phone and radio voice communications brings event data to a combination of systemic and human event processors. For example, as the capacity of an airport is reached, a verbal discussion might determine that flowing excess traffic to later arrival times is an optimal fix to the problem. However, because this overly human EDA is missing the full event picture, the people using their brains as event processors might actually compound the problem by pushing flights to a time of day when refueling capacity or gate capacity is severely limited.

Having defined the problem, let's now imagine that we have been tasked with designing an EDA that can have a tangible impact on the ripple effect. Let's call it FEDA for flight event-driven architecture. FEDA is an EDA that brings together the key players in airline flight control and enables them to share flight event data in real time. Throughout the rest of the chapter, we explore how an FEDA might ideally mitigate the ripple effect. To maximize the learning opportunity, we simplify certain aspects of the flight control problem and focus on architectural issues rather than deeply realistic descriptions of the various systems involved. However, even if you are a seasoned FAA programmer, you might still find the following exercise to be thought-provoking.

Objectives for FEDA, the Airline Flight Control EDA

Any successful IT program must begin with identification of major objectives and buy-in from key stakeholders. In the case of FEDA, there are two types of stakeholders: direct and indirect. Direct stakeholders would include the airlines, the FAA, airports, aviation service providers such as refueling and maintenance, weather services, information technology service providers to all parties, and key personnel in each group. Indirect stakeholders would be passengers and crew, who are affected by airline flight control but do not exercise any influence over it. For FEDA, we will concern ourselves only with direct stakeholders.

Functional Requirements

The good news for an idea like FEDA is that there is a simple overall goal for the project, and a high degree of alignment in desiring the goal among the stakeholders. Everyone wants to cut down the financial impact and stress of the ripple effect. In specific terms, we see two groupings of project objectives for FEDA: functional and architectural requirements.

- **Real-time awareness, for both human and machine users of FEDA, of airline flight control events that affect each FEDA stakeholder**—FEDA needs to give stakeholders a better idea of what is going on with the flow of flights than they could get by picking up the phone or assessing multiple data inputs manually. In this context, a stakeholder could be either a person, such as an airport operations manager, or a system, such as a gate scheduling program.

- **Autonomic response**—FEDA should have some level of autonomic response capability. The EDA cannot rely solely on human decision making and event processing. If that were the case, FEDA would simply be a costly version of the current manual system. FEDA needs to be able to make, or at least recommend, routing and scheduling options for flights and airport operations. Then, based on human approvals, FEDA should have the ability to communicate specific routing and scheduling information to each stakeholder system seamlessly. For example, if a backlog of arriving flights has been described by FEDA, FEDA should have a level of integration with airport operations and support services' systems so that those systems can receive complete updated schedules automatically from FEDA.

- **Extensible, customizable front ends**—FEDA should contain a number of basic functions at the outset, but the EDA and its related front-end interfaces, both human and machine, should be extensible and open to customization for specific stakeholder needs.

- **Extensible for new stakeholders**—FEDA should have application programming interfaces (APIs) capable of easily adding new types of system users. For example, an airport shuttle service or baggage handler union might also want to have better knowledge of flight schedules so that it can optimize its own operations.

FEDA's design must allow for defining and provisioning the system to new user types.

- **Advanced bottleneck awareness**—For FEDA to have high value, the system needs to show conflicts and potential delays before they happen. In other words, FEDA must be able to "think ahead" and develop airline traffic flow scenarios and describe their potential impacts on each stakeholders' operations.

- **"What-if" modeling at the stakeholder level**—FEDA should be able to give stakeholders the ability to run what-if scenarios on impending traffic flows and scheduling. The system should allow for a local playbook type model that can be stored for future use. Ideally, the system will enable systemic learning, giving users the opportunity to review past scenarios and understand how optimal flow can be achieved in the future.

- **Bottleneck resolution capacity**—FEDA should do more than just report potential delays and map out a playbook for easing the resulting ripple-effect congestion. The system should contain a set of functions for stakeholders to use in resolving ripple-effect flight backlogs in a way that is fair and optimal to each entity. For example, as Steven Waslander has suggested in his research, the airlines might benefit from the ability to buy and sell traffic flow factors to discover and realize an optimal financial result from a particular traffic pattern. FEDA could enable this type of flight delay and airport capacity "auction."

- **Interstakeholder communication capabilities at the system level**—For FEDA to deliver better airline traffic results than the current semiautomated, phone- and computer-based systems, each stakeholder in FEDA must be able to communicate with each other at the system level. Data about airline traffic patterns and potential schedule changes must flow from system to system within FEDA as data. FEDA should not be reliant on a person transmitting data to another person in the system to achieve a result. Of course, human users can modify data in the system in real time and override FEDA's scheduling algorithms for a myriad of reasons, not the least of which would be safety.

- **Reliability, security, reporting, and audit**—It's a given that FEDA must be highly reliable, scalable, and secure. Any system of this type has to meet strict standards for performance and security. The system needs to enable extensive reporting and potential integration with analytics tools. And, it must be able to pass the test of auditors who want to assure stakeholders that the data in the system is confidential and accurate.

■ **Bottleneck analytics**—Over time, FEDA should be able to show analysts where bottlenecks occur in the overall flight traffic system and highlight potential solutions. With a root-cause analysis, for example, FEDA might be able to show that recurring delays stem from a lack of gate capacity at a specific airport. Such data could be used to justify additional investment in gate facilities at the airport to relieve congestion.

Figure 7.3 shows how FEDA works in resolving a ripple-effect delay situation by involving the air traffic stakeholders in a multitrack business process flow. FEDA is at the heart of this process flow, collecting and synchronizing air traffic and other operational data and distributing it to stakeholder systems (FEDA client applications and human users). FEDA also collects, synchronizes, and distributes the collaborative bid/resolve communications that occur among the stakeholders as they interpret real-time event data and make operating decisions based on the ripple's impact on their business.

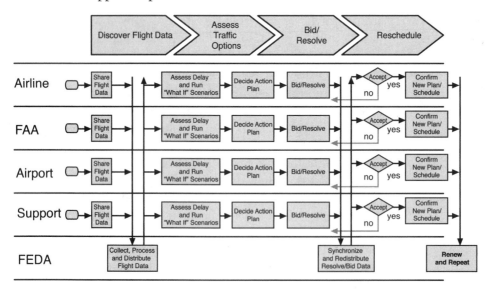

Figure 7.3 Multitrack process flow that illustrates the interactions between FEDA and its stakeholders in resolving a ripple-effect problem.

System Requirements

FEDA will naturally encompass hundreds of heterogeneous systems across a comparable number of organizations. To work, FEDA must comprise a set of system requirements that enable such a broad level of integration. To that end, it's a given that FEDA will be based on SOAP XML Web services functioning in a service-oriented architecture (SOA) type architecture. As such, FEDA should mesh with most of the developing SOA initiatives that are likely to be under way at the stakeholders. In addition, FEDA should include the following high-level system requirements:

- **Data transformation**—FEDA will fail if it requires stakeholders to modify their current data models. FEDA needs to contain extensive data-transformation capabilities, as well as an extensible data dictionary, for smooth interoperation of component systems.

- **FEDA should be highly extensible**—The EDA should be designed for a high level of component reuse. For example, a weather event service should be able to flow event data to event listeners of multiple types, including those not immediately envisioned for the initial deployment.

- **Processing of relevant airline flight control events at the local, stakeholder level**—FEDA connects thousands of independent event streams, from regional and international airports and a myriad of other systems. FEDA must be designed at all levels—from local implementation to global architecture, to enable event origination at the smallest level of granularity and locality.

- **Cost-effective integration**—FEDA must have the capability for existing and new stakeholders to connect with the airline flight control EDA at a reasonable cost.

- **Minimal impact on existing systems in their day-to-day operations**—FEDA must "do no harm" to existing systems. Rather, it should expose event data as event services by riding on top of existing systems.

High-Level Architecture

FEDA is going to be a complex EDA. To make sense of it, we think it is wise to describe the architecture in two steps. First, we will outline a high-level view of the EDA. Then, we will plunge into detail. Figure 7.4 shows such a high-level architectural view. As we can see, event data originates at the top of the diagram, with the systems of the respective stakeholders. The control towers and FAA systems are the event producers that generate a set of event streams that describe flight departures and arrival times. The airline systems produce their own comparable event streams. Fueling and maintenance services produce event streams that describe their progress in servicing flights on the ground, while weather services generate event data about conditions that might affect flight operations.

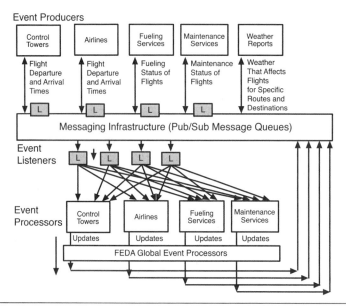

Figure 7.4   An optimal high-level architecture for FEDA.

Event data flows to the messaging infrastructure. The event producers publish event information through event (Web) services. Event listeners subscribe to the event streams published by the event services. Through the messaging infrastructure, the event listeners flow event data to the event processors as instructed by the subscription settings of the event processors. For example, Southwest Airlines operations at LAX would not subscribe to event data that described flight capacity at London's Heathrow airport. Yet, Southwest would certainly be made aware of any major outage at Heathrow that flowed back by ripple effect all the way to LAX. FEDA is a global system, and all subscribers (event processors) are able to see information that affects their operating conditions.

The information architecture issue here is how to present data to stakeholders. It would be impossible and undesirable to have every airline operations center view every single event in the entire world every second. There needs to be a primary operational field of vision for a specific airline at a specific airport. At a secondary level, FEDA needs to provide stakeholders with situational information that might affect their operations.

FEDA has multiple sets of event processors that perform functions related to their location and stakeholder. At the level of the individual airport, including the airlines that operate there and their respective service providers, FEDA event processors provide basic visibility into the flow of inbound and outbound flights. Working to the degree of automation that is user-specified, they can help stakeholders optimize their operations in that airport. The local level FEDA event processors power scenario modeling, interstakeholder communication, and the bid/resolve functions that allow stakeholders to pay, or get paid, for shifting traffic flow. In essence, the local level (airport) event processor lets the stakeholder ask, "What does an event pattern mean to me? Is there a bottleneck forming downstream from me? What would a thunderstorm mean to my flights/fueling schedule/maintenance planning this afternoon? What should I do about it? Accept, modify, resolve/bid?"

At the airline level, FEDA has to have the capacity to aggregate traffic flow data to reflect the scope of flight operations relevant to the airline in a particular scenario. For example, a regional carrier such as Alaska Airlines might set its FEDA event processors to track air traffic flow through Mexico, Los Angeles, San Francisco, Portland, and Seattle, where a large number of its flights travel multiple times a day. An airline will inevitably have multiple points of control in FEDA, usually at the local airport level, but an airline should also be able to synchronize its FEDA event processors and drive traffic decisions across as many local points of control as it needs.

At the global level, the global processing tier shown in the figure, FEDA aggregates all event data, and stakeholder inputs—which themselves become events—processes them into usable pattern data, and then reflows that data back to the stakeholders as a new event stream. The stakeholders can then adjust their plans accordingly. In this way, FEDA is an event loop, constantly refreshing itself to provide stakeholders with the latest model of what is happening in their airspace and on the ground. From the individual stakeholder perspective, others' actions contribute to my event pattern. My actions contribute to others' actions—and then we engage in a feedback loop.

Globally, FEDA also performs analytics across multiple localities and stakeholders, discovering bottlenecks and their causes. Each FEDA event processor employs its own algorithms to investigate, model, and interpret the event stream it is presented with. FEDA would ship with certain algorithms out of the box, but there would also be a development kit to enable stakeholders to add new algorithms of their own or tweak existing ones. Ideally, FEDA would have a facility for sharing algorithms as Web services through a systemwide Universal Description, Discovery, and Integration (UDDI).

FEDA is a multitiered EDA, with each tier functioning as an event producer, event listener, and event processor to the extent that it is required. The local level produces event data, but also listens for new event data from the global FEDA event processors that have a systemwide view. The tiers are dependent on one another, though any tier can also receive event data that is wholly new. For example, a terrorist threat that shuts down all airports in the United States would be a new input at the global level flowing down the local tier. FEDA is also a complex, implicit EDA—implicit because it harvests event data from the ongoing operations of stakeholder systems.

Enabling Technology Factors

Creating and running FEDA would be an extremely challenging job. On a technological level, FEDA is a highly complex architecture involving thousands of different systems administered by hundreds of separate stakeholders. The key to pulling it off is to drive functionality and adoption without tightly coupling stakeholders' component systems. Some of the other key enabling technology factors include the following:

- **Common data model**—Although the component systems of FEDA, the systems that drive airline, airport, and support service operations, need not change to participate in FEDA, FEDA still needs to operate on a common data model. To make this work, FEDA needs to function using a broad set of standards-based data transformation capabilities. Event data produced by local systems using their native data model and format must flow into FEDA after being transformed into a FEDA-friendly data model.

A key enabler of this would be a FEDA data dictionary that lets developers implement data transformation at the local deployment level.

- **Agreement among stakeholders regarding event definition**—For FEDA to work, the stakeholders must agree what constitutes an event. For example, capacity of a fueling service must be harvested from existing systems (or manually input)—in a way that is rendered uniform across the system, for example, 737s per hour, not litres per minute.

- **Federated, standards-based messaging infrastructure**—FEDA needs to transmit millions of messages among its thousands of constituent systems. To do this, it will require a standards-based messaging infrastructure. Given the current state of the industry, that will likely mean enterprise service buses (ESBs) from multiple vendors and open source providers. The ESBs need to be federated so that messages can flow freely and easily between event producers, listeners, and processors that are attached to the ESBs. Included in such a messaging infrastructure would be the following specifications:
    - A standards-based message format, such as SOAP
    - Reliable, secure networks
    - Mediation capability between divergent ESBs—ESB solutions from different sources do not necessarily share identical implementations of the standards. In addition, some of the networks that connect to FEDA will inevitably run different message transport protocols (for example, Java Message Service [JMS] and Hypertext Transfer Protocol [HTTP]). To work, FEDA must be able to mediate between these potentially incompatible systemic components.

- **Firm governance guidelines**—The governance and administration of FEDA needs to accommodate the local and global requirements of the system itself as well as those of the stakeholders.

As you might have noticed, there is an organizational aspect in each of these technological factors. Local and global control, federated message, agreement as to event definition, and so forth are all both technical and organizational in nature. We deal with the purely organizational issues later on in this chapter.

What FEDA Might Look Like in Real Life

Being a complex, implicit EDA, FEDA brings together the output of numerous systemic components. As Figure 7.5 shows, even in a still simplified view, FEDA is a monster of architectural complexity. For each stakeholder, we have a set of core systems functioning as event producers through event Web services, an ESB(s), event listeners, event processors, and n-layers of integrated subsystems that feed their own event streams into ESB as well. Some of these stakeholders themselves might have immense enterprise architectures. For example, each airline would have global operations systems and airport local systems functioning as event producers. Ideally, stakeholders with such complex and multilayered systems would use ESBs and SOA for integration, simplifying the task of publishing event data to FEDA using SOAP XML.

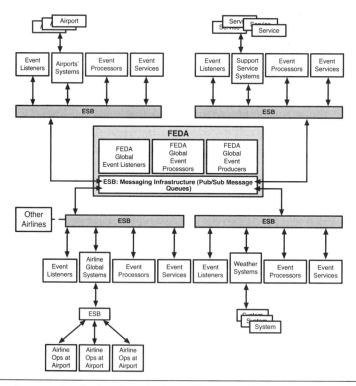

Figure 7.5   A more detailed and realistic architecture for FEDA, showing the multiple enterprise service buses (ESBs) and systems, event listeners, producers, and processors involved.

FEDA itself is based on an ESB model, which is set up to receive all stakeholder event stream data from their respective event Web services. FEDA functions as an event listener, event processor, and event producer, flowing event data back to stakeholder systems by publishing event data onto its ESBs. FEDA is also based on SOAP XML Web services for its messaging functions. It publishes its event stream back to the stakeholders using Web services to the ESB.

ESB Federation

FEDA relies on ESB federation to function. SOAP messages published by a stakeholder must be able to travel freely from the originating event Web service through to any event listener Web service consumer on FEDA's ESB. Going in the other direction, SOAP messages originating from FEDA's event services (the updating loop) must be understandable at the event listeners' resident on the stakeholder side. And, this mediation must be achieved without adding a sticky layer of integration on top of all of the other moving parts in FEDA. If that were the solution to the mediation issue, FEDA would become too costly and complex to manage.

For example, in Figure 7.6, let's imagine that there is an event Web service on the airline side that publishes data about flight arrival times. The SOAP messages from that Web service originate from a .NET application and flows to an open source ESB over HTTP. The SOAP message is then routed to FEDA, and then through FEDA to an Oracle ESB for consumption by a J2EE Web service consumer on the support stakeholder systems. The message must be able to travel across these different SOAP implementations and transport protocols—in this case, from SOAP on HTTP to SOAP on JMS. As anyone involved in the SOA field knows, not all vendor platforms are identical when it comes to standards implementations. Some run SOAP 1.1, some run SOAP 1.2, and so on. It is an essential requirement that Web services providers and consumers operating on separate ESBs and platforms, as well as networks, be able to interoperate smoothly. Specialized solutions are typically needed to enable this functioning.

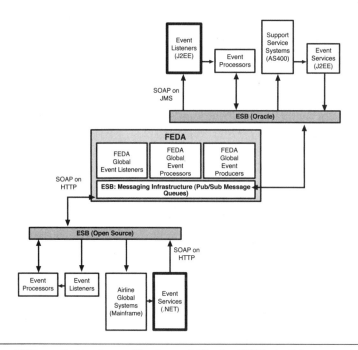

Figure 7.6 ESB mediation is a critical capability for FEDA. In this example, the event Web service on the airline side originates from a .NET application and flows to an open source ESB before being routed to FEDA, and then through FEDA to an Oracle ESB for consumption by a J2EE Web service consumer at the support stakeholder systems. The message must be able to travel across these different SOAP implementations and transport protocols—in this case, from SOAP on HTTP to SOAP on JMS.

Data Transformation

The data that flows to FEDA from the event producing Web services comes from underlying systems that were, in all likelihood, never designed with EDA in mind. In the example shown in Figure 7.6, the airline's operational data about flights is generated from a mainframe computer running a COBOL application on CICS. The mainframe is exposed to the ESB as an event Web service using a Microsoft .NET application. FEDA, in turn, must receive data in a standardized form or the system will never work. As a result, each FEDA stakeholder must have the capability to transform its own system data into a form that FEDA can use and understand. In concrete terms, this means that FEDA must be sent SOAP XML messages that match an agreed-upon schema. This can happen in a number of ways, but typically, each stake-holder would utilize the data-transformation capabilities that came with their particular ESB and SOA platform.

For example, the airline's mainframe might characterize a flight arrival time in the following way:

Field Name	Flight Number	Origin	Destination	Scheduled Time	ETA
Data	1234	LAX	SEA	0900	1000
Field Definition	*4 integers*	*3 characters*	*3 characters*	*4 integers*	*4 integers*

On the other end, at the support services, such as refueling, which need to plan their schedules based on flight schedules, the systems need to see data that will be understood by the following model:

Field Name	FN	Dep	Arr	Sched	ETA
Data	UA1234	LAX	SEA	050107,-6	050107,-5
Field Definition	*10 characters*	*3 characters*	*3 characters*	*GMT standard*	*GMT standard*

Let's look at the differences in the data sets and data models. For the airline, the data is described in a format standard to mainframe systems. The airline knows who it is, so it doesn't need to say, "United Flight 1234." It just says FlightNumber=1234 and it knows what that means. The mainframe also knows what day it is, so it doesn't have to keep track of the date in this particular data set.

FEDA, in turn, needs to receive the data about flight arrivals in a universally understandable, standardized form. It must be able to consume a SOAP XML message that contains the following data:

Field Name	Carrier	Flight No	FAA Num	Dep Loc	Arr Loc	Scheduled Arr	ETA
Data	UAL	001234	634524	LAX	SEA	0501070600	0501070700
Field Definition	*3 characters*	*6 integers*	*6 integers*	*3 characters*	*3 characters*	*10 integers*	*10 integers*

As you can see, FEDA modifies the data model for flight arrival time by splitting the carrier and flight number, and adding a separate FAA flight identification number that is standard across all carriers and airports. FEDA also has mostly different field names. FEDA isn't trying to be difficult by picking different names for the same data—for example, "ArrLoc" instead of "Destination." However, in addition to being an EDA, FEDA is an application connected to a database itself. The event processors and event producers that make FEDA work at the core need to have a working data model, and the one that FEDA's designers pick needs to be enforced throughout the stakeholders.

To resolve discrepancies between data models and enforce its data model in a standard way across stakeholder systems—without affecting the way those systems work internally—FEDA's designers need to define and publish a standard SOAP schema for use by stakeholders.

FEDA would share the schema it needed through a Web Services Description Language (WSDL) for the flight arrival event Web service. FEDA would direct stakeholders to the WSDL by pointing to it on the FEDA registry, or UDDI. To turn the published SOAP schema into a usable event Web service, the stakeholders would utilize several functions of their SOA platforms and ESBs. They would use the WSDL in their Web services development tools (e.g., Eclipse or Visual Studio) to expose their operational systems as event Web services. Because they were based on the WSDL and the SOAP schema it embodied, the event Web service would conform to the FEDA standard. In addition, the stakeholder would likely need to take advantage of the data-transformation capabilities of their ESB and SOA platforms to achieve the translation between the desired FEDA data model and their own native data model.

With the data-transformation layers of the ESBs involved, the body of a SOAP message communicating a flight's arrival time would resemble the following, regardless of the data model used in the underlying systems:

```
<carrier>UAL</carrier>
<FlightNo>001234</FlightNo>
<FAANum>634524</FAANum>
<DepLoc> LAX </DepLoc>
< ArrLoc > SEA </ ArrLoc >
< ScheduledArr >0501070600</ ScheduledArr >
< ETA >0501070700</ ETA >
```

Carrying State

EDAs communicate changes in state. In the example we are working with, United Airlines Flight 1234 from Los Angeles to Seattle is an hour late. The hour delay is the change in state that FEDA needs to communicate to its stakeholders. The challenge, though, is to make such a state change understandable and actionable in a complex, implicit EDA that cuts across multiple stakeholders and systems. In a silo application, there is probably no need to communicate a complete set of data relating to state. In fact, it would be a waste of network bandwidth and developer resources. In the example, the United Airlines systems might communicate the delay of flight 1234 from 9 to 10 o'clock with an eight integer message that said, "12341000." The systems involved, such as those of United's local airport operations or payroll application, would understand, based on syntax, exactly what 12341000 meant. This is not a good setup for an EDA, however.

As we have noted earlier in the book, conventional application integration usually involves a high level of preconception from one system to another, resulting in tight coupling. If the payroll system at United is configured to understand what the message "12341000" means when it arrives from the airline's operational system, that payroll system has to maintain a high level of preconception about the operational system. It has to know, for one thing, that the system represents United Airlines, and not any other. It has to know what day the operational system has in mind when it simply says 1000, for 10 o'clock. In this last instance, there might be a hard-coded calendar somewhere in the enterprise architecture that synchronizes all of United's systems on a common time framework. The tight coupling results from the reality that an external system that wants to integrate with United's operational system and payroll system would need to understand the condensed message syntax used to communicate changes in flight time as well as the tightly coupled time stamp involved. Although it would not be a superhuman challenge to integrate in this way, the costs and complexity of integrating a large number of airlines with comparable data models and high levels of preconception would be prohibitive.

If the messages about flight times only need to remain in the tightly coupled world of United Airlines, there is no problem. When other stakeholders need to know about state change, we run into trouble. The scheduling system for a fueling contractor at LAX might have no way of understanding what 12341000 meant. How would the system know it meant United Airlines flight #1234? How would they know what day the flight was arriving, and so on?

In a complex, implicit EDA, the messages that communicate changes in state need to contain complete information about the state change. In our example, instead of saying "12341000" to indicate that United Flight 1234 was an hour late, FEDA would need to receive, and transmit, the complete SOAP message shown above. The United systems that normally communicated "12341000," would have to employ a data-transformation capability to fill in the blanks and transmit the complete SOAP message that detailed the name of the airline, the FAA number, the destination, and so on, to the other stakeholders as well as FEDA itself. It might help to think of this process as data enrichment as much as data transformation.

SOA Governance for FEDA

Because FEDA spans both a large group of separate stakeholders and a new set of technologies, the system requires two levels of governance. There is organizational governance, which manages how the system is used, who controls it, and so forth. We discuss that shortly. On a technological level, FEDA requires strong governance of the Web services and SOA that comprise its numerous component parts. The following section touches on the emerging specialization of SOA governance, which has achieved a certain prominence with the rise of Web services in the IT industry.

IT governance is nothing new, but Web services, with their universal accessibility and standards-based messaging, are so inherently chaotic and wild that they require a thorough and disciplined approach to governance. Simply put, SOA governance is the set of technologies, processes, and practices that provide assurance to system owners that the SOA is performing as it is intended to in terms of security and reliability. Of course, realizing this goal can involve some highly intricate patterns of implementation, but the objective should remain clear. To make FEDA, which is an EDA and an SOA, secure and reliable, it takes a strong governance solution.

SOA governance is a broad subject, one that could probably fill a book of its own. To keep the issue focused, we concentrate on the ways in which policies, or rules, for the SOA/EDA are defined and enforced. Policy is the essential ingredient for governance. In the context of SOA/EDA, you will typically hear policy referred to as Web services policy. For example, there is an emerging standard known as WS-Policy Metadata Exchange, or WS-MEX. WS-MEX is a standard for communicating governance policies that apply to Web services in an SOA or EDA.

Security and governance has a tendency to put new labels on old, familiar concepts. A policy is, in essence, a rule. Some policies are clearly identifiable as rules, as in access control or encryption policies that mandate adherence to a specific procedure. Other policies can be seen as rules implicitly. For example, a Quality of Service policy, or service-level agreement (SLA) might specify a threshold of acceptable performance for a Web service. The EDA can function if the SLA is not honored, but the policy stating the desired service level will have been broken. The trick in that case, of course, is to be aware of the SLA violation.

The work of SOA governance, then, involves the definition and enforcement of Web services policies. Definition of policies is a two-part process. At a high level, the stakeholders in the EDA—in our case, the people and organizations that come together to build FEDA—must decide which policies they want to define, and then flesh them out with specific policy detail. For example, FEDA's governing body (more on this later) must decide whether they want to encrypt traffic on the EDA. Encryption might be desirable, as it would thwart possible eavesdropping by malicious parties. However, the desire for encryption would have to be balanced against its cost, complexity, and systemic performance drag. Is FEDA flight data as sensitive as health records? This is the kind of high-level policy definition decision that must be made. From this process comes a list of Web services policies that FEDA needs to define in detail.

Detailed policy definition involves adding meat to the basic policy required. If there is going to be encryption, what kind will it be? How will the keys be managed? Will all messages require encryption, or just those of a small set of FEDA component systems? Keep in mind, also, that policy definitions tend to change over time. Ideally, FEDA will have a dynamic policy definition capability, where policies can be modified as needed on a continuous basis.

After FEDA has defined its Web services policies for its SOA/EDA governance, it needs to enforce those policies. After all, it is meaningless to have a policy that cannot be enforced. It would be a waste of time, or even dangerous, to allow FEDA stakeholders to develop and deploy event Web services on FEDA that were not subject to the policies specified for governance. For example, if a FEDA event service lacked a failover capability, and the event service failed, then FEDA would be blind to the output of that event service. The result would be a great diminution of FEDA's capacity to manage traffic flow. If such break-downs occurred early in FEDA's life, the whole system might appear flawed and fail to achieve broad adoption.

FEDA needs a way to make sure that the governance-related poli-cies it has defined get enforced when the system is deployed. FEDA has to have a high level of confidence that the Web services that run on its ESBs and those of it stakeholders are running in accordance with stated policies. What this involves, typically, is the use of a dedicated software agent to enforce policy. We explore this in detail in the next section.

Finally, FEDA needs to have the ability to audit policy enforcement. For many reasons, ranging from practical management issues to compli-ance and risk management, FEDA has to be able to generate and exam-ine high-integrity reports on its system usage and Web service policy enforcement. To continue with our previous example, if flight arrival time SOAP messages are required to be encrypted, FEDA needs to have an audit log that shows that each and every SOAP message was encrypted. The production of audit-worthy logs is the only way that FEDA will be sure that the policies it defines are being enforced to an acceptable level. Now, to answer the question that is surely (there she is again!) on your mind, how do you actually develop and deploy an EDA with these sophis-ticated governance capabilities? The answer is that you have to design governance right into the EDA itself, as part of the architecture.

SOA/EDA Governance Reference Architecture

Returning to the issue of SOA governance and infrastructure that we introduced at a high level in Chapter 5, "The SOA-EDA Connection," let's now see how these ideas connect with a practical EDA example. Figure 7.7 brings back the SOA governance and infrastructure reference model from Chapter 5, at least the bottom portion, which contains the SOA man-agement solution, UDDI registry, and policy metadata repository.

To refresh from Chapter 5, we govern the runtime SOA/EDA by defining policies and storing them in the policy metadata repository. As Web services are deployed, the policies that govern them are bound to them through their listings in the UDDI registry as metadata trans-ported from the metadata repository. The standard used to make this binding of policy to the Web service is WS-Policy, which transmits policy metadata to and from the metadata repository in policy attachments. In practical terms, the registry and metadata repository might be tables in the same database running on the SOA management solution.

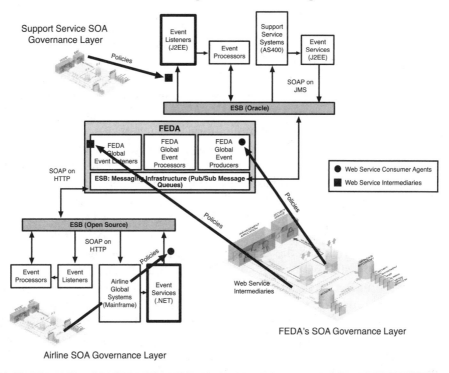

Figure 7.7   SOA governance reference architecture, at runtime, showing the relationship between UDDI registry, policy metadata repository, SOA management solution, ESB, Web services, and Web service consumers.

(Courtesy of SOA Software)

Actual policy enforcement at runtime comes from the provisioning of intermediaries that stand in front of the event Web services and agents that act as gateways for outbound SOAP requests emanating from the Web service consumers. The intermediaries and agents get their instructions from the Web services management solution, which itself gets its policy information from the registry and metadata repository.

For FEDA, there would ideally be one central registry and metadata repository to govern all the Web services that make up FEDA, whether or not they are actually part of the FEDA system itself. In reality, however, the individual stakeholders would probably have their own SOA governance infrastructure, registries, and metadata repositories. That is only logical because not every Web service existing in the enterprise architecture of a stakeholder would necessarily be connected with FEDA. The challenge in that situation would be to have some type of federated governance so that FEDA Web services policies could be defined and enforced for stakeholder Web services that touched FEDA. In particular, that might mean a federation of registries. Let's look at our example and see what that means.

In our example, shown in Figure 7.6, the airline publishes a flight time though an event Web service (event producer) that is available through the airline's ESB. From a governance perspective, the stakeholders will have a number of criteria by which they want to monitor and control their Web services, including security, reliability, and performance. Take access control, for example. The airline needs to (or should want to) control who has access to that event Web service. That access control is governed by the airline's SOA governance layer, shown at the lower left of the diagram. The UDDI registry that lists the flight time event Web service and the policy metadata repository for that service are both controlled by the airline. The consumer of the flight time Web service is located within FEDA, and as such is governed by FEDA's SOA governance layer, shown at the lower-right corner of the diagram. FEDA, in turn, publishes the flight data back out to other stakeholders, who themselves will have some type of SOA governance layer. The UDDI registries and metadata repositories need to be federated to work together providing uniform governance policy across the entire FEDA system. Let's look at several other governance activities that will require UDDI federation.

Basic performance monitoring of Web services is a policy matter. In a critical system like FEDA, Web services must be managed for Quality of Service (QOS) or service-level agreement (SLA). For a call-and-response Web service, the SLA might stipulate the expected response time for an invocation of that Web service. The response time threshold is stored as a data point in the metadata repository and deployed to the intermediary that governs the Web service. If the Web service response fails to meet the service-level agreement, the intermediary will know this, and notify the SOA management solution that the SLA has been violated. Typically, an SLA violation will trigger a Simple Network Management Protocol (SNMP) alert to whatever system management console (for example, Tivoli Enterprise Console, Unicenter, Microsoft System Center, HP Openview). In this way, the QOS of Web services in a large, complex SOA/EDA like FEDA can be monitored by central system administrators.

Figure 7.8 shows what a system administrator might actually see when monitoring Web services that are in production. This figure is taken from a real SOA management/governance product, the SOA Software Service Manager. (Disclosure: Two of us are affiliated with SOA Software, but we do not want you to think we are playing favorites. The console view shown in the figure is comparable to many similar solutions on the market today.) The console displays Web service performance metrics and charts whether the Web services are functioning within the service-level agreement. The console also highlights alerts and service discovery. The tabs for other functions of the solution allow for provisioning of intermediaries and programming of governance policies.

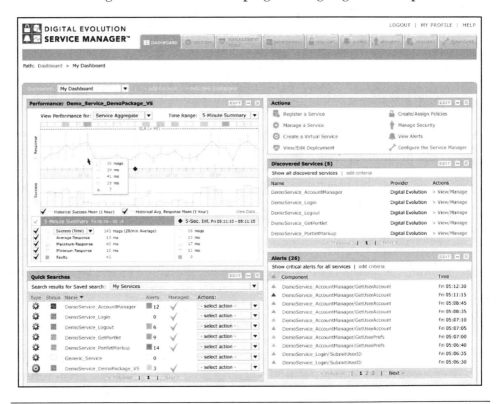

Figure 7.8   SOA Management Solution—This screen show shows a typical Web service management/SOA governance solution at work. The console provides a real-time view of Web performance and adherence and deviations from service-level agreements. At the lower right, alerts for service level and security issues are displayed for system administrators to see.

(Courtesy of SOA Software)

The flight time arrival Web service should have an SLA. The SLA for this service might include confirmation of message delivery to the ESB, response time, as well as a live/dead message for the Web service that is monitored by the SOA management solution and enterprise console. Many ESBs have a built-in feature for reliable and persistent messaging, so enforcing an SLA for message reliability might be automatic. The intermediary is programmed, through the metadata repository, to listen for the heartbeat and report in to the SOA management solution if the heartbeat flatlines.

Routing and protocol transformation are another area where policy enforcement is needed to ensure reliability and performance of Web services. As the SOAP messages travel across the three ESBs and platforms that make up FEDA and the stakeholders' individual architectures, they must be transformed and controlled at each step. In addition to the data transformation we discussed earlier, the SOAP messages must be changed to travel on HTTP to JMS. They must be modified to be acceptable to an Oracle platform, having been generated on a .NET platform, each of which has minor discrepancies in standards implementation that require mediation. In addition, the three governance layers involved must achieve a mutual understanding of optimal routing, failover, load balancing, version control, and security.

Dozens of security parameters must be considered in this example, but in addition to access control, the owners of the stakeholder systems and of FEDA must think through nonrepudiation, audit logging, certificates, signatures, and keys, if encryption is an issue. With the kind of risks associated with airline traffic, including safety, liability, and terrorism, the stakeholders might want to opt for highly secure data transmissions, including signatures and encryption, so that no one can eavesdrop on message traffic or modify a message in transit.

Let's go deeper and see how policy enforcement actually works. Figure 7.9 shows a simplified view of FEDA, but one that expands the view of Web service intermediary governing the flight arrival time event Web service. The intermediary consists of a pluggable pipeline architecture. As the SOAP messages travel from the Web service consumer, which is an event listener in FEDA, to the event Web service, located on the airline's ESB, they are intercepted by the intermediary. The intermediary runs the SOAP message through a series of policy enforcement pipeline components.

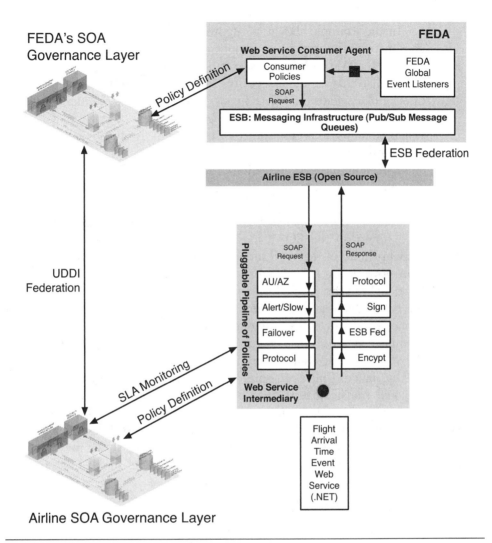

Figure 7.9   Expanded view of the Web service intermediary, showing the pluggable pipeline architecture of the intermediary. There is a pipeline of policy enforcement components for both the Web service request and response. The policies that are enforced by the intermediary as well as the actual selection of pipeline components meant to be deployed are controlled by the SOA governance layer of the respective stakeholders. To work with FEDA, there must be federation between the governance layers, mostly their UDDIs and policy metadata repositories.

In the example shown in Figure 7.9, the inbound SOAP message goes through four pipeline components. In the first pipeline component, AU/AZ, the Web service consumer is authenticated and authorized. To accomplish this essential security step, the pipeline component in the intermediary reads the SOAP header and establishes the identity of the consumer. Then, by communicating with the SOA governance layer, which contains an access control list and identity store—or integration with those types of systems at the stakeholder level—it either clears the authorization and authentication of the consumer or rejects the SOAP request.

Then, the SOAP message passes through a pipeline component that monitors the performance of the Web service. The intermediary places a time stamp on the SOAP message, which is then used to track the response time of the Web service. Performance data flows back to the SOA governance layer from the intermediary, creating a performance log. The Web service performance data from the intermediary is used at the governance layer to issue an alert to system managers if the Web service is slow or not working at all. The intermediary's pipeline on the inbound SOAP side also contains a failover component, which redirects the SOAP message to another instance of the Web service if the original one has failed. Finally, the pipeline flows the SOAP message through a protocol transformation step because the Web service that is being requested is on a different transport protocol from the Web service message that originated the SOAP request. The SOAP message changes as it moves through the pipeline. In this example, the SOAP message that emerges from the pipeline looks different from the one that entered the first pipeline component.

There is a pipeline of policy enforcement components for both the Web service request and response. There are pipeline components to process the inbound and outbound SOAP messages. They are not necessarily the same components, either. In some cases, there is a pipeline at the consumer agent as well, such as in situations where the SOAP request needed to be encrypted. What if it's a one-way service, which simply publishes event data to the ESB without requiring a specific invocation? In that case, you can still define and enforce governance policies using an intermediary. The intermediary only has a one-way pipeline, though. For performance monitoring in a one-way situation, some SOA designers specify a "heartbeat," where the Web service emits a standard, time-stamped SOAP message to the SOA governance layer at regular intervals. In that way, the governance layer knows if the Web service is down.

The policies that are enforced by the intermediary as well as the actual selection of pipeline components meant to be deployed are controlled by the SOA governance layer of the respective stakeholders. To work with FEDA, there must be federation between the governance layers, mostly their UDDIs and policy metadata repositories.

One point that's worth making here is to highlight the utility of the SOA governance solutions. Each stakeholder in FEDA can have its own SOA governance solution for use in whatever Web service and SOA construct it wants. That same SOA governance solution can also be adapted for use by the EDA. There is no need to acquire a separate SOA infrastructure or governance solution to build an EDA or participate in an EDA. The standards make it possible. As long as the Web services used in the EDA and the governance solution used to manage them are based on standards, the stakeholder's main SOA can be extended into an EDA with relatively modest effort and additional investment. Of course, getting to that first rung of the SOA governance ladder might take some time and money, but once there, the EDA possibilities present themselves.

Event Web Service Life Cycle

It might seem as if we are going out of sequence by discussing runtime governance of our SOA/EDA first, and then describing the Web service life cycle. However, based on our experience, we believe that comprehensive SOA governance is a necessary requirement to implement before development of constituent Web services can be undertaken. Of course, you could develop your event Web services first, and figure out how to govern them later, and indeed many SOA/EDAs work this way, but it is far from optimal. Web services are inherently chaotic and open, so ideally they should be controlled very tightly at all stages of their life cycle. In FEDA, with its multiple, independent stakeholders, the need for strong governance is all the more crucial as each stakeholder develops and deploys Web services and exposes them to FEDA.

SOA Governance: A "Must-Have" for Web Service Life Cycle

To illustrate the importance of governance to the Web service life cycle, let's take a look at the life cycle of a completely ungoverned Web service. Of course, no serious IT professional would ever do such a thing, but the contrasts that become evident between governed and ungoverned Web services can be quite educational. If a developer at the airline in our example wanted to create a flight arrival time event Web service, he or she could do so using a number of Integrated Development Environments (IDEs) or tools that are generally available. For instance, he or she could use a Microsoft Visual Studio .NET or IBM's Rational Eclipse based IDE and expose the program functionality of the airline's flight scheduling system as a SOAP Web service. After generating a WSDL document that enabled any developer anywhere to create a consumer for the Web service, he or she could publish the Web service's location on a publicly accessible UDDI.

In an ideal world, only FEDA stakeholders with legitimate business would create consumers for the flight arrival time event Web service and subscribe (listen) to its output. Each FEDA stakeholder who wanted to access this Web service would contact the owner of the service and make sure that the provisioning of the service would not overtax the infrastructure supporting the functioning of the service. If there were a performance problem, the stakeholder and Web service owner could be in touch and resolve the relevant issues. Alas, this is not how the world of IT works, even with the best of intentions.

You can get into several levels of trouble with an ungoverned Web service, or even a semigoverned one. In broad terms, they fall into two groups: security and performance trouble you can have as a result of planned connections with upstanding and well-intentioned professional colleagues, and security and performance trouble you can have from inadvertent dealings with bad or irresponsible strangers. We look first at the trouble you have with people with whom you want to connect.

If you simply publish a Web service without any governance, or with deficient governance, even legitimate users can cause showstopping security and performance problems. In terms of security, you would lack authentication and authorization, so you might be allowing access to the Web service to unauthorized people. Remember, a pure Web service is open to access through Port 80 on the firewall, so literally anyone can come in and use it. Even if you restrict access to the Web service to users from trusted domains, you still have little or no control over who is actually accessing the service. Web services are machine to machine in nature, so they don't recognize human users without the help of a governance solution. The "user" of a Web service is another application. You might not care, but you should because not everyone should be allowed to access your Web service, even if they work for a trusted entity.

Ungoverned, you are also open to risks of repudiation. Without a certificate or auditable Web service transaction log, you are vulnerable to the accusation that your Web service did not deliver results for a request. Or, you might be unable to charge for the use of the Web service (if that is your arrangement) because you have no proof of the occurrence of an invocation of the Web service.

And, in the ungoverned SOA, the data you are transmitting to consumers of your Web services is vulnerable to eavesdropping and modification in midstream. Without a digital signature and/or encryption, you cannot prove that your SOAP message arrived at the consumer with integrity and confidentiality. Even while working with trusted partners, there is room for misunderstanding and conflict if there is little or no assurance of integrity and confidentially of message traffic.

In the realm of performance, the ungoverned Web service is vulnerable to a number of risks. If the provisioning of the Web service cannot be controlled, it is easy to run into a situation where the load on the Web service is unsustainable—a problem that can result in slow performance or even a crashing of the infrastructure supporting the service. In addition, if you have ungoverned Web services, they are highly vulnerable to outages caused by version changes or lack of failover. A complementary issue here is routing and protocol transformation. If the SOAP message needs to travel across networks that run on incompatible transport protocols, such as JMS and HTTP, the Web service might not work properly, or at all. Certainly, if the location of the consumer or Web service changes, there is a great risk of the connection being broken from this kind of problem.

So, with all of these security and performance problems evident even when working with trusted partners, imagine how severe the exposure to risk can be when confronting the idea of malicious users. In our age of threatened "digital warfare," you could envision a lot of scenarios where people might want to wreck a system like FEDA. Overloading Web services, unauthorized access, compromised messages—all of these look a lot more disastrous when contemplating the actions of bad people.

The bottom line here is that you must develop your Web services with governance in mind. Or, to be more complete, the best practice to follow is to design and implement a comprehensive SOA governance solution before embarking on any Web service development. If you don't, you are courting disaster. To put this into a practical framework, we want to introduce a concept now known as the "loop" of SOA governance.

Closing the Loop

Whether you realize it or not, when you develop and deploy Web services with an SOA governance solution, you are engaging in a loop of policy definition, policy enforcement, and audit. As shown in Figure 7.10, the activities of defining governance policies for a Web service at design time, enforcing them at runtime, and auditing whether the defined policies were actually enforced are all connected. Best practices dictate that you should want to enforce the governance policies that you define and that you should have a high-integrity audit log of Web service transactions to validate the enforcement of your policies.

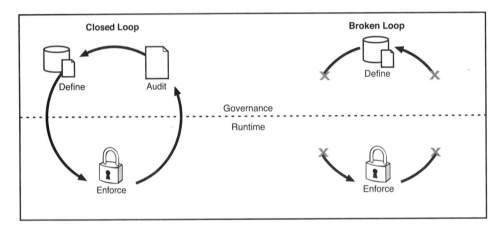

Figure 7.10   The loop of SOA governance. Policies that are defined for a Web service at design time need to be enforced at runtime. The enforcement should be fully auditable, an outcome that is best ensured through the use of a "closed loop" of SOA governance, where design time, runtime, and audit are completely integrated. (Courtesy of SOA Software)

The optimal way to ensure enforcement and auditability of Web service/SOA governance policies that you define is to develop and deploy your Web services using a "closed-loop" approach to SOA governance. In a closed-loop SOA governance model, whatever policies you define for a Web service at design time are automatically enforced at runtime. The audit capability of the closed-loop SOA governance model (typically built into the SOA governance solution that is utilized) provides a record of the deployment and can ensure that policies are enforced as intended.

This might seem obvious, but practice shows that it is not always so evident. What a lot of IT professionals are discovering lately is that it is all well and good to define governance policies for Web services at design time. However, upon promoting those Web services to production, there is a risk of a drop-off in policy enforcement. A lot of smart people are actually working with a "broken loop" of SOA governance, whereby they "define and hope" that policies will be enforced. There is a surefire way to get to a closed loop, though, and that involves integrating design-time and runtime UDDIs, and their respective policy metadata repositories.

If you are curious about how this actually works, take a look at Figure 7.11, which shows a closed-loop SOA governance model in action. In this situation, Web services that are being developed are given defined governance policies that are stored in the design-time UDDI and policy metadata repository. When the Web service is put into production, the integrated runtime UDDI and policy metadata repository pick up those defined policies and enforce them. The integrated UDDIs enable the creation of an audit log that reports on the policy enforcement. Again, the standards of WS-Policy and WS-MEX make this possible. The trick, though, is for the integration of design-time and runtime UDDIs to be solid. Some solutions on the market today favor a metadata replication approach and this has a risk of disaggregation of policy metadata between design time and runtime.

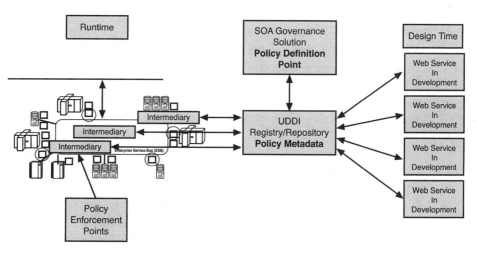

Figure 7.11   A closed-loop SOA governance model is attainable when the design-time and runtime UDDIs and policy metadata repositories are integrated.

Back to FEDA

Now, we are going to assume that FEDA builds in a closed-loop SOA governance model, with integrated design-time and runtime UDDIs. In addition, we are going to assume that FEDA stakeholders will be required to federate their design-time and runtime UDDIs and metadata repositories with FEDA's for the purpose of ensuring a closed loop. What this means, in our example, is that when the airline develops the flight arrival time event Web service, it defines the governance policies for it in a UDDI/repository that is integrated with the airline's runtime UDDI/repository. The airline's runtime UDDI/repository is, in turn, federated with FEDA's runtime UDDI/repository. The intermediaries and agents that are deployed to enforce those policies are instructed by the federated UDDIs/repositories. As a result, there will be an assurance that the governance policies defined for the flight arrival time Web service will be enforced as desired, and that there will be an audit log available to prove it. As new Web services are rolled out across FEDA, the intermediaries and agents will be able to discover them and automatically bind them to runtime policies that have been specified at design time.

After all this, you might be thinking that this SOA governance stuff is a heck of a lot of overhead to deal with. And, you would be right, except that it is truly mission critical. As we have discussed, it would be irresponsible or downright self-destructive to compromise on governance. Keep in mind that FEDA will have hundreds or even thousands of stakeholders and potentially tens of thousands of Web services—there can be no expectation of stakeholders knowing each other or agreeing to work together. Even with good intentions, there is a lot of room for trouble unless governance is ironclad.

The good news here is that the parallel emergence of strong standards for governance and mature governance solutions makes this seemingly daunting task fairly livable. All the major platform players who would be the likely solution providers for FEDA's working parts are aware of the criticality of governance through the full Web service life cycle, so you can have a high level of confidence that the platforms used for FEDA would contain governance features. Of course, you would have to know how to use them, and what the best practices include, to make it all work correctly. This chapter should give you an introduction to what's involved. The complexity of governing FEDA at a technological level, though, is also a good segue to the even more nuanced issue of how the system should be governed by the people and organizations involved.

Program Success

As you have read through the sophisticated and complex technologies required to attain a fully functioning FEDA, you might have wondered just how it was all going to happen on a human, organizational, and financial level. The truth is, succeeding with a project of FEDA's size and scope is only partly a matter of technology. Even calling it a project is probably a misnomer. FEDA would likely be its own organization. In a basic sense, FEDA would be no different from any other large multi-stakeholder IT endeavor, with which the airline industry is already familiar. However, the nature of EDA and SOA bring some additional challenges to the realization of FEDA as an organizational success. The following section looks at some of the prominent risks associated with FEDA and some ideas on how those risks might be best mitigated. The goal is to achieve success with FEDA from design, launch, and sustained operation over the long term.

Project Risks

There are myriad risks to undertaking a massive IT initiative like FEDA. Not only does FEDA bring together a large collection of stakeholders who have not all collaborated before (if they had, FEDA might not be necessary), but FEDA also simultaneously introduces a variety of new technologies. For some stakeholders, FEDA might be the first time they are working with production-level Web services connecting outside their own enterprises. Some of the major risks include the following:

- **Build it, and they won't come**—FEDA must have a high level of participation if it is to have a chance of success. If even a small number of major airlines balk and don't participate, FEDA will fail. FEDA must have a high membership rate from as many stakeholders as possible.

- **Build it, but it doesn't work**—This might seem obvious, but technological risk is a huge factor in the success or failure. At each stage of FEDA's life cycle, technological performance is a non-negotiable requirement. FEDA cannot fail and then be brought to proper functioning over time. It must launch in good working order.

- **Build it, but it is unmanageable**—Organizational risk could be deadly to FEDA. With all the stakeholders involved, FEDA will depend on a strong organizational governance model and agreement among stakeholders about how the system will be managed, maintained, and modified. FEDA will need to have robust rules about stakeholder conduct, conflict resolution, Quality of Service, financial obligations, limitations of liability, and so forth. These rules need to be enforced through an organizational structure that all stakeholders accept.

- **Build it, but it is insecure**—A security breach could weaken the chance for FEDA's success at launch or long-term viability. FEDA must be designed for security from start to finish, and have security standards and policies that stakeholders can embrace for the long haul.

- **Build it, they come, and then half of them leave**—As they say in Hollywood, the only thing worse than a bad movie is half a bad movie. FEDA does not need the participation of every single stakeholder to succeed, but if a sizeable portion of airline traffic players opt out, the system will never attain its potential for utility. Defections of key stakeholders could turn into a stampede, ultimately ruining the system.

- **Build it, but go broke**—Whether it's excessive development costs or ongoing maintenance budgets that are too rich for stakeholders, financial risk threatens FEDA's success. This is a multitiered risk. At the minimum, the project needs to be managed well enough to avoid financial surprises or cost overruns. On a more substantive level, though, FEDA needs to create financial value for stakeholders or it will be quickly abandoned. How much is too much to spend on FEDA? We will try to answer that question. Whatever the number is, though, FEDA must be worth it for stakeholders. A related risk to this problem is the potential for a single vendor to gain too much control over FEDA and start using its position to charge excessive fees for system maintenance.

Mitigation of Risks

With these risks in mind, consider the following approaches to risk mitigation and ensuring success for FEDA. Let's start with the organization of FEDA itself. In our view, an EDA of the magnitude of FEDA should comprise its own independent organization. Whatever its structure (corporation, partnership), FEDA needs to be able to make and enforce rules for stakeholders. A well-designed and properly managed organization can drive mitigation of almost every significant area of risk to the project, including technology risks.

Technology risks are, of course, based mostly on technical specifications and best practices, which we have outlined throughout this chapter. However, the realization of such specifications across multiple stakeholders is mostly a matter of organization and governance, not technology per se. FEDA might specify use of SOAP XML, but only a credible governing body can enforce use of the standard.

Organization

There are many possible styles of organization for FEDA, though three possibilities jump out as good candidates for running such a complex IT solution. One approach is to create an organization with a strong, respected leader. For example, there might be a retired airline president or Air Force General who can assume a mantle of leadership and bring the stakeholders to agreement and productive collaboration. Another workable approach is to develop a highly democratic organization with leadership shared across stakeholders based on their investment into FEDA. This approach requires good leadership as well, though it is less reliant on a star personality to make it all click. Yet another approach is to find a suitable industry organization that could sponsor FEDA and make it part of its larger organizational matrix. That would obviate the need to create a wholly new entity and infrastructure for FEDA, which might be appealing to the stakeholders.

FEDA's organization need not be overly large or cumbersome. It needs a steering committee, for sure, to run the project itself, but also probably the organization as well. Under the steering committee, there should be a committee, or team, responsible for each of several key project areas, such as software development, architecture, standards, security, infrastructure, finance, rules, and stakeholder management. Ideally, representatives of major stakeholders would sit on relevant teams and the steering committee. One of the main goals here is to develop a system where stakeholders feel that they have a say, or at least have a chance to have a say, in how it all works.

As a mirror of the stakeholder organizations, the teams and steering committee should allow for participation of stakeholder employees from different levels of their respective organizations. The steering committee is a likely place to find executive representatives of stakeholder firms, while the teams would find a good fit for stakeholder developers and other IT pros, including vendors.

The FEDA organization will need a mechanism for agreeing on the rules of the system. We are not big advocates of needless bureaucracy, but as with so many other aspects of a project like this, with so many stakeholders, there has to be some kind of structured and enforceable governance. At a minimum, there should be some kind of "constitution" or bylaws for the way that FEDA is run, even if it is part of a larger organization. This agreement—it should have a legally enforceable dimension as well—should specify the rules of FEDA, the process of adopting new rules or changing existing ones, penalties for noncompliance, and so forth. The best approach would be to give the steering committee final say on the content of the constitution, with input from the subcommittees and leadership, representing the interests of the stakeholders.

Financially, FEDA needs to be self-sustaining. Running FEDA will not be cheap, so key stakeholders will have to be ready to contribute to its operating budget. Minor stakeholders should also be required to pay for access to FEDA, but on an equitable basis. One of the main functions of the steering committee will be to set budget levels and manage financial commitments from stakeholders. FEDA should also undergo an external audit to satisfy all stakeholders that their funds have been used appropriately.

FEDA will also need, in all likelihood, to have a number of full-time employees, supplemented by contractors. Whether or not FEDA has a high-profile industry executive at its helm, the FEDA organization needs an executive director and support staff. FEDA should have a chief architect, head of development, and head of infrastructure, all with supporting staff as needed. Though much of the day-to-day work of developing and running FEDA would probably be handled by vendors, FEDA would be well served by having a dedicated group of full-time people responsible to the organization and its stakeholders for implementation of their plans and rules and expenditure of funds.

One interesting aspect of FEDA governance that came out of our brainstorming was the need for an agreement among the stakeholders not to exploit FEDA for their individual commercial gain. Many FEDA stakeholders are fierce competitors and there might be a temptation to use data from FEDA to gain an unfair advantage in the marketplace. For example, an airline might use FEDA data to plan ways to throw delays at a competitor on a particular route, or publicize FEDA data to make a competitor look bad. All of these types of issues must be addressed.

Project Life Cycle

Though FEDA is much more than just an IT project, the way that the design, development, and rollout of the system is managed, in project terms, can serve to mitigate many of the risks associated with the whole endeavor. At the beginning, the development of FEDA is a project, for sure, though in a broader organizational context. As such, it must be approached with all the rigor and best practices of a demanding enterprise IT project.

We all know about project management, so we will not belabor basic project steps here. Rather, we want to highlight certain aspects of FEDA that need special attention because of the nature of EDA. The newness of the technologies and the broad set of stakeholders make effective project management all the more critical and challenging.

As we go through some of the established project life cycle steps, keep in mind that the project itself will be sponsored by the kind of organization we have previously identified for FEDA. At a high level, best practices would dictate that FEDA's initial rollout proceed according to a project life cycle that resembled the following:

1. Consensus Building
   a. Agreement among stakeholders to pursue FEDA
   b. Agreement to form FEDA organization and ratification of its makeup
   c. Preproject training
2. Discovery
   a. Technological audit of stakeholders
   b. Stakeholder requirements gathering
   c. Core FEDA requirements gathering
3. Drafting of Project Plan
   a. Project life cycle outline
      i. Pilot deliverables
      ii. Beta deliverables

      iii. Stage 1 requirements
         1. Core FEDA functionality
         2. Stakeholder integration capabilities
         3. New stakeholder on-ramping software kit
      iv. Stage 2 requirements
         1. Advanced analytics
         2. Multilanguage UI capability
   b. Assignment of responsibilities to individuals and vendors
   c. Vendor RFIs and draft RFPs
   d. Draft Enterprise Architecture Plan
      i.   Web services standards specifications
      ii. SOA governance specifications
      iii. SOA platform selection guidelines for stakeholders
   e. Draft infrastructure requirements
   f. Draft security plan
   g. Draft training plan for stakeholders

4. Review and Discussion of Project Plan
5. Approval of Project Plan and RFPs
6. Solicitation of Vendor Bids
7. Review and Approval of Vendor Bids
8. Pilot Development
9. Review of Pilot and Modifications to Project Plan
10. Stage 1 Development
11. Beta Release and Review by Stakeholders and Core FEDA Team
12. Stage 1 Test
13. Stage 1 Deploy
14. Stage 2 Development, Test, Deploy
15. Annual Review and Follow-On Project Planning

One notable difference between FEDA and a conventional IT project can be found in the first step we suggest for the project. Before embarking on FEDA, there needs to be agreement among the stakeholders that the basic idea is a good idea, and that the suggested organizational structure will work. Then, there needs to be a training program to get stakeholders up to speed on what they are actually going to be doing. It would be a mistake to start writing a plan and RFPs without the ones paying the bills—and using the system—having a deep understanding of the EDA approach. As EDA matures, this step would become less critical. One aspect of consensus building that might need attention, too, is to present FEDA to stakeholders as a system they will own. The risk is that stakeholders will perceive FEDA as a vendor-driven sales pitch: a big budget that they want to get approved—this would be disastrous because it would cause all sorts of unnecessary tension and faults in the execution plan. The challenge is for the leadership of FEDA to assert the broad ownership of the project and assign roles to vendors without giving too much leverage to the vendors.

After consensus, we have discovery, which culminates with the creation of a thorough project plan for FEDA. This document should reflect the sum total of FEDA's design, project milestones, and organizational guidelines. As the governing document of the project to design, develop, and implement FEDA, the project plan must be approved by FEDA's governing body and reflect the intent of the project managers to honor the wishes of that governing body in technological, organizational, and financial terms.

The development cycle looks like a standard IT project, and it is not much different, except that there is a threshold of success in FEDA, or any multimember EDA, that is pretty high compared with most projects. It's a new technology, a new paradigm, and multiple stakeholders all at once. Our recommendation in this kind of situation would be to invest deeply in piloting the idea and getting feedback and enabling broad learning at these early stages. The time spent on this approach early on can pay dividends later as the system goes live.

Risk Mitigation Recap

Returning to the original risk list, let's see how the organization of FEDA can mitigate risks of many different kinds:

- **Build it, and they won't come**—If the organization does its work of managing the expectations of stakeholders, ensuring fairness in organizational governance, technological neutrality, and financial responsibilities, the risk that FEDA will become an orphan is greatly reduced.

- **Build it, but it doesn't work**—By managing the project plan carefully and exercising sound oversight over the vendors and technology leads on FEDA, the organization can mitigate the risk of technological failure.

- **Build it, but it is unmanageable**—The organization can set the tone for manageability of FEDA, and it can also lay down specific rules, SLAs, and contractual terms to make FEDA manageable.

- **Build it, but it is insecure**—If the organization takes its responsibility for setting security policy and standards, and creating a tone of seriousness and accountability about security, the security risk(s) can be mitigated. The organization should also provide external audits for security to assure stakeholders that FEDA is secure.

- **Build it, they come, and then half of them leave**—The organization has the power, if it chooses, to ensure the ongoing success of FEDA. This might be the greatest challenge of all—to provide a continuing basis for reliability, value, and fairness among all stakeholders.

- **Build it, but go broke**—The organization should endeavor, from the very beginning, to ensure financial responsibility and fairness into the design of the system and the structure and governance of the organization itself. By exercising fiscal responsibility, demonstrating value for stakeholders proactively (for example, showing value generation reports) and managing vendors effectively, FEDA can survive for the long haul in financial terms.

In each case, it is the organization that has the power to mitigate the risk, even if the risk itself it not organizational in nature. Technological, security, and financial risks need to be looked at through the lens of organization. Only the organization can provide the important human dimension of mitigating these risks and ensuring success for FEDA.

Success Metrics

Before work can begin on even the most preliminary aspects of creating FEDA, the leadership of the organization must have a deep understanding of the reasons why FEDA should exist. FEDA is meant to solve a set of problems. For FEDA to make sense to its backers, any charter for a FEDA organization, and any project plan or vision statement, needs to identify how FEDA will solve those problems. And, although it might be generally understood that FEDA is intended to alleviate airline traffic congestion, the best-practices approach to undertaking such a large IT endeavor dictates that the plan for FEDA include specific success metrics.

FEDA's plan should contain a set of quantitative objectives that FEDA can help realize. These objectives might include a reduction in delayed flights, a savings of fuel used in taxiing, improved customer satisfaction ratings, a decrease in crew overtime, and so on. The reason why it is essential that such objectives be defined at the outset, and built into any organizational and project plan, is that FEDA is a costly program, and it must make economic sense to its stakeholders.

It is hard to put a dollar figure on FEDA, but the kind of work we envision for it would probably put the total cost for first year and launch in the range of 50 million dollars, with an ongoing commitment of perhaps 10 million dollars per year. That is a lot of money, especially for financially pinched airlines. FEDA needs to justify itself, first at the beginning, but then on a continual basis.

The good news is that the savings are not that difficult to identify. For example, the airline industry in the United States alone consumes over $30 billion in fuel. If FEDA can help realize even a 1% decrease in fuel consumption through improved efficiency of traffic flow and reduced airliner waiting times, that's a $300,000,000 savings for the stakeholders! The key, though, is to embed these success metrics into the fabric of the complete work of creating FEDA and its sponsoring organization.

Conclusion

Success with FEDA means overcoming myriad challenges and executing well on a highly complex technological and organizational plan. We could only touch on a few of the high-level issues in this chapter. However, we hope that you take away at least one significant concept for program success with a large-scale EDA: the completeness of vision required for success.

Delivering a successful FEDA involves the realization of an idea that spans technology, organization, and finance. FEDA is more than the sum of its parts. It is an advanced technology, but it is also more than that. It is a sophisticated multistakeholder organization, but also more than just people. It exists for financial reasons, but money is merely a metric for FEDA, not its sole reason for existing.

The key to success lies in leadership. In this case, and so many others that you might encounter in your work, a complex event-driven architecture brings together many people, technologies, and agendas. Only very solid leadership at the individual, team, and organizational level can ensure success throughout. To undertake FEDA without being sure of the leadership involved would be to court problems and expose the program to undue risk. On the other hand, with capable leadership in all critical areas, FEDA can develop and prosper over the long term, regardless of the challenges and risks it faces.

Chapter Summary

- The challenge of managing airline traffic flow presents a great opportunity to explore how an EDA can help solve a complex real-world problem with multiple stakeholders. With thousands of flights a day operating in the United States, disruptions to air traffic caused by weather, for example, can create very costly delays to airlines through a ripple effect where a disruption at one airport causes backlogs of flights in other cities and cascading delays that can take hours or even days to clear up. With fuel costs now so high, even modest improvements in flight traffic efficiency can be financially very rewarding for airlines.

- An event-driven architecture is a good candidate for solving the air traffic management problem because the problem itself is composed of multiple sets of events that originate in separate entities and are tracked by separate information systems. If one common system could have knowledge of the many different event streams that create air traffic congestion—weather, flight delays, mechanical problems, and so forth—and that knowledge could be accessed by all stakeholders easily, then the worst kinds of disruption could be avoided.

- This chapter sets up a hypothetical project called FEDA, or Flight EDA, which would gather all event streams needed to provide stakeholders with information they could use to manage flight operations. In this chapter, we take the perspective of those who would be responsible for creating FEDA, and examine the high-level requirements and realistic issues that would arise in the development of such a system.

- The goal of FEDA is to create real-time awareness of flight conditions that can be used both by airline personnel, the FAA, and flight support services, as well as by the information systems of each stakeholder group. It would need to be able to respond to flight traffic situations both autonomically and through human decision making.

- In functional terms, FEDA would need to be highly extensible, allowing for adaptation and use by unknown stakeholders. It would need to enable modeling of what-if scenarios for users and contain a capability for stakeholders to conduct trades of flight schedules. Of course, it would need to be highly reliable and scalable.

- FEDA would expose applications used by each stakeholder as SOAP Web services and surface them through ESBs. The FEDA system would consume these flight information Web services through event listeners, process the event information, and publish the information back to stakeholders in aggregated and digested forms. FEDA would be an event processing loop, where stakeholders could change event parameters in real time and thus reiterate the event overview for all to see.

- One of the most critical aspects of developing FEDA is the resolution of SOA governance issues. For FEDA to function, it must provide a high level of control over access and integrity of the Web services it consumes. At the same time, FEDA's governance must be flexible enough so as not to impede system adoption and expansion. One possible approach is to deploy intermediaries that authenticate and authorize the Web service consumers based on a central SOA governance policy registry. In addition, FEDA needs to have ESB federation capabilities, as it will inevitably be exposing and consuming Web services on ESBs and SOA platforms from multiple vendors. All must work together seamlessly to make FEDA a success.

Endnotes

[1] www.airlines.org data

[2] USDOT—Bureau of Transportation Statistics (www.bts.gov)

[3] Ibid.

CHAPTER 8

Case Study: Anti–Money Laundering

In the 1968 hit comedy, *Take the Money and Run*, Woody Allen tries to rob a bank by handing the teller a note that says, "Give me your money. I have a gun." The problem is, the teller can't read his writing, and thinks the note says, "I have a gub." The teller asks Woody Allen to have a bank executive initial the note before he can complete his robbery. All joking aside, though, this scene offers a great take on the difficulties that banks face in developing and enforcing sound security rules that can weather the tension between large bureaucratic enterprises and rapidly changing business conditions. In the area of anti–money laundering, which has become a serious area of concern in the age of terrorism, banks are under more pressure than ever to find effective and low-cost solutions to this pervasive crime.

Money laundering is the cash register at the end of a myriad of criminal processes—it's how crooks bank their ill-gotten cash and make it look like legitimate income. *The Wall Street Journal*, citing a KPMG study, estimates that money laundering is a *trillion* dollar crime worldwide.[1] In this chapter, we take a look at the problem of money laundering, and the ways that banks approach combating it. In particular, we dig into the information technology aspects of the anti–money laundering solution, and suggest ways that event-driven architecture (EDA) can help in the fight.

An SOA-based EDA, with its ability to gather data from disparate sources in a rapid cycle, has the potential to power effective and dynamic anti–money laundering detection. In this chapter, we explore the ways in which EDA can make this happen, with emphasis on EDA's potential to drive business rules processing and internal controls of both the detective and preventive nature. We also revisit the idea of "carrying state" in transaction messages as well as the organizational aspects of such an ambitious program.

Learning Objectives

- Seeing EDA as a key part of a solution to a very pressing and complicated problem

- Understanding how EDA can facilitate the enforcement of business rules that need to change continually to keep up with sophisticated criminals

- Seeing the potential for EDA to help international multithreaded compliance

- Understanding how EDA connects with the implementation of internal controls, both detective and preventive, as well as continuous monitoring and auditing

- Understanding the governance issues inherent in a complex, multistakeholder EDA

Cracking a Trillion Dollar, Global Crime Wave

Money laundering is the act of hiding illegally earned money from the police or tax authorities by making the illicit funds appear as if they originated from legitimate business activity. Typically committed with the unwitting assistance of a bank, money laundering is usually the final step in the commission of some other crime. Money laundering is a necessity for criminals because they need to have some way of explaining the source of their income to police or tax officials who might see financial assets as evidence of criminal activity.

For example, in the movie, *The Godfather*, Don Corleone starts an olive oil business to mask his criminal empire. Whatever money he earns, he tells anyone who wants to know, comes from his olive oil business, GencoPura. Of course, the olive oil business does not generate the income to support Don's lavish lifestyle. Instead, Don Corleone places his illegally earned money into the olive oil business's bank accounts, where he "launders" it and makes it look like legitimate income. Don Corleone, in addition to being a mobster, is also a money launderer. Let's take a look at how Don Corleone might launder his funds today.

Money laundering is a three-step process that is designed to evade many types of detection. At the government level, money laundering needs to mask criminal activity from law enforcement. At the bank transaction level, money laundering needs to slip under the noses of a variety of regulations and controls that are meant to ferret out such activity. The money launderer can get caught in either trap, so each step of the laundering process is carefully performed to evade detection.

The first step in a common money-laundering scenario leveraging bank deposit services is known as "placement," where illicit funds are deposited in a business bank account. If one makes a cash bank deposit greater than $10,000, the bank is required to report the transaction to the government. Why? Because it is suspicious activity, especially if the depositor repeats the behavior many times. For this reason, money launderers typically have to place deposits in chunks of less than $10,000. Or, they have to figure out other ways to place the money into the business bank account. Don Corleone could have his bookkeeper write a bogus invoice for a cash purchase of olive oil, book the transaction as a "sale," and then deposit the cash into the GencoPura bank account. Thus, he would have placed the illicit funds.

The next step is called "layering," wherein funds are moved from bank to bank, and consolidated. This masks the trail of funds, and makes it hard to detect patterns of criminal activity. In some cases, layering is accomplished by the extending of bogus loans to offshore entities that will never repay the funds.

Finally, in the "integration" step, the funds are reintroduced to the financial system. For example, when Don Corleone writes himself a paycheck from GencoPura, where he has placed and layered illicit funds, he is paying himself with "clean money," which he has successfully laundered.

There are many variations on these three steps, but the intent is always the same: masking the origin of illegal funds from criminal activity. One pattern that we focus on in this chapter is the phenomenon of loan repayment as a laundering technique. In this pattern, the money launderer takes a loan to purchase an asset, such as a car. Then, he uses illegal cash to pay off the car loan and then sells the car to a used car dealer. The check he receives from the used car dealer is his clean money that he can report as legitimate income.

The Size and Scope of the Money-Laundering Problem

The *Wall Street Journal* article mentioned previously also references a UK government study, published in February 2007, that describes how al-Qaeda money "…Can be raised in one country, used for training in a second, for procurement in a third, and for terrorist acts in a fourth region."[2] Think about that. Not only is money laundering estimated to be a trillion-dollar crime annually, but it also enables vast criminal and terrorist operations.

To put it another way, we want to share with you a conversation we had some years back with a prominent figure in the national security establishment. This man, who had been a highly decorated combat veteran in Vietnam, said, "You have to go after terrorists the way you go after guerillas… you have to hit them where they take refuge. And for terrorists, their refuge is the international banking system."

From a societal perspective, as well as a legal one, there is a strong incentive to fight money laundering. The easier it is to launder money, the more crime can "pay." With the terrorist dimension, lives are at risk. The risks of not detecting, preventing, and prosecuting money laundering are extreme, with far-reaching implications for the institutions that are unwittingly involved in the process. This is particularly urgent for banks.

A Banker's Nightmare

Banks face multiple levels of risk from money laundering. They have direct financial risk, in the form of fines, penalties, and liability from accidental involvement in money laundering. If a bank employee is actually involved in aiding money laundering, these risks are greater. The bank also faces risk to its image if it is portrayed as being involved with crime, even if the involvement is unintentional.

As an example of how serious and real this risk can be, Marianne Pearl, widow of slain reporter Daniel Pearl, sued Habib Bank, Pakistan's largest bank, in July of 2007, blaming them for the torture and murder of her husband in 2002. Specifically, her lawsuit alleges that a charity, the al-Rashid Trust, which banked with Habib Bank, was a front for al-Qaeda. And, the suit says that terrorists, backed by the bank, "…carried out the kidnapping, ransom, torture, execution, and dismemberment of Daniel Pearl and broadcast those images worldwide."[3] The coverage of the lawsuit also notes that U.S. regulators had announced earlier in 2007 that the bank had agreed to bolster policies aimed at detecting abuses by terrorist financiers, money launderers, and other criminals.[4]

To be clear, this is not a problem limited to banks that operate in countries that are under tight scrutiny for terrorism. There are undoubtedly other banks that have relationships with Habib and could easily be implicated in this kind of investigation. And as we know, money laundering is a global crime that affects banks in virtually every country. The risk, as you might imagine, is that the bank you work for could be traumatized by a criminal investigation, or even just the suspicion of the crime. Habib Bank might be completely innocent of the charges, but for many it will be viewed as the "terrorist's bank" for years to come.

On a financial level, banks face numerous levels of risk from money laundering. If they are guilty of participating in money laundering, the banks face fines and penalties. They might have liability to crime victims and tax consequences. These kinds of improprieties can trigger shareholder lawsuits and bank regulator and SEC investigations. There might even be criminal defense costs to bear if bank employees knowingly committed crimes. And, there is the financial cost of damage to the bank's reputation.

To mitigate these risks, banks engage in a costly set of controls and countermeasures, many of which are intended to comply with the substantial body of regulatory laws that govern the banking industry. These costs are rising, too, as the money-laundering problem grows more severe and global in scope. The KPMG study estimates that anti–money laundering compliance costs rose 60% from 2006 to 2007.

Unfortunately, even these added outlays for compliance and controls haven't really made much difference in money laundering, though perhaps they have kept the problem from getting even worse. The core problem for banks is to find a way to comply with regulations and enforce controls that span multiple national jurisdictions. Anti–money laundering is a matter of global multithreaded compliance. Banks must be able to detect and prevent criminal money-laundering schemes that could begin with placement in one country, layering in another, and integration in a third. There are solutions to these challenges, but most of them come with high price tags and tactics that can strangle innovation and agility.

How Banks Can Help Stop the Bad Guys

As we think about how anti–money laundering works at a bank, let's consider some of the obvious internal controls. Without taking an unnecessarily deep dive into this fairly arcane accounting subject, we can grasp the intent and practical aspects of internal controls. If you run a bank, or any business, for that matter, you have a strong interest in knowing exactly how much money you are making, how much you have, and what your financial obligations are. The basic test of how well you have done at this process is to examine your financial statements for accuracy and integrity. If your income statement says you earned a million dollars, you should be able to verify that you indeed earned that million and that actual currency equaling a million bucks was put in the bank. Getting there involves designing and implementing processes, procedures, and rules—also known as internal controls—that govern the financial aspects of your business.

When you work with a bank, you participate in their internal controls on many levels. For instance, when you present your ID to cash a check or require a bank officer's signature to receive a large cash withdrawal, you are working with the bank to control that no one other than you is withdrawing funds from your account. The bank invented these controls to keep you happy and prevent liabilities for themselves. (For those of you who love compliance, be aware that internal controls are at the heart of the much-maligned Sarbanes-Oxley Act.) Anti–money laundering is largely a matter of designing, implementing, and auditing internal controls that prevent and detect this crime.

There are two types of internal controls. A preventive control stops an infraction of the rules from occurring. A cash register lock is a simple example of a preventive control. The lock prevents an unauthorized person from opening the cash drawer. A detective control is one that an auditor or manager can use to look back at transactions and detect if an infraction of the rules took place. The cash register tape, which summarizes the day's cash transactions, is a detective control. If the day's total does not match the cash found in the drawer, the detective control will trigger an inquiry into why the two amounts do not match. If the detective control is well designed, it will also help identify the transactions and people who are responsible for the discrepancy.

Combating money laundering involves many preventive and detective controls. For example, to prevent money laundering, banks obey a federal law that requires depositors of more than $10,000 in cash to fill out a form disclosing the deposit. This law is both a preventive and detective control. By adding a governmental gate to large cash deposits, it deters money laundering. By creating a record of the names of large cash depositors, it helps detect money laundering.

The $10,000 disclosure law is a good illustration of how complying with a law creates an extended set of rules and business processes for a bank. As you could imagine, determined money launderers will find ways to get around this rule, so the internal controls must be good enough to catch money launderers who are too clever to deposit $9,999.99 every day at the same bank branch, and even that practice could evade detection if there were no internal controls or laws in place. How do you catch a crook who has ten associates depositing random amounts of cash ranging from $5,000 to $10,000 in ten different branches under ten different business names? That's where this gets interesting, and that's when it becomes an information technology problem.

Catching bad guys who use banks to launder money is a very tricky business, and one that is constantly changing. The most effective campaigns against this crime involve multiple levels of risk mitigation, including internal controls, training, cooperation with law enforcement, and communication with other banks. The most central feature of all these efforts, though, is the concept of business rules. Preventive controls require business rules, such as requiring disclosure of large cash deposits. Detective controls hinge on examination of transactions for violation of business rules, such as failures to disclose large cash transactions. Law enforcement and interbank cooperation results from "if, then" business rules that require notification and collaboration if certain conditions—such as a person making numerous foreign cash transfers—are met. Business rules are the connection between antilaundering controls and information systems. Business rules manifest as application logic that precludes unauthorized access to systems and flags suspicious transactions, and so on. As we move forward and learn about the role and potential of IT and EDA in anti–money laundering, we will be dealing almost continually with the design, application, enforcement, and audit of business rules.

IT Aspects of Anti–Money Laundering

Though many of the approaches to fighting money laundering are not reliant on technology—such as observing a nervous glance from a customer at the teller window or noticing that a tough-guy biker type seems to own a nail salon with an inordinately high cash flow—almost every serious and effective practice for catching money launderers involves checking for violations of business rules on banking systems or investigating patterns of transactions that are suspicious. Anti–money laundering is deeply rooted in IT, including many situations where IT supports a human practice or business rule.

Today, most banks employ a hybrid of IT, human, and organizational practices and processes to enforce business rules and investigate patterns of transactions that might indicate that money laundering is taking place. These practices range from systemically embedded rules, such as programming logic that precludes settling a large cash deposit without disclosure of the depositor, to sophisticated data analytics that can ferret out money laundering from millions of seemingly unrelated transactions. And, almost every antilaundering effort involves auditing, both continuous and periodic.

To see how IT and EDA fit in to the antilaundering process, we should clarify the difference between periodic and continuous audit. Most auditing done today is periodic, meaning that auditors look back over transaction records for a previous period of time and try to find evidence of money laundering. Experienced fraud examiners have established practices that can find criminal activity in the subtlest of clues. Figure 8.1 shows the systemic aspects of this kind of audit. In this example, the auditor examines data outputs from the mainframe-based bank transaction database and the distributed systems that log disclosures of large cash depositors. The auditor looks for exceptions to the business rule that mandates that large cash depositors fill out the disclosure form. An exception is an indicator that money laundering might be going on. The depositor who failed to fill out the disclosure will be investigated in greater depth.

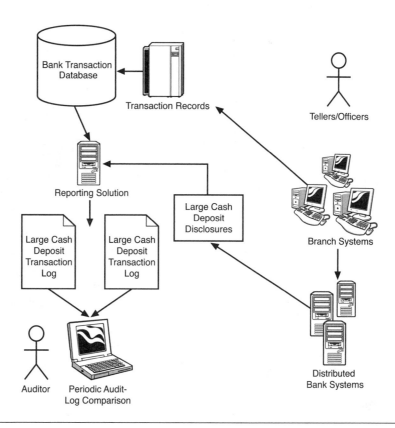

Figure 8.1 Periodic auditing to catch money launderers involves the auditor examining data from different systems and looking for exceptions to business rules. In this case, the auditor looks for records of large cash deposits where the depositor has not filled out the government-required disclosure form.

A continuous audit, in contrast, works with relatively live data, perhaps even real-time transactions. As depicted in Figure 8.2, continuous auditing typically involves integration of the involved systems using an enterprise application integration (EAI) solution, and also the deployment of an exception monitoring solution. With this setup in place, the exception monitoring solution can check transactions for their compliance with business rules in real, or near real time. The exception monitoring solution can alert auditors or other responsible staff for suspicious rules exceptions as they occur, or in timely reports. Most credit card fraud detection systems work in this way, as another example. This process is sometimes referred to as continuous monitoring.

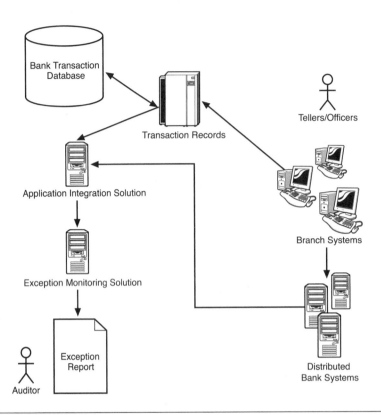

Figure 8.2   Continuous auditing against money laundering invariably requires some type of application integration (EAI) solution to be deployed to tie together the functioning of the systems that support the transactions under scrutiny. An automated exception monitoring solution checks for violations of business rules that might indicate money laundering.

There are pros and cons to both approaches to auditing, though we will see as we move forward that an SOA-based EDA has the potential to help both overall. A periodic audit is inexpensive from an IT perspective. The auditor can work from data exports from transaction systems or even paper printouts. And, periodic auditing is flexible from an IT perspective. The auditor can pick and choose what data sets he or she wants to audit and work with system output that does not require sophisticated integration. For example, the auditor could request a record of all cash deposits over $10,000 for a set period of time, and compare that record with the deposit disclosure records. Any deposits that lacked a disclosure would be good candidates for further investigation. The advantage of this situation from an IT, and cost perspective, is that it is a lot less expensive to generate reports that an auditor can examine than to conduct application integration that matches up such rule exceptions as they occur. This latter setup could enable continuous auditing. If you factor in the idea that the auditor can change the parameters of data output that he or she wants to see at any given time, the cost differential between simple periodic auditing and continuous monitoring become even more significant.

Continuous auditing has several major advantages over periodic auditing, though the approach comes with its own drawbacks. For one thing, in contrast to a periodic audit, a continuous audit can flag crime as it is occurring, not after. From a law enforcement perspective, this is a big plus. Being able to say crooks ran a billion dollars through our bank last quarter is not as good as catching them red-handed.

However, setting up continuous auditing is generally a lot more expensive than conducting periodic audits. The typical approach to continuous monitoring relies on proprietary application integration, and this pattern rapidly becomes unwieldy as it scales. Figure 8.3 expands our simplified example and shows the dependencies involved in implementing exception monitoring across multiple systems. Because money laundering can occur through a range of transaction types—such as loan repayments, offshore transfers, and so forth—multiple business rule sets must be checked for exceptions to catch suspicious behavior. At one bank, it starts to look like Figure 8.3. Imagine, then, what this approach to continuous auditing would require, in systemic terms, for achieving awareness of transactions at multiple banks in multiple countries. It quickly becomes impossible to manage, or at least pay for.

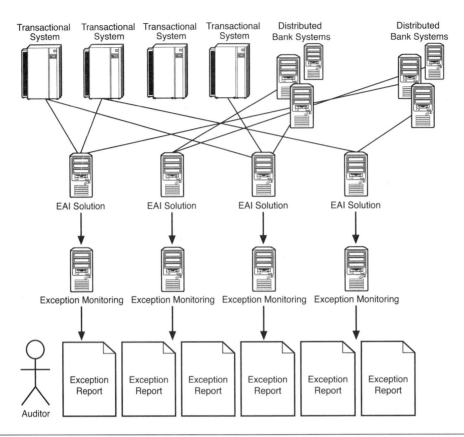

Figure 8.3 Implementing continuous auditing to detect money laundering across multiple systems and multiple rule sets can produce a complex and costly application integration challenge. Dependencies and incompatibilities between systems lead to a potentially inflexible enterprise architecture.

The costs of fighting money laundering are rising rapidly, and their increase is largely attributable to IT expense. As the *Wall Street Journal* article states, the cost of anti–money laundering has risen 60% from 2006-2007. Though part of the cost is training of employees to recognize patterns of crime, the article goes on to say, "Another cost is the computer systems that monitor transactions. The [KMPG] study found that a big challenge for banks is monitoring an individual's transactions and accounts across multiple countries. 'A significant proportion of banks could not carry out this type of monitoring,' KPMG said, noting that less than a quarter of those surveyed with an international presence are capable of monitoring individual customer money flows."[5]

In addition to pushing up costs of compliance and detection, adding the integration layers required for continuous auditing, at least under a conventional EAI model, also results in a lack of agility for banks. The banking industry is dynamic, with many mergers and acquisitions and strategy shifts. Indeed, as the KPMG report says, "Adding to the challenges is the increase in cross border banking mergers. They can introduce the headaches linking existing computer systems and meeting new standards and laws where the combined bank operates."[6] Ripped from the headlines, as we say! The IT costs of global multithreaded compliance are a huge "headache…" Banks are continually buying each other and expanding into new territories and lines of business. Each merger increases the risk of money laundering and also makes it harder and more costly to combat using an integration-centric continuous monitoring approach. For example, if a bank expands into investment services, it increases its risk of money laundering through the purchase of investment instruments. Mitigating this risk involves the implementation of additional layers of business rules and exception monitoring. Ultimately, the anti–money laundering efforts can impede business strategy, or they get relegated to subordinate priority in favor of the business needs, and the exposure to money laundering increases. What can be done about this? And, does EDA have a role to play in easing this seemingly impossible situation? The answer is yes. Let's move forward and see how.

EDA as a Weapon in the War on Money Laundering

If banks had some way of being aware of all of the financial transactions that make up most money-laundering schemes, they would be more effective at fighting it. Now, of course, banks have a high level of awareness of the transactions that take place within their enterprises. And, groups of banks and interbank networks, such as wire transfer facilitators, have a record of the funds they move about. The real problem in combating money laundering is a lack of understanding about the associations between transactions. It is the connection between two seemingly unrelated transactions that could indicate an occurrence of money laundering. For this reason, EDA has great potential to help detect and prevent this crime.

The Ideal Anti–Money Laundering EDA

Money laundering is a crime that occurs through a series of transactions, or a pattern of financial activity that creates a set of events. If software connected to an EDA can detect these suspicious transactions or patterns, the banks can have an easier time figuring out what is going on. At a high level, the ideal vision of an antilaundering EDA might look something like Figure 8.4. Figure 8.4 depicts an EDA for a single bank. Any system that could generate an event relevant to detecting or preventing money laundering—that is, one that is part of a detective or preventive control—publishes event information to the message backbone(s), which we call the *event cloud*. The rules engine(s) examines multiple event streams and historical event patterns to detect money laundering that is about to occur, or has just occurred. What we're calling *rules engines* for the purpose of this discussion use event producers to send notifications to any necessary party, such as antifraud personnel, auditors, law enforcement, and so on.

Putting this high-level EDA vision into the context of an actual money laundering pattern, let's imagine that we work at a bank that wants to monitor suspicious debt repayments. Rapid repayments of loans are a sign of possible money laundering. As shown in Figure 8.4, which adds some specific event data to our idealized model, a series of events hints at money laundering if they can be correlated and examined in near real time. In the example, a person named John Doe takes out a car loan in the name of a business he owns, and then pays off the loan three days later. Could he be laundering money? For the purpose of our example, he is—so let's see how our EDA could be used to detect or prevent this kind of activity.

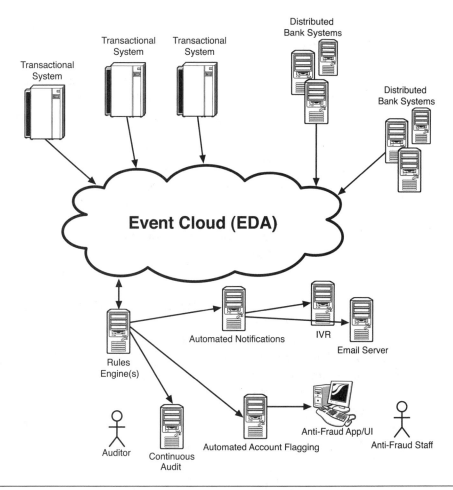

Figure 8.4 The high-level vision for an EDA-based anti–money laundering solution has all of a bank's systems publishing event data—transactions, account creation, debt repayment, and so on—into an "event cloud," to which a set of rules engines subscribes. The rules engine, which functions in this case as an event listener and event processor, feeds suspicious transaction data to a set of reacting systems, including a continuous audit program, an automated account flagging application, and whatever automated notifications are required, such as for law enforcement.

In the normal course of events, at a bank where application integration and audit are limited, the bank might not notice a few suspicious things about Mr. John Doe and his car loan. A casual observer might think that he just refinanced, or asked his mother to pay off the note... so the trick is recognizing that this particular payoff is suspicious. If we were able to use our EDA to listen to events related to customers, we would recognize that this transaction is suspicious. So, the trigger event might be when John Doe pays off his loan three days after it was established. The small business systems generate an event that indicates that John Doe owns four businesses, each in a different Standard Industrial Classification. (Code mismatching between business types, account holders, and transaction types is a classic sign of fraud.) The loan processing system generates an event confirming that John Doe has paid off the car in three days. The checking account system publishes an event indicating that John Doe has written 50 checks to "cash" this year. The branch systems generate an event indicating that he paid off the car loan in cash. The loan origination system generates an event indicating that he has bought eight cars recently for his four businesses. And, the loan securitization system publishes an event indicating that each car was pledged as collateral for each car loan and has been released as collateral upon repayment.

These and other events trigger publication to the bus. Some information is always reviewed, whereas others might be dynamically selected (either at random or due to some initial pattern match), and an anti–money laundering listener decides which ones to look at. After being picked up, the system might publish events back to the bus looking for specific data, then correlate this information and make some kind of a decision as to which events get published back to the bus. Multiple listeners could pick this event up—some, for example, might flag accounts to be monitored more closely, others might automatically block wire transfers, and so on.

As the EDA publishes event data to the subscribing event processors—in this case, the rules engines—these processors can then, in turn, publish their own event data that flags suspicious transactions connected to John Doe. Figure 8.5 illustrates this flow. The takeaway here is to see how the EDA can be dynamically extended to different tasks by different stakeholders. These stakeholders don't have to be associated with each other to perform these functions. In this case, for example, the person who runs the rules engine application can configure it to publish suspicious loan repayment transactions. This person does not have to know, or even care, what will be done with the output of the rules engine once the subscribers access it. That is the beauty of EDA. The reality is that money-laundering detection and prevention changes constantly, especially in the context of a large bank. In a large bank, a debt refinancing marketing program could spark a large number of suspicious loan repayments, which all turn out to be totally legitimate. How many "0% credit card payoff" solicitations do you get in the mail every week? Initiatives like this could easily create many false positives from a detection perspective. The rules engine that flags suspicious repayments can work without preconception of these programs and publish suspicious transaction data to the enterprise service bus (ESB). Another rules engine can subscribe to these events and weed out the repayments that are caused by a debt refinancing promotion.

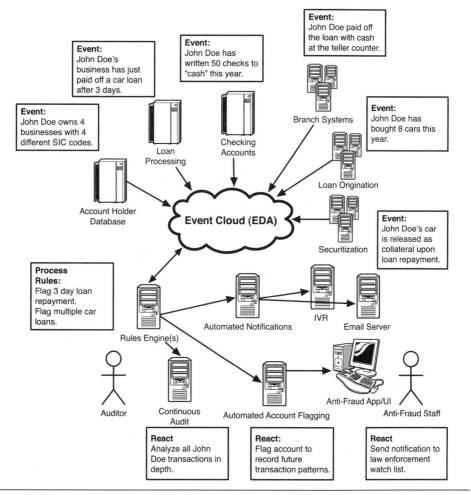

Figure 8.5 Adding specificity to the high-level model. Each of the bank's systems publishes event data that is consumed by the rules engine. Taken in total, a suspicious pattern of loan repayments emerges, triggering alerts to antifraud staff and auditors.

Figure 8.6 shows a simplified version of a global EDA approach to anti–money laundering. Multiplying our single bank, with its event cloud, worldwide, you could use an EDA approach to create regional event clouds—ESB clusters, in reality—to aggregate event data from across multiple banks. Antifraud systems and rules engines could parse event data and discover potentially suspicious transactions. In the end, you have a set of event clouds that connect with one another using the Web services standards. The net result would be a way to handle global multithreaded compliance.

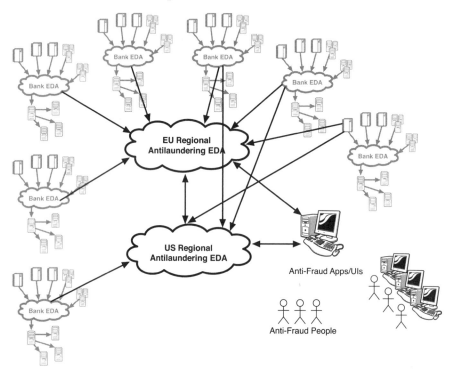

Figure 8.6   Global anti–money laundering using EDA involves connecting multiple event clouds, or ESB clusters. Though the standards can facilitate this, the practicalities of getting such a complex structure off the ground are quite daunting. However, even with a partial solution, the banking system might have an improved method of reporting on global compliance.

Before we celebrate our solution, we need to go up a few more levels and see how challenging the EDA approach to fighting money laundering can be from a global perspective—not to mention the other regulatory issues to be addressed in such an approach. Even in this stripped-down version, you should be able to see how complicated and costly such a solution could be. Nevertheless, this approach is an interesting case in which to discuss AML handling across multiple banks in a standard, reliable way.

How an Anti–Money Laundering EDA Might Actually Work

The good news about EDA as an anti–money laundering solution is that it can be deployed gradually and have a measured impact as it grows. In contrast to the FEDA system for the airlines, which needed to deploy pretty much in a fully grown state, a bank's anti–money laundering EDA can be developed to tackle one set of money laundering at a time. For our descriptive purposes here, the incremental approach fits well. We take a deeper dive into the loan repayment pattern of money laundering that we have begun to explain in the John Doe case and show how an EDA can be built to solve this particular type of fraud. As we go through it, though, we also highlight ways that the EDA can be extended subsequently to combat a broader array of frauds.

Figure 8.7 shows an architectural view of the event producers in the antilaundering EDA. In this case, where the bank is trying to detect suspicious rapid loan repayments, it uses common (perhaps existing) Web services to function as event producers that publish event data about loan repayments and related transactions to the ESB. As the figure shows, the event Web services are not specifically designed to be part of the EDA. Rather, in keeping with the architectural principle of minimizing preconception among EDA components and reducing central controllers, this EDA relies on event data produced from workday activities that already occur in the relevant systems. In the example, the loan processing systems generate event data about loan payments through a Web service called `PostPayment`. The checking account system produces event data through a Web service called `DebitAccount`, and so on.

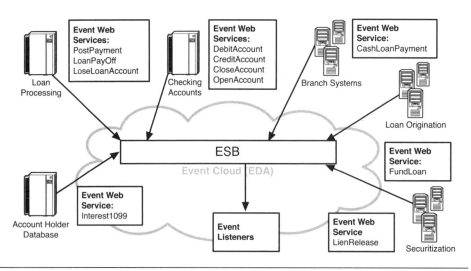

Figure 8.7 Event producers involved in detecting money laundering from rapid loan repayment.

As these systems process their workloads, the Web services send messages containing state information, published as event data, in SOAP XML. Thus, if John Doe pays off a car loan with cash at a branch teller window, the teller processes the receipt of the payment through a loan payment processing application that was developed using Web services, a business process modeling (BPM) tool, and an ESB. In the service-oriented architecture (SOA) world, this would be called a SOBA, or service-oriented business application. (See Table 8.1 for a breakdown of event Web services that are part of the loan payment SOBA.) The Web services used by the SOBA generate the state change information that the antilaundering EDA can consume and process. As you can see, the Web services used in the loan payment processing SOBA are the very same ones we call event Web services in Figure 8.7. As with so many EDAs, the regular workday Web services used for business processes do double duty as event services.

Figure 8.8 shows the business process model (BPM) view of such a loan payment processing SOBA, and the Web services that it invokes. The teller receives the cash payment, inputs the payment details into the loan processing application, posts the payment, and issues a confirmation to John Doe that his loan has been paid off. The remainder of the business process model requires that the loan processing application close the loan account and release the collateral from the loan. If the bank is using a suitable SOA platform to develop this SOBA, they might be able to generate a Business Process Execution Language (BPEL) document that orchestrates the Web services into the business process model.

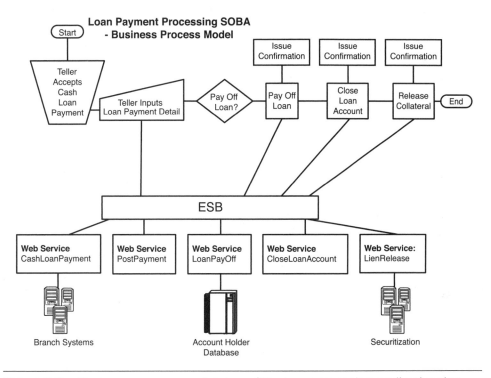

Figure 8.8   Business process model view of the loan processing application that generates state change data used by the antilaundering EDA.

Table 8.1 Breakdown of Event Web Services That Are Part of the Loan Payment Processing Service-Oriented Business Application (SOBA), and a Description of Their XML Output

Web Service Name	System Owner	Underlying App	OS	Language	Output	State Change
CashLoan Payment	Branch Ops	Teller Console	Win NT	C++	XML: Date, Loan Number, Payment Amt, Payoff Y/N	Cash payment Loan paid off
PostPayment	Loan Processing Ops	LoanWorks	AS 400	C	XML: Date, Loan Number, Payment Amount	Payment posted
LoanPayOff	Loan Processing Ops	LoanWorks	AS 400	C	XML: Date, Loan Number, Payment Amt, Payoff Y/N	Loan paid off
CloseLoan Account	Loan Processing Ops	LoanWorks	AS 400	C	XML: Date, Loan Number, Close Account Y/N	Loan account closed
Securitization	Collateral Portfolio Management	SecureLoan	Linux	J2EE	XML: Date, Loan Number, Release Collateral Y/N, BorrowerID	Collateral released

As each Web service in this loan payment processing SOBA is invoked, it sends a Simple Object Access Protocol (SOAP) message to the consumer using the ESB as its messaging backbone. From an EDA perspective, these SOAP responses are notifications of state change emanating from an event Web service. To reiterate, there are no specific event Web services in this case. However, the EDA uses the SOAP messages of the day-to-day SOBA to discover the state changes it needs to produce event data and generate an event stream.

However, and this is a very important idea to grasp, the Extensible Markup Language (XML) schema of each Web service in the SOBA needs, to some great extent, to conform to the event data needs of the EDA, or the EDA won't work. For the best of reasons, many messages used in application integration are extremely succinct. For example, if the SOBA developers are working off their standard EAI playbook, they might design a SOAP request for `CashLoanPayment` that says, in effect, "for this account number, *yes*, we have a cash payment." The application that is exposing the `CashLoanPayment` Web service (the loan processing system) understands what this means and handles the message accordingly. There's nothing implicitly wrong with this. But as we have discussed, this type of abbreviated XML schema creates a high level of preconception and dependency between the Web service and its consumer. The consumer and Web service need to know a lot about each other to work together, which tightens the coupling between the two. This is antithetical to good EDA design, partly because EDAs revolve around loose coupling, but also because there is no description of state change contained in the message. An event listener would have to be very dependent on specific application integration patterns to discern the state change occurring here. In contrast, if the event listener can parse the SOAP message, it will have a much easier time understanding exactly what change in state is occurring, and be able to flow this event data into the event processor with less dependency on the EAI patterns. The event processor can look at the XML and understand that a given loan was paid off in cash on a certain date without having to know very much at all about the EAI patterns involved. Of course, there is some degree of dependency. The event processor needs to know the XML schema, and it needs to know the syntax of the SOAP message and what an element like `PayoffYN` (for example) means. There needs to be a data dictionary and XML schema sharing. However, the richer the state change data flowing in the SOAP messages, the simpler it will be to develop a dynamic, efficient EDA.

To help make the EDA development work better, the respective EDA and SOA teams can take advantage of the BPM and BPEL platform tools. Though not essential, these capabilities can smooth the way toward getting an EDA off the ground leveraging an existing SOA or SOBA. The BPM approach is helpful because it allows those responsible for the EDA and the SOA to collaborate and gain understanding of the others' designs, needs, and outputs.

On their own, the data contained in these SOAP messages does not tell antifraud staff or rules engines much about possible money laundering. Taken together, though, they can present patterns that can be identified as suspicious. The event processors, which might be rules engines, look at sets of messages that they flag based on their anti–money laundering criteria.

As the event listeners and event processors detect suspicious activity, they set off a cascade of secondary event processors and event listeners. For example, when the event processors flag John Doe's loan repayment as suspicious on the grounds that it was (a) a cash payment and (b) paid off within a short period of time, the event processors should then run a query to see whether several additional suspicious aspects of money laundering are also present. It should query event listeners on the ESB to find out if there was collateral for the loan, and whether it was released, and also query to see if John Doe has paid off a loan for cash in the past. If these two queries return positive results, John Doe should be flagged and brought to the attention of antifraud staff. This flow of flagging and query is shown in Figure 8.9.

There could be a good reason for John Doe to be paying off loans in cash. He might be in a cash business, for example, or he might just be someone who likes dealing with cash and recently took advantage of a home refinancing program. At some stage, a person must get involved to sort out what is going on. The point at which a person needs to get involved is a measure of how efficient the EDA is. People tend to be expensive, in terms of their time and availability. Ideally, the EDA will be good at flagging real money launderers, and skip false positives. False positives are costly because they consume antifraud resources. In fact, the false positive (and perhaps false negative) rate is a good metric to include as you evaluate the success of an anti–money laundering EDA.

Again, though, the takeaway for this is the activities of the antilaundering EDA are independent and loosely coupled with the functioning of the bank's operational systems that feed the event data into the ESB. The antilaundering EDA needs to be dynamic and flexible, able to pivot rapidly to investigate ever-changing business rules and patterns of detection. It needs to be adaptable to changes in internal controls. If the EDA can only adapt to internal controls by requiring significant changes in underlying systems and their points of integration, the EDA will be very inefficient and probably not work well at all. Let's keep this concern in mind as we look at the specific challenges of getting an antilaundering EDA up and running in real life.

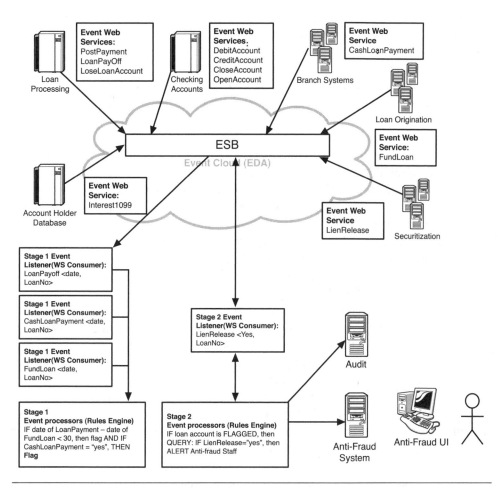

Figure 8.9 This expands Figure 8.8 to show the event listeners and event processors that flag suspicious loan repayment transactions and pass them along for further queries and possible alerting of antifraud staff and audit.

Building an Antilaundering EDA Solution

Now that we have had a look at how an antilaundering EDA might work, we can think about what would be involved in creating a working, effective EDA that would help fight against money laundering throughout a bank and all its operations and among other banks. Are you ready for another code name? Imagine that we all work for a bank that wants to use EDA to help in its fight against money laundering. Our project will be known as the Event-Driven Internal Controls Tracking System or EDICTS.

The goal of this section is not to repeat the basic EDA precepts we have elaborated on before. It is a given that EDICTS will consist of loosely coupled Web services, lack of a central controller, and so forth. Our goal in this section, rather, is to highlight certain essential requirements that would make EDICTS a worthwhile use of time and resources. In particular, we look at ways of solving the challenges of adaptability, relevance, and continuing success of the endeavor. One risk faced by new technologies is a long-term failure if a paradigm is not adopted with a long-term view. Many great ideas flourish at launch but then languish as IT and line-of-business managers return to activities that they perceive to be of higher priority and neglect the benefits of the new approach. The result of this cycle can be a relapse to firefighting mode and bandied solutions to chronic problems. We don't want this to happen to EDICTS!

As a change of pace, we describe the organizational and business issues at the same time as we develop the technological plan for EDICTS. Rather than breaking them out separately, as we did in the previous chapter, in this case we want to illustrate how these factors are interdependent. As we have often learned the hard way, there is really no difference between business needs and IT needs, no separation between politics and technological solutions. The greatest project in the world will either fail or evade funding if it doesn't satisfy the thorny and overlapping requirements and agendas of all stakeholders. And, as we hope to point out in this story, even stakeholders who lack direct power in the organization can be quite influential when it comes to validating the idea and delivery of an innovative technological solution.

Designing for Long-Term Success, Step 1: Optimizing Ownership

Let's face the reality that we are already far out on a limb if we are designing a system, and hitting up execs for budget, that falls into the compliance and security category. Despite the clear risks associated with money laundering, it is not always clear which stakeholder holding the purse strings at a bank is responsible for risk-related expenditures, particularly when they cross product and channel lines as this one does. The struggle for funding and endorsement can be even more difficult if the solution involves a new technology approach such as EDA. One of the biggest challenges, then, is to be relevant to stakeholders from the out-set, in terms of functionality, nomenclature, and outputs. EDICTS will fail if it is not relevant to all its major stakeholders. Relevancy must be designed in from the very beginning.

With relevancy in mind, let's make an assumption. If EDICTS is intended to help auditors and antifraud staff do their jobs, but it is established as a wholly separate system that these people will have to master, it will be severely challenged. Instead, we think the best practice for this type of solution is to assume that it should be embedded into the existing workflows and practices of its key stakeholders. For this reason, we came up with the EDICTS name. The idea of controls is built into the solution's identity. The requirements, features, and functionality of EDICTS should relate to established antifraud and antilaundering internal controls practices. In addition, the descriptions of EDICTS, its proposals, requirements, and documentation should reflect the language and mind-set of information security professionals, auditors, and antifraud specialists. As a first step, let's list the stakeholders and understand their needs for EDICTS, as shown in Table 8.2.

Table 8.2   EDICTS Stakeholders and Their Needs for the Solution, as Well as Their Day-to-Day Business Jobs

Stakeholder	Day-to-Day Work/Needs	Expectations and Needs for EDICTS
Senior bank executives (representing shareholders and Board of Directors as well)	Managing the bank for maximum return to shareholders and long-term growth of asset value, including formation of strategic alliances and mergers and acquisitions Ultimate responsibility for support and leadership of AML operations, including the risk assessment, risk mitigation programs, and internal controls	EDICTS needs to manage the risk of money laundering to an acceptable level EDICTS must balance AML efforts with costs and impact on business

continues

Table 8.2 (continued)

Stakeholder	Day-to-Day Work/Needs	Expectations and Needs for EDICTS
Senior operations executives	Running the bank as a profitable business, including staff productivity, cost control, vendor management and outsourcing Ultimate responsibility for execution of AML operations, including risk mitigation programs and internal controls	The bank should be able to implement a cost-effective EDICTS program EDICTS should have no impact on ability to outsource or make operational changes in an acceptable time cycle
Account executives and loan officers	Ensuring high-profit banking clientele, ease of doing business, long-term client engagement, strict but streamlined loan underwriting	EDICTS should have low impact on loan underwriting and quality of customer experience EDICTS should be effective at weeding out crooked accounts
IT management (CIO, CTO)	Ensuring high performance and reliability, securing IT for bank operations Using IT as a strategic asset	The bank must be able to implement EDICTS cost effectively and without disrupting other business-critical IT initiatives
Chief enterprise architect	Defining and implementing enterprise architecture SOA enterprise architecture planning and implementation SOBA general architectural specifications	EDICTS should work within the defined framework for SOA and SOBA at the bank
Information security management (CISO)	Developing and delivering information security policy, standards, guidelines, and procedures Managing IT security risk assessment and mitigation plan, including antilaundering Advising management on IT security aspects of compliance	EDICTS should aid in risk mitigation while not exposing the bank to increased risk through its design and implementation

Stakeholder	Day-to-Day Work/Needs	Expectations and Needs for EDICTS
Security management (CSO)	Ensuring security for the bank (physical, data, electronic fraud suppression) Interfacing with law enforcement	EDICTS should aid in the protection of the bank from security risks and help with detection, prevention, and prosecution of money laundering, including that which involves internal bank employees
Branch banking staff and managers	Conducting banking business with customers	EDICTS should help in the performance of AML duties without impeding the efficiency of the work process or degrading customer experience
Bank back office staff and managers	Processing transactions, loans, and operations	EDICTS should help in the performance of AML duties without impeding the efficiency of the work process or harming customer experience
Antifraud staff and managers	Executing antifraud programs, including anti–money laundering Executing internal controls framework for antilaundering	EDICTS must deliver a net gain in effectiveness of antifraud activities
Internal audit (chief audit exec)	Examining operations for evidence of fraud and waste Determining internal controls framework (COSO) and auditing for compliance of bank operations with IC framework Designing and conducting an internal audit program, based on risk assessment and risk mitigation programs and internal controls	EDICTS should map easily to existing internal controls EDICTS should deliver a net gain in effectiveness of internal audit's controls and countermeasures against money laundering EDICTS should help provide a streamlined way for external audit to test and certify the effectiveness of internal controls against money laundering

continues

Table 8.2   (continued)

Stakeholder	Day-to-Day Work/Needs	Expectations and Needs for EDICTS
External audit	Assuring shareholders and other stakeholders that the bank's financial statements are accurate	EDICTS should help provide a streamlined way for external audit to test and certify the effectiveness of internal controls against money laundering
Law enforcement	Investigating suspected money launderers and prosecuting them, with aid of bank	The bank should be able to use EDICTS to provide reliable evidence of money laundering EDICTS should help law enforcement investigate suspicious persons who might be laundering money
Bank customers	Needing a high-quality, cost-effective banking experience	EDICTS should not impede the banking experience or add costs
Bank vendors	Delivering on expected workload to bank according to contract and/or service-level agreement Passing required audits (e.g., SAS 70)	EDICTS should not add to difficulty or costs of providing services to the bank
Government agencies	Seeking compliance with antilaundering laws and regulations Inspecting/auditing banks for compliance	EDICTS should produce reports on antilaundering activities in conformance with regulations
Bank industry groups	Defining and gathering consensus and participation in industry-standard, antilaundering practices	EDICTS should be in conformance with industry rules, norms, regulations, and standards

Table 8.2 breaks out EDICTS' stakeholders and describes their regular business roles and expectations and requirements for EDICTS. What you should be able to see in this table are forces of simultaneous alignment and tension between the vision of EDICTS and the working responsibilities of the stakeholders. Yes, of course, everyone has an interest in, and incentives for, reducing money laundering. Yet each stakeholder has existing job functions and incentives that are in conflict with EDICTS. For example, while the branch banking staff might find EDICTS to be helpful in flagging suspicious accounts and customers earlier in the money-laundering cycle than existing controls can ensure, these same staffers might rebel if EDICTS slows down their system performance to the point where customers are dissatisfied with their level of service.

In a similar vein, the information security and corporate security groups have a strong interest in curbing money laundering. However, like any other business unit, they are limited in terms of headcount and resources. If EDICTS is designed in a way where it requires additional personnel, that could cause a conflict. Even if funds are made available for hiring, there could still be trouble with EDICTS. For instance, there is often a disruptive lag time between the identification of an open position and the hiring of a suitable person. In the case of an EDA, hiring the right professional might be quite challenging. If EDICTS generates "empty seats" that must be filled, and those seats cannot be filled in an adequate time frame, the whole launch and operation of EDICTS could suffer, possibly even detracting from other antifraud efforts. At the design stage, EDICTS program managers should be aware of this potential execution risk and try to plan ahead for its solution.

Identifying the best owner for the overall EDICTS program is ultimately one of the key ways to solve the tensions between stakeholder needs and EDICTS requirements. If EDICTS is hatched as a pet project of the chief architect and managed by the IT Department, it might fail to launch properly. The group that owns EDICTS must be vested with an incentive for its success from a business perspective. This idea is not unique to EDICTS, and can be transposed to other situations in corporate life where an EDA adds needed but not absolutely essential functionality to a business operation. The truth is the bank could survive without EDICTS, even if the program will make everyone's life easier. Determining who should own EDICTS, and where the program should "live" after its launch, is of great importance for its long-term success.

It's not obvious who should own EDICTS. The CISO might be a good choice, but CISOs typically don't manage systems for the long haul. Rather, they usually advise IT and business management on security policy. The best place for EDICTS is probably the antifraud business unit. They are the people who are most responsible for fighting laundering, even if the obligation filters out to many other groups and people. That being said, a number of other groups still need to take significant responsibility for the success of EDICTS from a technological, financial, and management perspective. Table 8.3 breaks out the roles and responsibilities of key stakeholders for the ownership and control of EDICTS.

Table 8.3   Breakdown of Roles, Responsibilities, and Accountabilities for EDICTS by Stakeholder Group

Stakeholder	EDICTS Role/Responsibility	EDICTS Accountability
Senior bank executives (representing shareholders and Board of Directors as well)	Executive Sponsor Leadership and highlighting importance Funding	Board level reporting on results of EDICTS Resolving major tensions between stakeholders Making EDICTS a priority by providing incentives for its successful adoption
Senior operations executives	High visibility leadership Steering Committee representation	Successful implementation by business unit
Account executives and loan officers	Getting trained on EDICTS	Reduction in laundering as a % of loan portfolio
IT management (CIO, CTO)	Delivery of EDICTS as a working system Steering Committee representation EDICTS development, testing, and long-term management	Reliable, secure EDICTS performance EDICTS updates performed as required
Chief enterprise architect	Architectural model for EDICTS Steering Committee representation	Architectural performance of EDICTS

Stakeholder	EDICTS Role/Responsibility	EDICTS Accountability
Information security management (CISO)	Security policies for EDICTS as a system Integration of EDICTS into Enterprise Risk Management (ERM) program Enforcement of InfoSec aspects of EDICTS Steering Committee representation	Measurable impact of EDICTS on InfoSec metrics Current and realistic standards and guidelines for EDICTS implementation
Security management (CSO)	Interface with law enforcement Integration of EDICTS with overall corporate security	Reporting on incidents and investigations triggered by EDICTS
Branch banking staff and managers	Familiarity with EDICTS	N/A
Bank back office staff and managers	Familiarity with EDICTS Local leadership on EDICTS	Reporting on levels of training and competency for EDICTS
Antifraud staff and managers	System owners Day-to-day operation of EDICTS Management of EDICTS life cycle Implementation of full EDICTS program at all levels of the bank Managing "up" to higher-level executive sponsors Setting agenda for Steering Committee	Reporting success metrics for EDICTS: Financial/antifraud/human/ERM Soliciting feedback from other stakeholders Managing IT role in EDICTS for optimal results
Internal audit (chief audit exec)	Periodic audit of EDICTS as a system Use of EDICTS as a continuous audit tool Advising stakeholders to make EDICTS audit-ready	Audit reporting of antilaundering results using EDICTS
Bank vendors/partners	Use of EDICTS standards where required (e.g., SOAP schema)	Compliance with EDICTS standards

The trick to getting EDICTS off the ground and running is aligning each stakeholder with the success of the program. This is far from simple, but it can be done. The antifraud unit will own EDICTS, but the program needs active buy-in at every level. EDICTS needs top-level executive sponsorship, which means, to a great extent, a long-term commitment to funding as well as resolution of agendas. The architecture and IT groups need to be given a clear mandate to execute EDICTS as well as the opportunity to have input on its requirements and technological implementation plan. This might mean that EDICTS is folded into a larger SOA corporate standard and project set. The information security and audit groups need to be on board with EDICTS and given the opportunity to have input on its nature. The extended business units need to participate in the launch and continued operation of EDICTS, so it would make sense to have EDICTS adoption built into the management plans and incentives of those units.

Another possible enabling factor for the launch of EDICTS could be the use of banking industry groups and standards bodies, as well as existing IT industry standards bodies. Though it is early in the technological life cycle of EDA, there are many industry organizations that set data compatibility standards for banks on a national and global basis. These groups, such as the European Committee for Banking Standards or OASIS, have already laid the groundwork for a program like EDICTS. For example, the emerging standards of SCA (Service Component Architecture) and SDO (Service Data Objects) are gaining attention from banks because of their ability to drive rapid adoption of service orientation.[7]

The thing to remember in this assignment of roles and responsibilities is that you are not dealing with a benign phenomenon. Money laundering is a serious crime and the failure to detect it could lead to major repercussions for the bank. As a result, careers could be at stake. If you were in charge of planning for the development of EDICTS, you would likely face more intense political wrangling than you would in a standard IT project scenario.

Designing for Long-Term Success: Step 2—Defining the Reference Architecture for the Development, Test, and Production

EDICTS will have an ever-changing requirements set because combating money laundering is a constantly shifting process, and one that touches many different areas of a bank's operations and network of partners.

In actuality, the EDICTS requirements set needs to pivot in two directions. In one direction, EDICTS needs to be capable of nearly endless updating in its extant functions. The specific way that a fully realized functional requirement works against money laundering will shift over time, so there needs to be a way to conduct subtle changes in the system with minimal cost and downtime. The second pivot involves extensibility. EDICTS needs to expand its scope of antilaundering. EDICTS needs to be able to add new antilaundering functions that involve previously untouched systems, in a cost-effective manner.

At a high level, with these two requirements pivots in mind, we can formulate a basic definition of EDICTS as the following: EDICTS should be a solution that contains both hot swappable rules processing components and a built-in platform for low-cost extensibility. EDICTS needs to be capable of centralizing business rules processing functionality in such a way that rules can be updated without undue stress or modification of dependent system parts. It should also have, built in, an interface or platform for continued extension that can be performed without undue disruption to the working parts of the system.

Given these two core assumptions—of updatability and extensibility—the way the requirements are implemented might still vary depending on the optimal setup within the bank. For instance, it might make sense to create a complete and isolated development and test environment for EDICTS, a dedicated hardware and network operation, and a dedicated software infrastructure such as ESB. Alternatively, EDICTS could be integrated into an extant, broader-based software development team and its Integrated Development Environment (IDE). Of course, this chapter is intended to provide a guide to thinking about developing an EDA, and individual results might vary. Indeed, your bank might have different needs, or you might have nothing to do with the banking industry at all.

Whatever the specific implementation looks like, though, EDICTS needs to have an architecture that contains the following components:

- **A modeling interface**—EDICTS' business owners, the architects, and the developers must all be able to collaborate in the modeling of the antilaundering logical flow in the form of a business process model.

- **A mapping of requirements to internal controls**—For the sake of relevance, and avoiding the creation of a duplicative workload, EDICTS' requirements should be rooted in the existing internal controls framework of the bank. EDICTS is a mechanism for implementing detective and preventive controls, so it makes sense to build its requirements gathering and implementation into the internal controls work stream.

- **A development interface**—The business process model should translate to the development of a software application that orchestrates the event listeners, producers, and processors, though without necessarily implementing central control of those elements.

- **A flexible rules engine**—Ideally, the business rules segments of the event processors should be independent from the rest of EDICTS in terms of hard-coding. The rules themselves, as well as the inner quantitative nature of the rules, will change constantly. To be dynamic, EDICTS should have rules components that can be plugged in, or unplugged, with relative ease. This might mean the use of rules Web services that can be deployed with few, or no, tightly coupled dependencies on the rest of EDICTS.

- **A planning and collaboration solution**—With its numerous and varied stakeholders, EDICTS needs to include some kind of collaboration tool. Whether this would be a stand-alone portal or application like Microsoft Groove, or a part of an existing collaboration workspace, would depend on the details on the ground at the particular bank. However, the requirement is still strong. EDICTS stakeholders need a place, ideally a virtual one, where they can share their workload, assign tasks, set schedules, engage in feedback sessions, and so forth, to drive the program forward on an ongoing basis.

Figure 8.10 lays out the reference architecture for EDICTS' development, test, and production environments and shows the connections to the stakeholder groups. Each stakeholder can monitor the progress of EDICTS at the development and test stage, an activity that essentially never ends given the perpetual upgrade mode of EDICTS. The SOA governance loop is a key concept to grasp in this architecture. Web services and their consumers need to be developed and tested with governance policy applied. Then, when they are deployed into production and set up on the ESB (or equivalent), those same governance policies need to follow them in an auditable fashion. In organizational and procedural terms, the EDICTS IT team and whatever group in IT that manages the SOA must be in tight synchronization. For practical purposes, as well as for the sake of project viability, they might even be the same people.

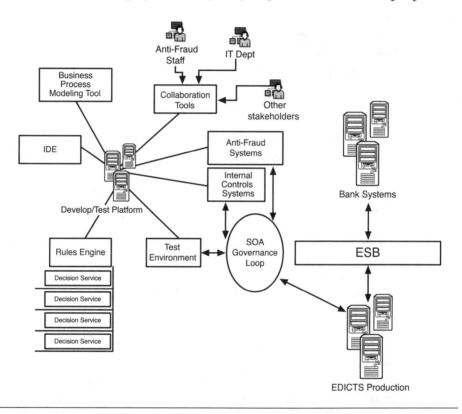

Figure 8.10   A basic reference architecture that shows how the planning, development, and production segments of EDICTS can work together. Before specific requirements are set, the stakeholders will need to agree on this architecture, which includes interfaces for collaboration between stakeholders as well as governance and deployment factors.

Designing for Long-Term Success: Step 3—Matching EDICTS Requirements with the Bank's Internal Controls, Risk Mitigation, and Compliance

Now that we have a workable reference architecture for EDICTS that maps to stakeholders, we can start defining actual requirements of EDICTS itself. Though it might have seemed counterintuitive, we needed to go through the elaborate stakeholder analysis, program ownership process, and reference architecture for development, test, and deployment before we can really look at requirements. Although in many standard system development situations, the evaluation of stakeholders can be conducted iteratively during requirements gathering, in the case of a complex, sensitive, and interdependent program like EDICTS, survival might depend on nailing the ownership and stakeholder mix just right at the outset. Also, in contrast to most system development efforts, where the owner is known at the start, EDICTS is so potentially broad that it's ownerless before it begins.

Continuing on our quest for long-term relevance, which translates into program survival, we suggest that the specific requirements of EDICTS map closely to the bank's existing internal controls over its financial operations. There are several reasons for this. For one thing, in keeping with our stakeholder alignment and interest in efficiency, we do not think it would be wise to create a wholly separate work stream and set of functions for the antifraud staff to master as they combat money laundering. The antifraud staff, and its corollaries in accounting, operations, and audit, also work from the same internal controls set. Plugging EDICTS into those controls gives EDICTS a seamless and practical connection to an existing and well-understood work stream.

To define requirements, therefore, we need to first understand the internal controls that mitigate the risk of money laundering. Most internal controls are based on a framework known as COSO,[8] which involves matching risks with control objectives and control procedures. (COSO is an acronym for Committee of Sponsoring Organizations of the Treadway Commission, a widely adopted internal controls framework for financial reporting.) For example, the COSO approach to the loan repayment money laundering trick for car loans might look like what is shown in Table 8.4.

Table 8.4 Internal Controls Framework, Based on COSO, for Example of Mitigating Risk of Premature Car Loan Repayment as a Money Laundering Tactic at the Bank

Control Objective	Risk	Control Procedures
Car loans taken out only for legitimate purchases of cars for personal or commercial use	Improper use of car loans to launder money through rapid repayment of loans and sale of collateralized vehicles	Establish procedures to prevent and/or detect repayment of car loans before 30 days of funding of loan Prevent writing of car loans to individuals or businesses who have prematurely paid off car loans in the past Establish procedures to detect premature cash payoffs of loan balances Establish procedures to detect patterns of premature car loan payoff and collateral sale fraud by individuals and businesses

Looking at this control setup, it might seem quite obvious to you or me that the bank needs to have procedures such as these in place to detect and prevent money laundering. However, what you need to understand is that the process described in the table, which in real life would include dozens or even hundreds of such control pairings, is designed to mitigate the risk of fraud systematically. Antifraud staff, working with auditors, first determine their control objectives. Then, they work through the risks to the attainment of those objectives, and finally, develop control procedures to mitigate the risks. If we are tasked with developing requirements for EDICTS, then we can take some comfort in understanding that a lot of the heavy lifting around EDICTS' antilaundering objectives and procedures for realization of those objectives has already been done for us. Our job, as definers of EDICTS requirements, involves figuring out the optimal way for an EDA to implement the control procedures already agreed upon by the antifraud staff, the line-of-business owners, and the auditors. Looking at it from another perspective, our work on EDICTS is a supplement to the existing work programs undertaken by these business groups. EDICTS can help them in their antifraud efforts without bogging them down in new, extraneous mastering of tasks and processes.

One final note on the importance of matching EDICTS requirements to internal controls: When the auditors (internal as well as external) conduct their audit of internal controls, they will be looking for evidence that the control objectives have been met through the control procedures. Once again, by matching EDICTS requirements to the existing internal controls, it is possible to add a high level of auditability right into the solution. It would be counterproductive, or even destructive, to the interest of EDICTS to require a new audit workload.

Figure 8.11 takes the EDICTS production system from Figure 8.10 and expands it into a basic reference architecture to show the major components needed to make EDICTS function in alignment with its internal controls mandate. At the core, we have the EDICTS management console. Like any enterprise application, EDICTS needs a control interface. This management console would contain both regular user and administrative functions. Regular users of the system, such as the antifraud staff, would use the management console to generate outputs necessary for checking the activities of detective controls. They would also use the management console to configure the pluggable business rules to match internal controls.

Administrators would use the management console to set up EDICTS and maintain it as a system on an ongoing basis. The administrative features would include capabilities for plugging and unplugging business rules, connecting event listeners with event producers, and interfacing with the SOA governance solution and SOA governance loop. Table 8.5 shows an approximation of the administrative interface of EDICTS. The table extends the COSO internal controls pairings shown in Table 8.4 and matches each control procedure with a set of event Web services and business rules.

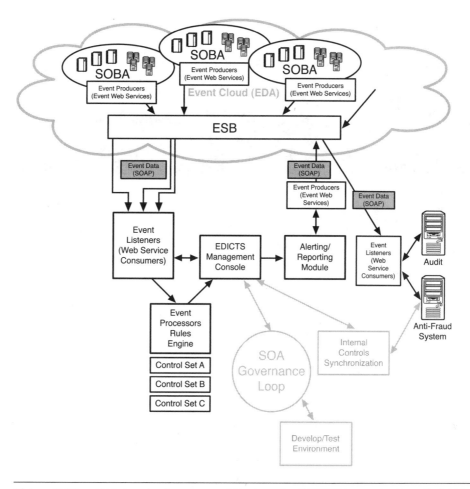

Figure 8.11 High-level reference architecture for EDICTS in production. Solid black arrows represent flows of production data. Gray arrows and shapes represent governance and metadata flows.

Table 8.5   Sample Requirements Set for EDICTS and Approximates for the Administrator Interface of EDICTS. (The table extends the COSO internal controls pairing and matches each control procedure with a set of business rules and event Web services.)

Control Objective	Risk	Control Procedure	Business Rules Applied	Event Web Services	Event Listeners	Reaction (could be a business rule)
Car loans taken out only for legitimate purchases of cars for personal or commercial use	Improper use of car loans to launder money through rapid repayment of loans and sale of collateralized vehicles	Establish procedures to prevent and/or detect repayment of car loans before 30 days of funding of loan	IF date of LoanPayment–date of FundLoan< 30, then **Alert antifraud staff**	LoanPayOff FundLoan	Subscribe to: LoanPayOff FundLoan	Invoke Premature PaymentAlert Web Service
		Prevent writing of car loans to individuals or businesses who have prematurely paid off car loans in the past	IF date of Loan Payment – date of FundLoan< 30, then **Invoke Web Service:** FindLoans ForAcct_ HoldSocSecNo IF (date of Loan Payment – date of FundLoan< 30) for AcctHolder>1 THEN **Alert antifraud staff**	FindLoans ForAcct_ HoldSocSecNo LoanPayOff FundLoan	Subscribe to: LoanPayOff FundLoan FindLoans ForAcct_ HoldSocSecNo	Invoke Suspect Borrower Web Service
		Establish procedures to detect premature cash payoffs of loan balances	IF date of Loan Payment – date of FundLoan< 30, then flag AND IF CashLoan Payment = "yes", THEN **Flag**	LoanPayOff CashLoan Payment FundLoan	Subscribe to: LoanPayOff CashLoan Payment FundLoan	Invoke Premature PaymentAlert Web Service
		Establish procedures to detect patterns of premature car loan payoff and collateral sale fraud by individuals and businesses	IF date of Loan Payment – date of FundLoan< 30, then flag	LoanPayOff CashLoan Payment FundLoan LienRelease	Subscribe to: LoanPayOff CashLoan Payment FundLoan LienRelease	IF loan account is FLAGGED, then QUERY: IF Lien Release= "yes", then ALERT Antifraud Staff

Table 8.5 is also a representation of the way that functional requirements for EDICTS could be documented. As we have discussed, the requirements for EDICTS will match internal controls. To make this happen, each COSO control objective, risk, and control procedure needs to be paired with functional requirements that spell out the specific Web services and business rules that will be used in enacting the control procedure. As EDICTS grows in functional scope, its requirements can be fitted to an expanding set of internal controls.

The Alerting/Reporting Module has two separate but related functions. It is able to send real-time alerts about suspicious transactions to antifraud systems. In addition, it can generate reports of EDICTS system activity, including logs of transactions and analysis of transaction flows with money-laundering patterns applied. In the first case, which is a real-time, or near-real-time process, EDICTS helps enforce preventive internal controls. By alerting antifraud staff, and systems, of possible improper activities, EDICT can prevent money laundering.

In the second case, where EDICTS is providing information about transactions occurring in a prior period, the system is supporting detective internal controls. Auditors can review the reports and analyze them for patterns of money laundering or transactions that might indicate money laundering occurring in another branch of the bank.

Though the reporting function can be run as a stand-alone application, we suggest that the alerting and real-time reporting capabilities of the module be designed as EDA components themselves. The alerts, which are an output of EDICTS, are generated by event producers and published at the ESB level. Any system that needs to receive those alerts, such as the antifraud systems, can subscribe through event listeners. Extensibility and flexibility are two advantages of this approach. As EDICTS grows, it might be desirable to connect real-time alerts to a whole range of systems, such as ATMs or loan processing systems, that might not even exist yet! The EDA approach gives EDICTS a lot of adaptability into the future.

Designing for Long-Term Success, Step 4: Integrating EDICTS with the Bank's SOA

In Figure 8.11, we depicted the banking systems feeding event data into EDICTS as service-oriented business applications (SOBAs). This might be somewhat optimistic, as in reality most of the bank systems will not be SOBAs, at least in the near future. However, we chose to represent them as SOBAs to emphasize the optimal nature of exposing event sources as Web services and to emphasize the importance of aligning the EDA development efforts with whatever SOA program is unfolding at the bank.

For optimal economy and reduction in incompatible architectures, EDICTS should be built in tandem with the bank's SOA. Though we have discussed the EDA/SOA connection through the book, in this chapter, we want to focus on several selected areas of relevance. In particular, we look at the value of joint planning by the SOA and EDICTS teams, compatibility of development environments and practices, and alignment of SOA and EDA governance.

Joint Planning with Enterprise Architecture Teams

As many of us learned the hard way, what appears to be a technology problem is actually a human or organizational matter. To make EDICTS a success, it must be designed in keeping with the SOA standards that are defined for the bank globally. We are assuming, of course, that there is an SOA at the bank, and that the bank has formed committees to define their particular SOA standards. In our view, this is a good assumption for any well-run financial institution.

The people who are building EDICTS need to be invited to participate in the SOA planning and management process. EDICTS needs a seat at the table, or at the very least, access to the bank's SOA standards. At the same time, the EDICTS team needs to know that they are expected to follow the bank's SOA standards.

For example, SOAP schema coordination is an area where joint planning between SOA and EDA teams can benefit both EDICTS and the bank's overall enterprise architecture. As an EDA, EDICTS relies on having Web services that carry event state within their SOAP messages. The SOAP schema that carries state might not automatically be the type specified or preferred by the SOA teams. In fact, they might have good reasons for not wanting such a schema. This is a matter to be resolved.

It might seem obvious that it pays to set up the SOBA with Web services that carry state in their SOAP messages. However, in reality, there are a number of barriers to achieving this objective, some of which are rooted in well-established principles of system design. For one thing, security standards might require that messages not contain excessive amounts of private customer data. It is more secure to send an abbreviated message, for instance one that contains only a portion of an account number, than a message that contains the account holder's name and account number. The exposure to the threat of message interception can be offset by the countermeasure abbreviated message syntax. The problem, of course, from an EDA perspective, is that you lose your state carriage in the message. At the level of infrastructure performance, the larger messages required to carry state can slow down the network traffic. Then, there is the simple issue of awareness. It is easily possible for developers to go about their work on the SOBA without realizing that they were supposed to create XML schemas that carried state in the SOAP messages. Once their SOBA is finished, tested, and deployed, it will be too late to go back and retrofit the SOBA's Web services to EDA state carriage format without incurring additional expense, use of resources, and time.

There are solutions to both of these problems, but each solution requires forethought, especially in advance of the development of service-oriented applications. If messages, especially those traveling outside of corporate networks, are forbidden from containing a high level of account detail, they might need to be encrypted (if link-level encryption is used, there is a whole class of security issues that need to be solved, such as replay attack vulnerabilities, and so on—but they exceed the scope of this chapter). Network performance issues need to be addressed, and so on. However, budget and enthusiasm for the extra security elements and network capacity might be limited and it would be unwise to assume that the performance drag brought about by an EDA will automatically be resolved by the network operations folks at your organization. Preplanning and joint team coordination are essential to ensure success.

Compatible Development Practices

It might not be reasonable to expect the various SOA and EDICTS delivery groups to standardize on one type of development environment and server architecture. Sharing development practices can go a long way to ensure that the bank develops its SOA using any number of Web service IDEs and enterprise service buses, or equivalent server technologies, so we should assume that EDICTS will be assembled out of components from that SOA. As we know, SOA creates connectivity between heterogeneous systems. However, as we also know, in reality there can be subtle differences in standards and technology implementations among different vendors that can cause frustrating and sometimes costly delays and hassles. It's good to be aware of issues related to IDE incompatibilities and adjust for anticipated issues in the shared development practices within your organization.

It's important to have a consistent process and toolset for checking code in and out of development—this can help streamline the life cycle (SDLC) of EDICTS, as it will flow with that of the SOA. Ditto for testing procedures. Uniform testing and release, as well as patch management, will cut costs and confusion from EDICTS. From a high level, it would make sense for EDICTS to be seen by IT managers as simply another SOA-related development project, not a unique or high-maintenance endeavor requiring special resources.

Having a single set of development skills, as well as test and deployment processes, will simplify the training process for both SOA and EDICTS teams. Ideally, the bank should not have a group of developers who are well versed in EDA techniques and a separate group that is familiar with Web services and SOA but not with EDA. There should be one pool of IT talent to draw from, a state wherein the bank can have the greatest degree of flexibility to apply staff resources to projects. Also, if the goal is to establish EDA-friendly SOAP schemas and other best practices in the SOA that can enable extensible EDA projects, then joint training and cross-training are all the more compelling to consider.

Coordination and Alignment of SOA Governance

Effective governance is crucial to ensuring that EDICTS can function properly and fulfill the challenge of being endlessly adaptable and dynamic. It is only with governance, which ensures that the system operates as intended, with secure and appropriate access to data, that EDICTS will have any integrity. However, the governance must also be flexible enough to adapt the many planned and unplanned future changes in EDICTS makeup.

It might seem counterintuitive to make governance the last item of a requirements discussion. In the SOA projects we have participated in, the discussion of governance comes, if not first, then right at the start of requirements setting. In the case of EDICTS, though, we felt it was necessary to establish all the stakeholder roles, reference architectures, and connections to internal controls before getting into the governance discussion. If we had not gone through these preliminaries first, the specifics of governance would lack relevance.

We should also assume that we are not going to develop a governance solution for EDICTS from scratch. That would be a huge waste of time and money, and probably wouldn't work that well, either. Instead, EDICTS should be governed by the bank's SOA governance solution, but with some adaptations.

Yes, SOA governance is SOA governance. But, with EDICTS, several factors need extra attention. For one thing, EDICTS is bound to connect to a great number of external users and systems. Whatever policy setting mechanisms are established for external access must be very thoroughly checked for secure provisioning of access privileges to EDICTS' Web services. In addition, EDICTS is not the typical application running with its logic controlled centrally. The invocation of its Web services is likely to be a lot more unpredictable. The nature of EDICTS results in more passive consumption of Web services than a conventional SOA, where consumers and providers are matched closely for the purpose of defining governance policies.

On another level, the SOA governance for EDICTS should map to the bank's internal controls. This is necessary for several reasons. It would be terrible if EDICTS accidentally exposed the bank to more security and control risk through deficient governance. And, the same internal controls that EDICTS is helping to enforce now include EDICTS by design. The owners of those internal controls need a way to validate that EDICTS is being well governed, and that its governance is in alignment with the control objectives and control practices. Further to this idea, EDICTS will probably be subject to different, likely stricter, audit requirements than other applications. The governance solution must be able to generate audit reports of system activity, as well as system findings and data, in a manner that satisfies the auditors.

Finally, the serious criminal nature of money laundering requires that EDICTS be secure from the inside out. As any experienced information security expert will tell you, internal threats, including personnel, can be the most difficult to mitigate. The EDICTS governance solution must have a layer of policy that enables extra security so that the watchers of the system can be watched themselves. Or, perhaps, the administrators who manage the EDICTS governance solution must be subject to strict segregation of duties. For example, there might need to be dual permissions required to provision access to the EDICTS governance solution. If that policy were not in force, an administrator could provision himself with access to the system and potentially modify it without being detected.

Though there are many equally valid approaches to governing an SOA and EDA, we will assume that the bank is using an SOA governance solution that utilizes a central policy store for policy definition and distributed agents for policy enforcement. With that in mind, but without going over every nook and cranny of Figure 8.12, let's take a look at some of the highlights of SOA governance that are relevant for EDICTS:

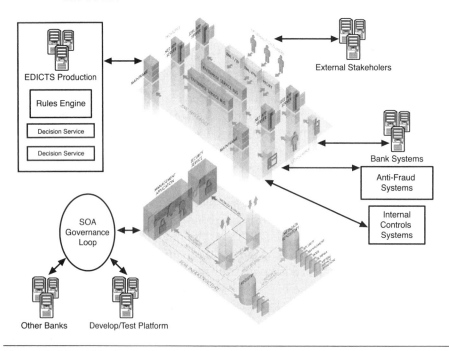

Figure 8.12   This figure shows the relationship between a comprehensive SOA governance solution, including Registry and policy metadata repository, and the working parts of EDICTS. Web services intermediaries intercept SOAP messages traveling from consumer and provider through ESBs and enforce policy. Design-time and runtime governance are managed through a closed-loop approach that unifies policy definition and enforcement across EDICTS' SDLC.

- **Registry/UDDI**—One aspect of EDICTS as a production system that is so pervasive it is difficult to diagram is the UDDI registry at the heart of the bank's SOA and EDICTS. As we have discussed earlier, every Web service in the bank, as well as those in certain partner organizations, needs to be listed in the registry for the SOA and EDA to function in a governable fashion. We are assuming, of course, that the UDDI registry connects with a set of SOA governance policies stored in a policy metadata repository. The UDDI surfaces through the management console so that administrators can connect EDICTS with necessary Web services, and also provision access to EDICTS' own Web services, in a way that is consistent with the bank's overall SOA governance approach.

- **Policy metadata repository**—The policy metadata repository, which might be joined at the hip with the Registry in some vendor implementations, contains the governance policies that need to be enforced for each Web service in the bank, including those that connect to EDICTS. The policies contained in the repository govern such factors as access rights for Web services, including secondary and tertiary access rights that are passed along as tokens from human users, encryption, ESB federation and mediation, and provisioning of access to external users.

- **Intermediaries**—SOAP intermediaries, both on the consumer and Web service side, are the policy enforcement points that assure system owners that the Web services are functioning as intended, in terms of security and reliability. There are several varieties of intermediaries available in the industry today, though most utilize a pipeline architecture that enables the administrator to switch policy enforcement on and off for both the outbound and inbound SOAP message flows. For example, in EDICTS, it might be necessary to encrypt a SOAP message that contains account holder information. The SOAP intermediary would cause the SOAP message to be encrypted and thus comply with the governance policy.

- **Performance monitoring**—With a large number of potential Web services necessary to make EDICTS function, it is essential that its constituent Web services be reliable. System administrators need to know if a service is slow, or down. And, if a service goes down, it needs to failover to another instance of the service, or, at the very least, let someone know that it is down. Performance monitoring is another type of governance policy. The policy metadata repository should contain performance monitoring policies for EDICTS' Web services. For example, EDICTS might require that bank Web services publish data every 60 seconds for the system to be up to date on the latest transaction flow. If a Web service is slow, or fails, the system administrator needs to know. This can take the form of an alerting process, such as Simple Network Management Protocol (SNMP) alerts to a system management console. Some SOA governance systems even have contract functions where Web service consumers and providers can come to an enforceable agreement regarding performance parameters. Beyond this, many SOA governance solutions offer the capability to map dependencies between linked chains of Web service consumers and providers. If these dependencies are not tracked properly when EDICTS is being developed, and especially as it is expanded, certain Web services could be subject to unsustainable load and break the system. In some cases, it might be possible, and desirable, to connect the SOA governance solution with network infrastructure management systems to optimize network performance in the EDA. In a large, potentially global EDA like EDICTS, network performance is a real issue, especially because the system could affect regular bank operations if it slows the network down.

■ **Closed loop**—The SOA governance loop seen in Figure 8.12 and others represents the concept of a closed-loop SOA governance solution. We recommend that EDICTS utilize a governance solution that enables consistent definition and enforcement of governance policy from design time through runtime. As Web services are developed, and then placed into position at design time, the governance policy that is specified for them should automatically continue with the Web service at runtime. For example, if a Web service requires encryption of an outbound SOAP message, the designer needs to be confident that the encryption policy will be enforced at runtime. The closed loop ensures that this will happen, and also provides an audit log to prove that the encryption is in effect. Closed-loop SOA governance for EDICTS relies on a continuously updated, unified UDDI registry that spans design time and runtime.

Chapter Summary

- This chapter walked us through the application of EDA on an application, enterprise, and cross-enterprise level.

- Money laundering, the crime of concealing illicit earnings in legitimate bank accounts, is a worldwide problem affecting many banks. Banks are required to be vigilant in detecting and preventing money laundering, and many of the controls they implement to avoid becoming complicit or liable in this crime involve enterprise information technology.

- Detecting money laundering requires banks to be able to observe suspicious patterns of transaction activity, including those that take place between multiple banks and even countries.

- Event-driven architecture has the potential to improve a bank's ability to detect money laundering by seeing and correlating transaction event data from transactions across multiple divisions of the bank, multiple banks, and geographic regions in real time. The EDA can be dynamic enough to allow fraud examiners to establish and modify money-laundering detection parameters in a short cycle time.

- In an anti–money laundering EDA, transactional systems within a bank would publish event data into the event cloud, either always or upon request, where it could be processed through rules engines that drive a continuous audit process. ESB would sit at the heart of these event clouds. Suspicious transactions could be flagged for follow-up by antifraud staff, or even referred to law enforcement.

- In a broader view, multiple bank event clouds could be harvested by regional or global event listeners and event processors that detect transaction patterns between financial institutions.

- Putting such an antilaundering EDA into effect is not a minor undertaking. To succeed, the system would need to factor in the needs and expectations of multiple stakeholders, and achieve buy-in prior to commencing the project. Senior management, for example, would need to commit to the success of such an ambitious concept, especially if it involves integrating with other banks. An antilaundering EDA would also require very close coordination between security professionals, internal audit, and IT.

- To work, an antilaundering EDA would need extremely effective, but also efficient, SOA governance. For the level of dynamic connectivity needed between component systems, the antilaundering EDA needs to make governance and control a seamless process. Otherwise, the system will bog down.

- Ultimately, an antilaundering EDA needs to be approached as a service-oriented business application (SOBA) within the bank's ongoing SOA program. If it is positioned as a separate system with its own infrastructure and governance, it would probably become too cumbersome and expensive to run, and it will fail.

Endnotes

1. Mollenkamp, Carrick. "Costs of anti money laundering soar." *The Wall Street Journal*, July 9, 2007.
2. Ibid.
3. AP. "Daniel Pearl's Widow Sues Terrorists' Bank." July 18, 2007.
4. Ibid.
5. Mollenkamp, Carrick. "Costs of anti money laundering soar." *The Wall Street Journal*, July 9, 2007.
6. Ibid.
7. Seeley, Rich. "SCA and SDO Become SOA Essentials for Banking System." SearchWebServices.com 4/7/07
8. For more information, visit www.coso.org

CHAPTER 9

Case Study: Event-Driven Productivity Infrastructure

Jerry Seinfeld does a routine where he wonders how mankind discovered that glue can be made from horses. He describes a scene where someone is trying unsuccessfully to stick two pieces of paper together, when, suddenly a horse rides by, causing an instant revelation of potential… "Hey, wait a minute!" he imagines the brilliant inventor saying. "How come I never thought of that before?" So it is, too, in IT. Sometimes, trends of technological innovation exist in parallel for a period of time before someone realizes that they can be put to work together, for a greater effect than either one on its own. There are some great examples of this from the history of technology, including the merging of recording technology and the telephone (creating the answering machine), the joining of the QWERTY keyboard with the cathode ray tube and the CPU (the modern computer), or the phone with the computer (networked computing).

Today, we are witnessing the parallel maturing of event-driven architecture (EDA) and productivity infrastructure, two separate, but potentially synergetic information technologies. Each is powerful in its own right, but together, they can create transcendent event-driven information processing environments. This chapter explores the potential integration of EDA with productivity infrastructure. In particular, we focus on the ways that productivity infrastructure empowers the human thinking and decision making that is often implicit in the process flow of an EDA.

Learning Objectives

- Understanding productivity infrastructure and its potential for integration with EDA
- Understanding the potential for enhancing the human decision-making capability within EDA through the integration of productivity infrastructure
- Connecting business process models from structured to unstructured process steps, spanning back-end systems and productivity tools, such as e-mail
- Understanding approaches to determining a target architecture for EDA-productivity infrastructure integration

The Often Inadequate Human Link in the EDA

As we have seen throughout this book, there are many instances where the corporate "nervous system" of EDA loops through a human decision-making process. In the airline traffic case, it was the flight operations managers who were called upon to make critical decisions about flight prioritization based on input from the EDA. In the anti–money laundering case, bank fraud staff were fed information about suspicious transactions for their review and decision on actions. This EDA-human connection makes sense much of the time. Indeed, there is often no substitute for a person, and his or her awareness of multiple influencing factors, in a business decision-making process. Artificial intelligence is suitable in some cases to make or support human decisions, but even in cases where decision making can be automated, there is frequently the need for a person to take responsibility for the decision. Alas, there is still no way to hold a computer accountable for the consequences of a decision that causes an airliner to crash or money to be stolen from a bank account. Given the inevitable presence of people in EDA-based decision process flows, one of the big challenges is relative inefficiency of human decision making.

Unlike computers, people are extraordinarily inefficient at decision making and are, in fact, quite high maintenance. Whereas a computer can execute a decision algorithm at any time within a fraction of a second, people need to be present (awake and focused) to make a specific decision at a specific time. This is not efficient, and in some cases, might be harmful to the business process that the EDA is meant to serve. And, in many cases, people need to make decisions in groups, a situation where the inefficiency of communication compounds the delay and quality of the decision. For example, if the air traffic EDA enables rapid decisions about prioritizing flight departure times, but the key decision maker needs to consult with a superior, who is out to lunch, the whole process could be delayed to the point where it compromises the whole intent of the system.

In other cases, people might need to access external sources of information to make decisions that feed into an EDA decision-making process. The bank antifraud staffer might have to review scanned document images to compare signatures on old checks before making a judgment call about whether to escalate a fraud investigation or notify law enforcement. This type of manual, or semimanual, process can cause harmful inefficiency for the EDA. In this instance, the antifraud staffer might have to manually write down the name of the suspected account, exit the EDA interface, open a records management application, and conduct a search for matching documents. After manually reviewing the documents, he or she might have to share the findings with other antifraud staffers or document review specialists before making a decision to escalate the case. Such a discussion could involve a combination of e-mail, phone, fax, or instant messaging. None of this is particularly horrible, but the cumulative effect of faults in the communication and manual process flows—spread out across multiple concurrent fraud cases—can result in a significant drag on performance and suboptimal antifraud efforts. The solution to these types of challenges is known broadly as *productivity infrastructure,* and it is maturing today at a rapid rate.

Overview of Productivity Infrastructure

Productivity infrastructure (PI) is an umbrella term to describe people's and organization's increasingly connected and synergistic use of phone, e-mail, Internet, PDA, intranet, extranet, and desktop productivity applications. What was once a collection of essentially siloed productivity technologies and workflows—phone calls, e-mails, searching the Web, creating documents, using a PDA, and so on—are now merging into a combined infrastructure that drives personal and organizational productivity. In brand-name terms, productivity infrastructure is integrating the functionality of product sets such as Microsoft's Office System, Cisco's VOIP solutions, IBM's Lotus suite, and Google's Docs and gMail services, just to name a few.

To understand the importance and impact of productivity infrastructure, let's use the creation of a sales proposal as a baseline example of the kind of unstructured type of workflow that typically challenges information workers to be productive. In contrast to structured tasks, such as those performed by customer service agents at a call center, a great deal of business work today involves unstructured tasks, which are unpredictable in terms of workflow step order, location of needed information, and stakeholder identities, roles, and responsibilities. In the case of creating a sales proposal, a number of different approval patterns, issues to be resolved, and decision makers might be involved at any given time. The processes, people, and underlying data and documents required to create the sales proposal might change from case to case. Though the process will contain the basic flow shown in Figure 9.1, in reality each situation will be slightly different. Managing this subjectivity within a tight time frame is the essence of productivity infrastructure.

Each step in the creation of the sales proposal, as shown in Figure 9.1, involves multiple people, often from different work teams, in the sharing of information, documents, and knowledge. The more efficiently the people involved in completing this multistep, multiplayer process can get their work done, the better off the organization will be in productivity terms. The impetus behind the development of productivity infrastructure is the drive to enable workers in unstructured information work to get more done in less time, with less expenditure of resources.

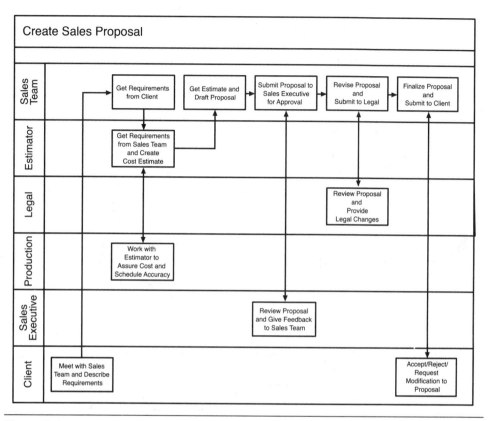

Figure 9.1 In the process flow of creating a sales proposal, multiple people and groups must collaborate and share documents and information, often in real time.

As Figure 9.2 shows, the steps in the sales proposal development process map to capabilities in the productivity infrastructure. In this example, VOIP technology speeds up the process of connecting the customer with the sales rep by automatically connecting a landline call to a mobile device. All participants in the process use e-mail to communicate, with relevant stakeholders able to share links to document repositories where proposal templates and other data are stored for common use. A portal user interface (UI) links stakeholders to the workflow management process as well as collaboration sites that contain blogs and wikis that publish up-to-date information needed for crafting the proposal. Social computing technologies like MySpace, FaceBook, and LinkedIn allow individuals to understand connections between stakeholders that might not be apparent through job titles or task assignments. Team sites enable stakeholders to make sure that their proposal is in alignment with team objectives and business goals, or clarify approvals required for the proposal. The real-time instant messaging or Web conferencing facilitates rapid resolution of open issues for the proposal.

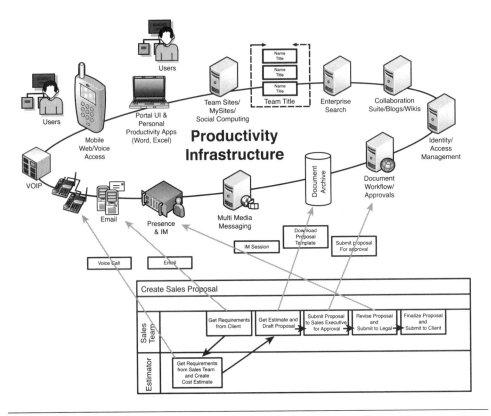

Figure 9.2   Productivity infrastructure, which links workflow, collaboration, e-mail, phone, mobile, document repositories, and Web 2.0 technologies, such as blogs, wikis, mysites, and social computing, can drive efficiencies in the unstructured, multiplayer, iterative process flow required to create a sales proposal.

If everyone involved in creating the sales proposal were sitting in the same room at all times, then there would be no reason for the investment in productivity infrastructure. In fact, that's how business worked until about 1890, when the telephone started to move people away from physical proximity to their business partners. Today, of course, the groups of people involved in getting business done are almost never all together, and certainly not in any reliable pattern or schedule that will allow them to get time-sensitive tasks done. And today, as we often find, it's not just being able to communicate with others in a collaborative process that makes things flow smoothly. To get the tasks accomplished, each participant needs to know who the other players are, who they report to, what their priorities are. On top of all that, participants also often need access to information that is not easily located without the assistance of others in the group. To make access to needed information available without requiring time-consuming conversations or e-mails, participants need to be able to search for and find what they are looking for on their own.

Productivity infrastructure has the potential to drive more efficient workflows for unstructured tasks, assuming it is implemented properly. The time cycle for completing the entire process flow for creating a sales proposal, for example, becomes shorter with good productivity infrastructure, and the time investment of each participant goes down as well. Ideally, the accuracy and quality of the final product improves as an added bonus. However, productivity infrastructure can be complex to deploy, as it can raise some challenging security, compliance, and interoperability concerns. We mention this here just to assure you that we are not all starry-eyed about the ease of deploying such a comprehensive and interconnected infrastructure, and neither should you be. Nevertheless, we do believe that productivity infrastructure, once in place, can be leveraged further using EDA.

The Potential Benefits of EDA-PI Integration

To see the potential for benefits of integrating EDA with PI, we should think about the advantages of linking the corporate nervous system of EDA with the comparable organizational nervous system of PI. With EDA, corporate systems can detect changes in state that affect business. Wherever the EDA needs human input, PI can speed up the EDA's reaction time to the state change. PI can also improve the quality of the human input because it can link people with data sources, and each other, with high efficiency. Ultimately, there is the potential for the creation of loops of interaction between EDA and PI, where state changes noticed by the EDA elicit reactions from people though the PI, who, in turn, input their own changes of state to the EDA.

As shown in Figure 9.3, the integration of productivity infrastructure and EDA can be understood by considering a simple business process model that involves inputs from two enterprise systems that must be evaluated by people. Event Web services on applications A and B publish data about their state to the enterprise service bus (ESB), and on to an application built using a Business Process Modeling (BPM) tool. The process model calls for people to assess the data presented by the states of applications A and B, and for them to make a decision about what the states mean, and then take action either by instructing application C or terminating the process without taking action. The PI is designed to notify the decision makers of the change in state. After the decision is made, the reaction to the change in state flows back to the EDA through an event Web service located in the PI.

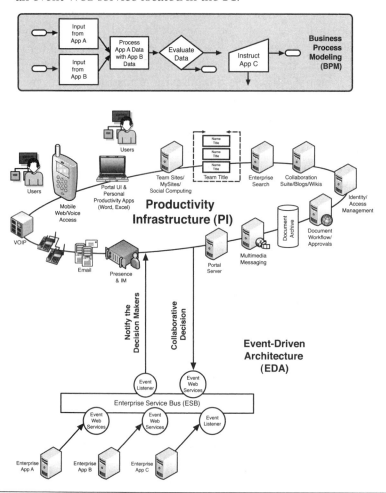

Figure 9.3 The integration of productivity infrastructure and EDA, connecting people and enterprise apps through an ESB and event Web services.

If there were just one person who could make the decision called for in the process, off the top of his or her head, there wouldn't be much need for the kind of elaborate setup called for in Figure 9.3. However, let's suppose that the decision being made in the process flow is complex, high risk, multistakeholder, and time sensitive. Imagine, for example, that it involves the decision to manufacture goods with costly inventory. The decision could have impact on financial statements, factory capacity, even labor unions, hence the decision to proceed could be a collaborative decision. In that kind of situation, a tight integration between the decision makers and the EDA could have a real impact on the business.

In the case of a manufacturer setting inventory levels, the time required to make a decision—the right decision, that is—is highly relevant to business success. If the manufacturer guesses wrong, and either overstocks an item whose product life is on the decline, or understocks a hot seller, the financial results will be less than optimal. In another example, preparation for a hurricane takes the coordinated effort of many disparate government agencies, safety personnel, health-care institutions, and so on. Because lives depend on the speed and accuracy of these efforts, you can see it's extremely important that these efforts are in sync and in constant communication of state changes. In these kinds of situations, even the difference of an hour or two, or the lack of a few critical nuggets of business data, can have an impact on the overall objective of saving lives or protecting the bottom line. Imagine, for instance, if you decided to order a truckload of component parts for the manufacture of a product that was later determined to be unneeded. It might not be the end of the world, but it would create an accounting and logistical hassle to return the order. Multiply this type of problem across a large, global company, and the effect on earnings could reach into millions of dollars of direct and indirect costs. Consider, for example, the necessity of engaging accounting staff unnecessarily due to faulty decision making.

In addition to offering a shorter decision cycle time, the integrated EDA-PI approach has the potential to enable a higher quality of decision than the current state of integration between PI and enterprise systems. Keeping in mind with this example that we are dealing here with decisions that cannot be automated through rules engines, consider the factors that affect the quality of decision making among multiple stakeholders. In our view, the quality of a decision depends on the financial and human consequences of the decision. The decision that saves lives and saves money is the best one. Of course, there is a range of quality decisions between best and worst, but the goal should be to strive for the best decision in the largest number of cases. This concept is known as the "decision yield."[1]

As anyone who has worked in a large, distributed organization could tell you, the quality of a decision depends on multiple interdependent factors, including knowledge of who the stakeholders are for a particular decision, equal simultaneous access to information, and equal understanding of information. Quality of decision making also depends on a productive engagement of stakeholders inside an organizational hierarchy. The higher level stakeholder might have the ability to overrule the correct decision through innate power, and the smarter subordinate might not have, or want, the opportunity to oppose the incorrect decision. Of course, productivity infrastructure cannot help an organization overcome this hierarchical flaw in process on its own. However, by providing open access to shared opinions and corporate knowledge, and real-time access to multiple points of view, the hierarchy effect can be mitigated in favor of discussion and group learning.

Integrating EDA and PI can improve the efficiency and quality of the information provided to workers who are tasked with making business decisions. Ultimately, this can result in reductions in overhead or increased utilization of staff for strategic business purposes. We felt this point was worth making because we have heard many dialogues about the value of service-oriented architecture (SOA) and EDA that make the assumption that there is a high-efficiency analysis apparatus available to parse the output of these systems. This is not necessarily so, and indeed, a lot of approaches to SOA dead-end into an empty seat called "stakeholders" and fail to generate good return on investment (ROI) as a result.

The productivity infrastructure itself can function as an event producer as well. A simple example might be an event announcing the presence of a stakeholder or that a new sales lead has been detected. Another example, which touches on an exciting new area of PI, is the concept of "active search" within the enterprise and its potential to function as an event producer from within the PI.

Figure 9.4 depicts an enterprise search solution allowing a productivity infrastructure to function as an event producer. To see how this works, we must first understand the process of an enterprise search solution, which is an increasingly common fixture in today's enterprises. Like a Web search engine, the enterprise search solution contains three core elements: a query server, an index server, and "crawlers," which read through documents and other data sources and feed their findings into the index server. The enterprise search index, like their corollaries in the Web search world, is a massive and exhaustive directory of information located within the enterprise. The enterprise search solution operates by taking queries from end users through a front-end UI (e.g., a search box in a portal interface), sending the queries through the query server to the index, and returning matching results back to the end user through the UI.

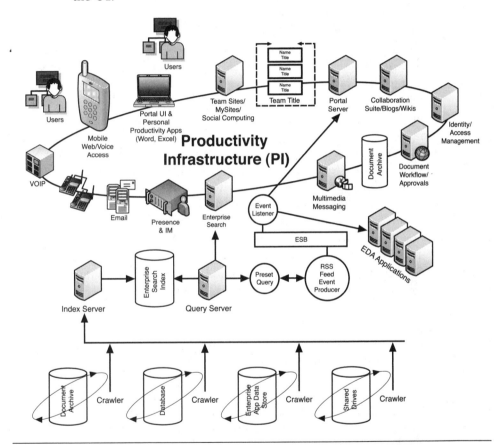

Figure 9.4 Active search involves the use of an enterprise search solution, which "crawls" repositories of unstructured data, indexes them, and then sends RSS feeds in response to preset search queries. The RSS feeds, which function to indicate the presence of specific information in unstructured data, can serve as event producers.

Some enterprise search solutions offer the ability to conduct active search, a process wherein certain queries are stored and continually rerun, with the search results being published to end users through RSS (Real Simple Syndication, a form of Extensible Markup Language [XML]). So, for example, an end user in a real estate development firm could use an enterprise search solution to query the company's internal document libraries for data that matches the keyword of a particular neighborhood. If the user types "Chelsea" into the search box on the portal UI, that query will return any documents or other indexed data files that contain the word "Chelsea," and the user could then learn about projects or people involving Chelsea. In an active search mode, the user could store the "Chelsea" search and instruct the search solution to issue him an RSS feed every day that contained the latest search results for "Chelsea" without the user having to run the query every day himself.

From an EDA perspective, it is possible to imagine how this active search function could turn into an event producer. The stored query, and resulting RSS feed, could be designed to publish changes in state that exist within unstructured data environments. In our real estate example, the query might feed into an algorithm that determines whether specific people or company divisions are working in Chelsea, a change in state that could drive action through the EDA. A customer relationship management (CRM) system attached to the EDA could flag the activity in Chelsea, based on the event data published through the enterprise search solution and PI, for follow-up by account executives in the neighborhood.

There is even the potential for EDA and PI to interoperate as looping, connected halves of a bigger EDA. Events published out through the EDA inform stakeholders and drive action through the PI, which, in turn, publishes back event data about stakeholder activities, presence, and data creation through the PI. Admittedly, this level of sophistication is fairly futuristic, even for this forward-looking book. However, we believe the potential for productivity improvements and information worker empowerment through the integration of EDA and PI are powerful and promising.

ProdCo, an EDA-PI Integration Scenario

To see how EDA and PI could be integrated, we will use the example of a custom manufacturing business. To optimize the learning experience, we are going to keep the example fairly simple and focus on the aspects of this hypothetical business that are most general to all businesses. This company, which we call ProdCo, could stand in for a mass of businesses that perform custom services on a job-by-job basis. Within ProdCo, we focus on the sales proposal and order fulfillment process to highlight the potential EDA-PI integration.

Sales Proposal and Order Fulfillment at ProdCo

The sales and fulfillment process at ProdCo is touched by a group of teams and individual stakeholders. To get a proposal out to a client and then fulfill the order, the Sales, Marketing, Production, Legal, Finance, and C-Suite executives need to be involved. Sales, of course, is the main point of contact with the client. Marketing engages in the process to assist with pricing and discount programs that might be tied to particular campaigns. Finance is involved to ensure that the pricing and costing of the job are appropriate, and that the HR aspects of the job are properly considered. Finance also weighs in with sourcing decisions and execution. Production is responsible for actually doing the work. The C-Suite has oversight, especially if the job is large or strategically significant.

Figure 9.5 shows the essential flow for ProdCo's proposal-fulfillment-assessment process. The sales team drafts the proposal and circulates it through reviews by Legal, Production, Finance, and the C-Suite. If there are revisions, the review cycle might repeat in whole or part. After the client approves the proposal, the job goes into production, and is fulfilled. Finance becomes involved again for sourcing of materials and overseeing labor expenses, as well as invoicing and collection. At the end of the process flow, the Finance Department publishes the results of the job—if it made or lost money compared with the estimate—and all other departments receive this information and update their own knowledge bases. Or not...

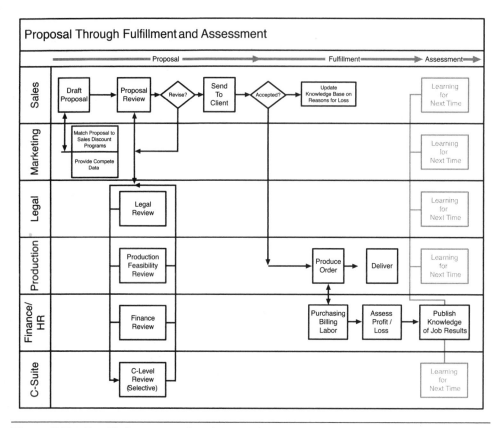

Figure 9.5   ProdCo's process flow for creating a sales proposal, fulfilling the job, and assessing its profitability.

There are a couple of design flaws in this process, though to be fair to ProdCo, it's about as good as it can be given the current state of technology. For one thing, the review loops for the proposal might be a lot more complicated and subjective than any process model can approximate. And, the assumption that the process flow makes is that everyone has access to relevant information on a timely basis. The Marketing Department might not know, for example, that certain types of projects lose money, so they ought to be dropped from the discount plan, and so forth. Most problematic, though, is that the process is very inefficient. The people and groups involved in this process waste time managing and finding the information they need to get the process finished as well as communicating with one another. A closer look at the way ProdCo has set up its productivity software and enterprise architecture can reveal some of the causes of this inefficiency.

ProdCo's Current Productivity Tools

Figure 9.6 shows how ProdCo has set up its productivity tools and enterprise applications. The Sales and Marketing teams have access to the CRM system, while Finance and Production use the enterprise resource planning (ERP) solution. Collaboration inside each team, and between teams, is a fairly ad hoc affair, with stakeholders e-mailing files back and forth and saving them on departmental shared drives that each team can access through a portal interface. It is possible for a non–team member to access a portal, but that person must first be granted access rights by a departmental administrator. Each team portal has calendaring capabilities, and everyone is able to schedule meetings using the e-mail suite. The C-Suite executives use a business intelligence dashboard that is fed by the finance staff because it does not tie directly into the ERP system.

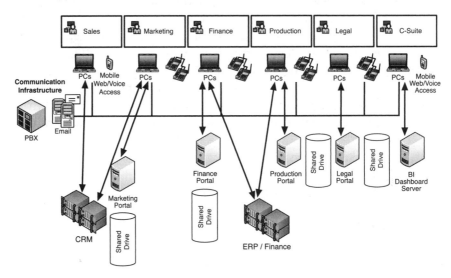

Figure 9.6   The ProdCo teams involved in creating sales proposals and fulfilling orders use two enterprise systems—CRM and ERP—and a slew of ad hoc productivity solutions, including shared drives, e-mail, and voice communication.

ProdCo's productivity solutions and enterprise applications are too siloed to be highly efficient. There is no efficient way to share information or documents across the entire company—at least in a way that does not open access to the document to every single employee, which nobody wants. Connections between systems are haphazard or nonexistent. So, for example, there is no way to seamlessly import the terms of a sales proposal into the ERP system. It must be reentered when the order goes into production. Approvals on each phase of a proposal, and its subsequent production phase, are conducted by e-mail and phone. The ERP system does have automated approval functions, where executives can sign off on purchase orders, overtime schedules, and so forth. However, the problem is that these approvers must often communicate with others, such as the Legal Department, before proceeding. The efficiency of the automated approval function is mitigated by the slow, unstructured process of human-to-human communication within the firm. And, there is no way to keep track of recurring patterns of unstructured workflow that could save time in the future.

For example, imagine that certain types of orders require materials to be sourced from Mexico. The procurement staff has learned from experience that in the summer months, the heat inside the trucks coming from Mexico is so intense that it can ruin the parts in transit. They know now either to order these parts in advance, or actually pay for a refrigerated truck. Of course, this is more expensive, though paying the expense is preferable to delays and missing parts. However, the procurement staff has no way to keep this relevant fact in front of all stakeholders at all times. The ERP system has a "notes" section, where the procurement staff can write down a reminder to order a refrigerated truck with that SKU. Yet, when the sales team wants to make a deal, or the Marketing Department wants to create a discount campaign, they do so without realizing that their margin is lower than normal on the item that includes the Mexican components. The C-Suite, too, might lack visibility into the issue, and wonder why margins are low on this type of product.

ProdCo's Proposed EDA

Being wise and forward-looking, ProdCo has decided to invest in shifting its architecture toward SOA and EDA. Figure 9.7 shows how this would work. ProdCo would install an enterprise service bus as an integration layer that exposes the functionality of both the CRM and ERP systems as sets of Web services. A portal server would provide access to the various department portals and also make certain CRM and ERP functions are available to users who didn't have access to either the CRM or ERP client. The departmental portals themselves would remain essentially untouched, though their provisioning could now be centrally controlled and extension of existing portals could be governed more thoroughly than before. Communications would remain a silo.

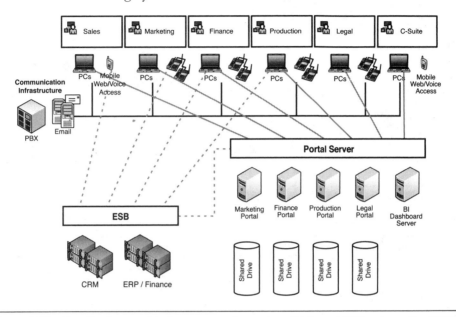

Figure 9.7 ProdCo is considering a move toward an SOA and EDA, where the CRM and ERP/Finance applications would be exposed as Web services through the enterprise service bus. The departmental portals would be accessed through a central portal server, though their content and administration would remain essentially siloed. The communication infrastructure would remain unchanged.

To appreciate how the EDA approach would work for ProdCo, let's look at a small part of the production process, the ordering of supplies based on a bill of materials. Figure 9.8 shows the flow for the bill of materials (BOM) process as well as the matchup between the process steps and the Web services enabled in the EDA. Certain steps, though, such as selecting the winning bids from the RFQ, are still human processes and cannot be fully automated. Other steps, such as requesting procurement, might be semiautomated, wherein the ERP system does all the work once a person has approved the request for RFQ.

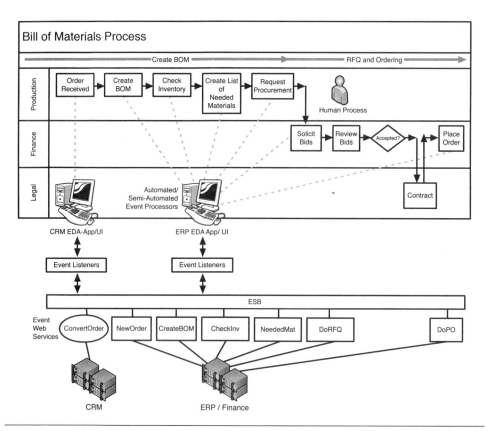

Figure 9.8   ProdCo's EDA exemplified through the process flow of creating a bill of materials and requesting quotes (RFQs) from suppliers.

As shown in Figure 9.8, the bill of materials process consists of several automated/semiautomated steps that work off the event Web services, as well as a few that are completely human. Sales proposals exist in the CRM system, but when a customer makes the decision to buy, under the new EDA approach, the CRM system's `ConvertOrder` Web service publishes the state change of the proposal from "Pending" to "Accepted." The event listener in the ERP EDA application receives this state change information and, in reaction, takes the order data from the CRM system and transfers it to the ERP system. This step could be fully automated, meaning it could occur simply because of programmatic instruction, or it could be semiautomated, where a person gets a signal through the UI that the order is ready to convert and the human action of clicking a button on the interface actually completes the transfer from CRM to ERP systems.

The process flow then follows a series of event-triggered service steps. The ConvertOrder Web service in the CRM system results in the creation of a new order for production in the ERP system. The NewOrder Web service publishes that its state is "New," which is listened to by the CreateBOM (Create Bill of Materials) Web service. The Web services CheckInv (check inventory) and NeededMat (Needed Materials) create a list of materials that are needed for the job but which are not in stock. The DoRFQ Web service is activated by the NeededMat Web service's publishing of its change of state (from Nothing to List). Each of these Web services can be invoked manually or through an automated process.

Sending the RFQs out to vendors, though, is a manual step even if the actual work is done by the system. A procurement person ensures that the RFQ goes to suppliers who are appropriate for the materials needed. However, even this could be a fully automated process that reacts to the event of DoRFQ by generating a Request For Quote electronically and sending it to preapproved vendors through e-mail or online notification calling them to a vendor portal.

Assuming the EDA is implemented correctly, it provides numerous advantages to ProdCo's operations. It renders the back end more flexible than a conventionally architected system. The EDA makes it simpler, faster, and cheaper to implement changes in the process flow for RFQs, and enables streamlined reporting and aggregation of data for consolidation of purchase orders and vendor management.

However, the human decision elements of the process flow are not much affected by the EDA. The act of soliciting bids from vendors is still either wholly or partly human, as is the selection of winning bids. It would be possible to automate both of those processes, though, and even include some fairly sophisticated rules sets to ensure best practices in procurement. Taking the human beings out of the picture for selecting vendors, for example, might occur if ProdCo could implement a set of business rules that awarded contracts to vendors with the lowest price, the best ranking for quality from production operations, and a consistent track record of on-time delivery. If this automation were implemented, the bill of materials process could proceed seamlessly without the messiness and delay of human actions. This area provides another great opportunity for ProdCo to expand its EDA innovation.

Returning to our example of goods from Mexico that melt in hot trucks in the Arizona sun (and we're not making this up, either; it happened to one of us), we can see that there are still instances where there is a need for subjective human knowledge to get to the best possible business result from a process flow, even with an advanced EDA in place. And, this is where the efficiency of ProdCo's EDA starts to falter.

As the automated, or semiautomated process of converting an order from proposal to sale, and the derivative bill of materials/RFQ steps cascade out from the entry of the sale into the ERP system, we still dead-end at a person—or group—that needs to decide which vendors get to bid on the order. In the best-case scenario, the vendor selection is done by an experienced person who understands all the subjective issues involved and acts promptly and decisively. In a less-rewarding scenario, the decision is made by a distributed group of people who might individually lack the knowledge of the subjective challenges to getting an optimal procurement accomplished. There are many scenarios in between, such as an inexperienced procurement person who cannot process the vendor selection quickly due to lack of information, or one who makes the wrong decisions based on lack of knowledge, or even a lack of awareness that certain types of knowledge are required to make the decision. In this situation, we see the promotion of the person who knows that one must request a refrigerated truck from Mexico, and his or her replacement being a person who doesn't have any idea that such a problem exists. The new person will proceed, with the best of intentions, to repeat a mistake that has long since been solved.

There are several aspects to this poor quality decision cycle. If the communication process that connects the people in the decision loop is detached from the EDA and procurement interfaces, the communication itself risks being inefficient and inaccurate. For example, imagine that the vendor selection process is dependent on people reading long e-mail threads from the bottom up, assessing the situation, and making recommendations. (Surely, we've all been there…) This communication pattern is less than ideal for rendering a consistent, rapid set of correct decisions. However, because of the subjective nature of most unstructured processes, such as selecting a vendor using group knowledge as the basis for the decision, e-mail threading is probably unavoidable. At the very least, it is clumsy and unreliable. Even if everyone involved is paying attention and very well informed, the process could bog down if one or more participants is unreachable (or unfindable)—to the extent that production orders could back up because of communication breakdowns in the procurement process.

ProdCo's EDA also lacks the capacity to store organizational knowledge. The specialized knowledge about the subtleties of procurement is not stored in a fashion where stakeholders can easily find or use the information. One enterprising person might create a procurement best-practices document that he or she can use, and perhaps even share with others. But, if that document is lost on a shared network drive, its contents might never reach other stakeholders who need it. If the creator of the document moves on, the document will likely disappear. A dedicated and well-managed procurement team could also create an intranet site on the portal server for collection of practices and settling of decision issues. This approach has some benefits over a totally uncoordinated procurement method, but it might still result in time lags and communication mistakes if the stakeholders still need to toggle back and forth between their intranet team site, e-mail, and the actual ERP system to make and implement decisions. At the very least, it is a largely unrepeatable pattern.

The integration of ProdCo's productivity infrastructure with its EDA is a major contributor to solving this dilemma, where lost knowledge, lack of knowledge, and poor communication mitigates the positive impact of an EDA and improvement business process management. PI integration cannot solve this problem all by itself, of course. There are myriad challenges related to training, knowledge preservation, best-practices documentation, and so forth, that are required to ensure good human decision cycles in a process flow. However, the chances of ProdCo attaining the best human decisions in the EDA environment are greatly enhanced by the integration of the EDA and the PI. Without this integration, the likelihood that ProdCo will optimize the organizational impact of the EDA is slight.

A Better Proposal: EDA/PI Integration

We might be displaying some hubris by characterizing EDA/PI integration as a better proposal. The truth is, it's a very new area and still quite theoretical. However, as we go through the potentialities of EDA/PI integration in the ProdCo case, we believe you will see some exciting possibilities for improving the way work gets done in practical terms, hence be able to apply these principles elsewhere.

Unstructured tasks, such as procurement staffers rounding up best-practices data from diverse stakeholders, tend to be messy and unpredictable. Given that reality, it is challenging to design any kind of technological solution that will consistently solve the problem and make the unstructured tasks faster, simpler, and cheaper to execute. In fact, there really isn't much in the way of standard language or practice to even describe the kind of problems that IT solutions need to solve for unstructured tasks. For this reason, we are going to attempt to work backwards from identification of unstructured task problems, to causes that can be remedied by EDA/PI integration, and build a solution approach from there.

First, what problems does ProdCo face with procurement, and which can be traced back to inefficient unstructured tasks and poor EDA integration? Wasting of time ranks high on the list because slower procurement typically translates into slower production. Then there is the loss of knowledge over time, which can result in slow procurement or other costly errors in production. Then, there are just plain mistakes made through poor communication or inadequate decision-making processes.

Backing out of these problems, we can get to a set of business objectives for the integrated EDA/PI. ProdCo needs to have rapid procurement that is accurate. They need high quality and consistent knowledge transfer as team members move in and out of roles. And, they need transparent, well-documented decision processes that result in accurate, timely procurement without imposing an undue administrative burden. This last point is relevant because it is nearly always possible to cure a process by larding it up with many onerous administrative tasks and parameters. The net effect, though, is usually counter to the goal of efficiency. Getting the right process in place without choking the team members with bureaucracy is a fine balancing act.

In Figure 9.9, we see how productivity infrastructure can help ProdCo's procurement staff collaborate with one another, as well as other groups, share knowledge, and communicate efficiently in the fulfillment of the RFQ process. In the early steps of the process, from "Order Received" through "Create List of Needed Materials," the procurement staff is notified of changes in order status and impending RFQ workflow. The specific mechanism of notification could vary, though it would probably be an e-mail alert or a change in an order status screen on the intranet. As the procurement staff needs to solicit and review bids, they can use the team sites and search features of the PI to find expertise that might rest with individuals throughout the company. In our example, if the procurement staffer searched for the name of the product that gets shipped from Mexico, he or she might be directed to a wiki or blog that communicates the salient details of shipment in hot weather that would enable even an inexperienced procurement staffer to avoid the problem that has plagued others. Once that kind of knowledge is extant and searchable, it is harder for the organization to lose. The Web 2.0 type of features that allow individual users to create their own material easily—but also securely—is an underpinning of successful PI. Ultimately, the EDA can be extended to facilitate these types of investigatory searches simply by connecting the `NeededMat` (Needed Materials) event producer with the PI search.

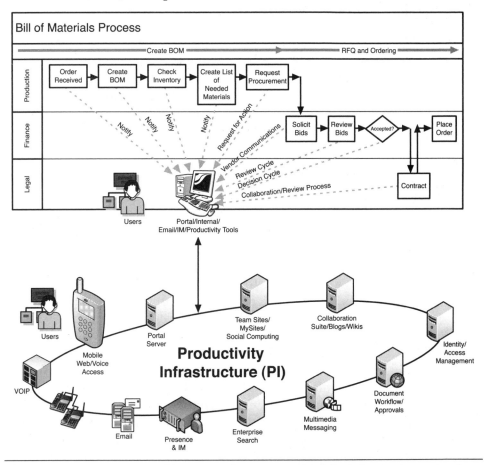

Figure 9.9   Matching the RFQ process flow to a productivity infrastructure, showing the connections between process steps and collaboration, communication, and knowledge sharing areas of the PI.

Stakeholders in the process can work on documents, such as contracts and RFQs, in a virtual collaboration environment and document management system. Throughout the process is communication, pervasive and real-time, through e-mail, phone, mobile devices, IM, and Web meetings. The net effect of this sophisticated PI is a faster procurement cycle with greater sharing of knowledge in real time and preservation of knowledge. PI has the potential to help ProdCo realize its business objective of rapid, accurate procurement.

You might imagine, based on robust productivity functionality shown in Figure 9.9, that even without integration of the underlying enterprise EDA applications, you would be ahead of the game. Having solid connectivity between stakeholders in real time, and streamlined access to documents and knowledge is a big boost to productivity, even without tight integration with ERP and CRM. However, as you start to tie sets of systems together, the benefits become striking.

EDA/PI Integration Requirements

What will it take to integrate ProdCo's PI and EDA? To keep it simple and focused, so we can learn, we look at the functional requirements for EDA/PI integration as they relate to the procurement example only. The following are the requirements that would drive improved productivity in the procurement process through connection between the underlying EDA-enabled ERP and CRM applications and the productivity infrastructure. In keeping with our custom in this book, we also assign this hypothetical project a name. We are considering integrating ProdCo's PI with its EDA, so the name PIEDA fits well. It sounds a bit like a geek fraternity, which in a sense, it is.

One of the first requirements that the PIEDA team will have to figure out is the interface. There are two basic choices: Integrate the productivity tools into the EDA-enabled ERP and CRM applications, or surface the ERP and CRM applications through the productivity infrastructure tools. Both options require the use of application programming interfaces (APIs) and custom tooling for implementation, though neither requires creating interfaces wholly from scratch. The major productivity suites are available with APIs and development kits that enable integration of interfaces and routing and transformation of messaging to and from enterprise systems.

The first option, which is shown in Figure 9.10, puts the EDA-enabled ERP app into the same UI as e-mail, document archive, search, and a team site with RSS feeds. In this kind of unified dashboard, the procurement staffer can work on specific RFQs and have a view of his or her e-mail, relevant documents, and team updates without leaving the ERP app. In the second option, the ERP app might appear as a sidebar in the e-mail client, for example. The best practice for this entire issue might be to do some research first, consulting the end users and showing them the mock-ups to get input on how they prefer to work before committing to one approach or another.

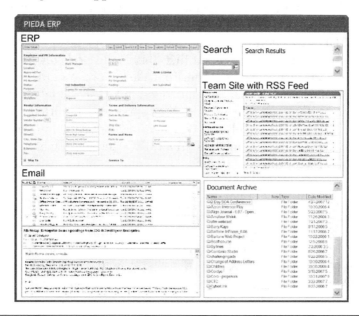

Figure 9.10 Wireframe mock-up of a composite UI for PIEDA, showing a single interface that contains ERP features, search, e-mail, team site with RSS feed, and a document archive.

As shown in Figure 9.10, one of the most basic features of PIEDA is the ability to automate notification of procurement process status changes to stakeholders. When an order is received from the CRM system, the end user is notified, perhaps through an IM or RSS alert. Same thing when the "Create BOM" process is executed in the ERP system—the procurement person is notified, and so forth, through Check Inventory, and Create List of Needed Materials. This real-time (or rapid) notification of end users of changes in state in the EDA serves to prompt action on the part of the end user. For example, if the procurement staffer is alerted that an order is going into the "Check Inventory" state, then he or she can consult the team site for background information on this type of order and be ready to handle the vendor selection right away. In this way, PIEDA connects the enterprise nervous system of EDA right to the human thought processes necessary for completion of the process flow.

Following the process flow shown in Figure 9.9, the next requirement for PIEDA we need to address is the request for action that occurs when the process reaches the "Request Procurement" stage. When the bill of materials has been generated, and the inventory checked, and the list of needed materials drawn, the procurement is now ready to begin. PIEDA will alert the procurement staffer that he or she needs to create an RFQ and solicit bids. At first, this would probably be an e-mail that requests that action be taken. To make the process efficient, though, the e-mail should contain an embedded link that will take the end user to exactly the right screen in the ERP app where the RFQ can commence. If the end user simply receives an e-mail notifying him that he needs to go to the ERP system and start an RFQ, and making him look it up (perhaps by copying and pasting a job number into a search field), we have not accomplished very much in terms of efficiency.

This innate linking from e-mail, blog entries, IM texts, and documents through to the actual job page on the ERP system is an essential requirement to make PIEDA worth the effort and expense.

As the RFQ and bids go through the review loops, PIEDA needs to keep decision makers close to each other and to the related documents. The ERP app needs to show the presence of stakeholders so that all the people involved in the process can connect with one another—either through IM, e-mail, phone, or by looking up information that was authored by a particular person or team. In other words, if a procurement staffer receives an alert that he must review a draft of an RFQ, the draft of the document should appear in the same interface as the alert. Then, the draft should show the presence of its authors, with their availability for IM, e-mail, or phone instantly visible. Alternatively, a user should be able to link on the mysite, teamsite, or blog of any document author or group of authors to learn more about what they know about the procurement process.

It should be possible in PIEDA to conduct a search through the documents, blogs, wikis, teamsites, mysites, and ERP business data to find relevant information about the procurement, or the project itself. Through an enterprise search interface, and back-end enterprise search engine, the end user needs to be able to look up any missing information about the procurement. In our example, if the procurement staffer searches for the component that needs to be shipped in a refrigerated truck, he or she should see the pertinent notes about shipment in the search results—or at the very least, get a search result that points to documents that contain the needed information.

A more sophisticated version of the enterprise search scenario described previously involves including people in the search results. If the end user conducts a search for the bill-of-materials components, the search results could contain both a list of documents related to the components as well as the authors, including their presence and knowledge contributions to the organization. That way, if a procurement staffer cannot find exactly what he is looking for, he can click on the results of a people search and connect to expertise either live or through a published knowledge contribution such as a blog or wiki.

Business intelligence (BI) should be a requirement for PIEDA. Though not perhaps a drop-dead necessity, BI gives stakeholders the ability to analyze data and create reports that lead to organizational knowledge. For example, it might not be known that a certain component gets destroyed by heat in transit. If a procurement staffer ran a report on job orders that exceeded planned costs, he or she might notice that certain types of orders that contained a specific component (which melted in transit) all resulted in poor financial results for their respective orders. Of course, such BI functionality already exists in many ERP systems. The challenge for PIEDA is to make it available to users automatically, through the portal front end of the productivity infrastructure. This availability helps expose the knowledge potential of the business intelligence. And, going further, with RSS feeds and subscriptions, it becomes possible to alert people of new knowledge without the receivers of the knowledge needing to know in advance to look for it. Finally, with an EDA-PI connection, the RSS feed itself becomes an event with the potential to trigger action.

The collaborative workflow for document creation needs to manifest through PIEDA. As end users create documents and revise them, they must be able to see who has contributed to the drafts and be aware of their presence if they need to contact them. The document management functions of PIEDA need to be able to route documents along approval paths, allowing for final approvers to be aware that drafts have been created for their review. The ability to set up an instant online Web meeting or conference call to review a document in real time should be built into PIEDA.

Bottom line, PIEDA needs to provide users with real-time (or near-real-time) access and awareness about events that occur in the ERP and CRM systems. PIEDA needs to give users access to the people who create documents and data inputs to the system. The goal is streamlined, rapid decision making that results in the best possible decisions. PIEDA needs to stimulate the creation and distribution of knowledge in an effortless manner. Users need to find or receive knowledge passively.

PIEDA's Target Architecture

Having outlined PIEDA's functional requirements, the challenge now is to relate them to a target architecture for the development of a working EDA. After all, the goal of PIEDA is to reduce the amount of random and unstructured communication between people as they manage the information in the CRM and ERP systems. Doing this means connecting events in those systems to automated and semiautomated actions in the productivity infrastructure. The first step in this process is to understand how the functional requirements map to events in the overall architecture.

Figure 9.11 shows a target architecture for PIEDA. Notable is the contrast to earlier EDA examples we have explored, which have one area of event processing. PIEDA has three. There are events produced, listened for, and processed at the level of the CRM and ERP systems, shown as Area C in the figure. In addition, the productivity infrastructure itself has a whole event processing setup, shown as Area A in the figure. This is an interesting discovery for anyone getting under the hood of a productivity suite: It has many event-driven features right out of the box. Whether you're dealing with Microsoft SharePoint and Office, IBM Lotus, or others, you will find a handsome complement of event processing going on inside the application suite. For example, SharePoint has numerous automated notifications of document draft changes and blog posts, and so forth.

The third area of event processing—Area B—is PIEDA's actual integration between areas A and C. As depicted in Figure 9.11, PIEDA's event processing area is contained within the portal server. However, it need not be. We have approached PIEDA as if it were going to be developed using standard APIs built into the portal server. When undertaking a project such as PIEDA, many different alternatives might, in fact, be more attractive. For example, it might make the most sense to build PIEDA on top of the ERP-CRM service bus or develop it on its own stand-alone application server. The bottom line, though, is it will have to be built. At this time, there is no out-of-the-box solution for the kind of functionality envisioned for PIEDA.

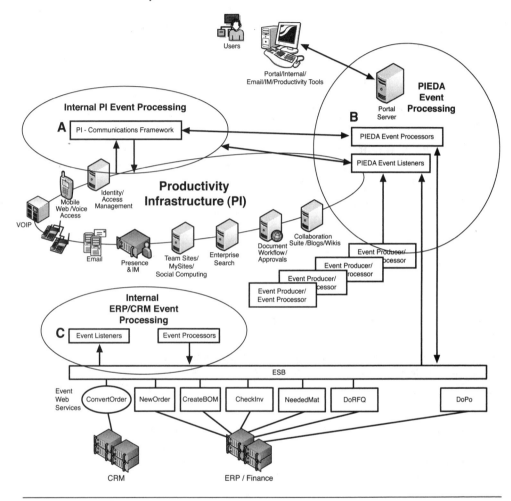

Figure 9.11   Target architecture for PIEDA, showing three separate areas of event processing: The CRM and ERP systems cycle event data between themselves (Area C), as does the productivity infrastructure (Area A). PIEDA (Area B) listens for event data from both, and produces its own events. All three event processing areas listen for each other's events.

Figure 9.11 is a rather complicated picture. However, PIEDA's beauty is that Areas A and C can operate quite well on their own, even if you take out B, the PIEDA event processing center. PIEDA is an incremental upgrade to the architecture, and the event processing capabilities of the PI and the back end are not reliant on it. We mention this because some might look at Figure 9.11 and decide that the effort is not worth the complexity. On the contrary, the productivity gains justify the work of making it happen. Plus, if it's done right, the complexity of PIEDA need not result in an excess of administrative load or inhibitions of process agility.

To illustrate how the target architecture for PIEDA fulfills the functional requirements, we'll walk through one specific example of the event flow. Using the requirement of "Request Procurement," let's examine the specific EDA functions that PIEDA needs to realize to make the requirement work. The requirement specifies that the ERP system inform the procurement staffer of the procurement need for a list of items. The flow of process steps shown in Table 9.1 describes how this requirement is fulfilled, adding in the events that are produced and listened to at each step.

Table 9.1   Connecting Event Producers, Listeners, Processors, and Reactions to Process Steps in "Request Procurement"

Step	Event Producer(s)	Event Listener(s)	Event Processor(s)	Reaction	Comment
Notify procurement staffer that procurement is needed	DoRFQ (Area A)	PIEDA (Area B)	E-mail Server (Area A)	Send e-mail that carries event state: Order Number SKUs needed	E-mail should contain dynamic links to underlying documents and presence information for stakeholders
IF collaboration is needed, create IM session to discuss RFQ	PIEDA Portal Server (Area B) CreateIM	PIEDA (Area B)	IM Server (Area A)	Create IM session that is populated with event state information	Requires XML carried on SIP

Step	Event Producer(s)	Event Listener(s)	Event Processor(s)	Reaction	Comment
IF documents are needed to support procurement, proactively link staffer with documents	PIEDA Portal Server, (Area B) working through Word Processor– PostDocument	PIEDA Portal Server (Area B)	PIEDA Portal Server (Area B)	Publish document update in document library on PIEDA	Document needs to contain author presence data, and links to author mysite and teamsite
Generate vendor solicitation e-mails VendSol	PIEDA Portal Server (Area B) Create	PIEDA Portal Server (Area B)	E-mail Server (Area B)	Create e-mail, populated with RFQ data	RFQ data should be in state carried through event publication

Once again, our old EDA friend—carrying state—surfaces in PIEDA. For an e-mail or IM session to be generated as a reaction to an event, the event processor must have access to the event state data in the event message. For example, if the user initiates the `CreateIM` command, which starts an instant message session with another stakeholder, the requirement is that the IM session will automatically contain data about the specific procurement under discussion, as well as links to the ERP system files as well as documents, that need to be discussed. To do this, the `CreateIM` command needs to contain a function that lets it search for already published event data about the procurement in question. In effect, `CreateIM` is a two-state command series that looks like this:

1. WHEN user initiates CreateIM command for procurement XYX, SEARCH message queue of events published for DoRFQ and FIND procurement XYZ data
2. INITIATE IM Session (through SIP), carrying XYZ data as XML bound to SIP

We use this IM example for a reason, namely that SIP to XML integration is not easy, and the standards involved continue to evolve. Binding SOAP to SIP is also challenging. Whichever method of integration is chosen, it needs to be flexible, allowing low friction for rapid changes in configuring IM session generation with changing business process models. It will take more than average effort to get it to work, but PIEDA should generate greater than average ROI.

The broader point is that PIEDA—Area B—needs to be a flexible switchboard connecting the event activities with Areas A and C to create ROI and justification of the whole project. If PIEDA is too rigid, and changes are time consuming or expensive, then the EDA PI integration will not serve its business purpose. Although this statement could be made about almost any application or architecture project, it is particularly true for PI. PI is inherently more unstructured and more unpredictable than conventional IT situations.

Implementation

Given the complexity of PIEDA, achieving the high degree of flexibility envisioned is a double challenge. Not only does your development team have to create an architecture that is wholly new, and do so with custom development, they must create an architecture that is highly flexible too. Some wise people might declare the challenge not worth it at the outset.

Although these wise people wouldn't be entirely wrong for wanting to avoid the hassle of entering uncharted waters, the good news is that PIEDA can actually be deployed in very small increments. Looking at Figure 9.11, you can understand that Area A already exists in some form. Virtually every sizable business in the world has an e-mail system, an intranet of some kind, and suites of productivity applications. VOIP and corporate IM are on the ascent as well. Building Area A from scratch is not an issue. Area C exists in its component parts, and exposing Web services and creating an EDA is a decision that is separate from building PIEDA. There would be a good rationale for creating an EDA at the CRM and ERP system level for its own sake.

We do not want to revisit EDA implementation in this chapter to the extent that it has been covered earlier. All of the multistakeholder buy-in and iterative design cycles discussed previously apply to PIEDA. The key takeaway for thinking about implementing PIEDA is to understand that Area B can be developed in stages. In fact, it can be deployed one feature at a time after a core set of EDA infrastructure pieces have been put in place. Unlike Area C, which needs a certain number of event producers, listeners, and processors to hit critical mass and function, PIEDA can start quite small. PIEDA can take one instance of event processing, such as "Request Procurement" and put it into full effect. This approach might even be the optimal way of getting it off the ground.

Given the fickle nature of human-machine interaction, which is truly at the heart of PIEDA, it would be wise to design, test, and deploy in tiny increments. Although the development team might think it's really cool to have an automated IM session generated, users might scoff at such a feature. To save time and resources, and ensure the highest level of success, PIEDA's implementation plan should include a thorough usability testing and feedback cycle. End users need to be included intensely throughout PIEDA's life cycle. This is especially relevant because PIEDA does not rely on prepackaged software, which usually undergoes its own round of usability tests and market research. In the future, though, PIEDA type platforms might become common. Today, though, it's an unexplored frontier. (Free tip for readers: If anyone is brave enough to stake a claim in this space, venture capitalists might find it interesting.)

Chapter Summary

- Most organizations have a large existing investment in a collection of productivity and communications technologies such as desktop file editors (e.g., Word, Excel), e-mail, instant messaging, content management, collaboration (e.g., SharePoint, Lotus Connections), VOIP, and so forth, that are known as productivity infrastructure. There is great interest in most companies to improve the utilization of these technologies, tie them more directly to business processes, and generate a strong ROI for the whole assemblage of disconnected parts. In this chapter, we look at ways to connect back-end systems exposed as event Web services to the end user in an event-driven productivity infrastructure.

- Advantages of integrating back-end systems and productivity infrastructure using EDA include the ability of end users to interact on a social computing basis and the ability for end users to search back-end databases, as well as enterprise applications and content repositories to get an integrated view of a customer.

- This chapter uses a case study where a company wants to improve the process that begins with a sales proposal and culminates with the fulfillment of a sales order. This involves a multistep process that begins with the mapping of the business process and then connecting those process steps with underlying applications and sources of data. Some of the data resides on back-end systems, while other parts of it are contained in various places within the productivity infrastructure. For example, information about a customer might reside on the CRM system, the ERP system, an e-mail archive, a collaboration suite, and a document repository.

- To make event-driven productivity infrastructure work, the CRM and ERP systems must be exposed as Web services up to an ESB, which is then connected through to an integrated solution that can consume these Web services and correlate them to activity in the productivity infrastructure. Thus, for example, when a user is preparing an e-mail about a customer, that user can start an IM session in real time that automatically references the customer, or look up CRM or ERP information about that customer from the e-mail client. Each step in the sales proposal to order fulfillment process maps to a set of event listeners that surface data about the customer in real time.

Endnotes

[1] Taylor, James and Raden, Neil. *Smart Enough Systems*. New Jersey: Prentice Hall, 2007.

Index

A

accidental architectures, examples of, 25

agents
  auditing, 149
  defining, 149
  domain agents, 151
  infrastructure agents, 151
  message backbones, 151
  simple agents, 150
  typing, 150

aggregation agents, 151

agility, SOA-EDA development, 135

airline flight control EDA case study, 159-160
  ATCSCC software, 161
  FEDA
    adding new users to, 168
    auditing, 169
    autonomic response, 168
    bottleneck analytics, 170
    bottleneck awareness, 169
    bottleneck resolution capacity, 169
    carrying state in, 181-182
    cost-effective integration, 171

customizable front-end interfaces, 168
data transformation in, 171, 178-180
enabling technology factors in, 174-175
ESB federation in, 177
event web service life cycles, 191-195
extensibility, 171
extensible front-end interfaces, 168
functional requirements, 168-170
high-level architecture, 172-174
local event processing, 171
minimal impact on existing systems, 171
mitigation of risks in, 198-199, 203-204
organization in, 199-200
project life cycle, 201-203
project risks in, 197
real-time awareness, 168
reliability, 169
reporting, 169
security, 169

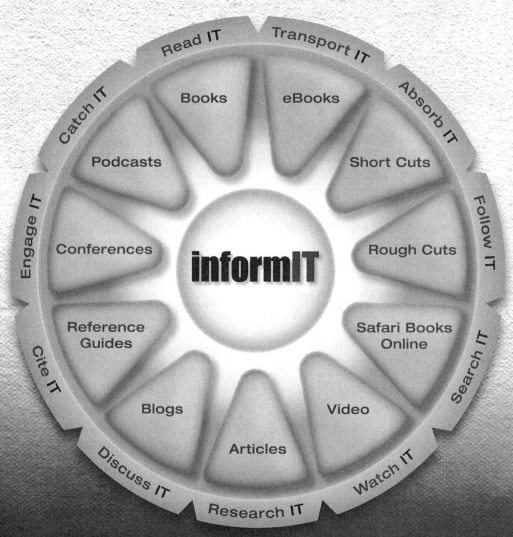

FREE Online Edition

Your purchase of **Event-Driven Architecture** includes access to a free online edition for 45 days through the Safari Books Online subscription service. Nearly every Addison-Wesley Professional book is available online through Safari Books Online, along with more than 5,000 other technical books and videos from publishers such as Cisco Press, Exam Cram, IBM Press, O'Reilly, Prentice Hall, Que, and Sams.

SAFARI BOOKS ONLINE allows you to search for a specific answer, cut and paste code, download chapters, and stay current with emerging technologies.

Activate your FREE Online Edition at www.informit.com/safarifree

> **STEP 1:** Enter the coupon code: VJGMPWA.

> **STEP 2:** New Safari users, complete the brief registration form.
> Safari subscribers, just log in.

If you have difficulty registering on Safari or accessing the online edition, please e-mail customer-service@safaribooksonline.com